3/08

"Most parents acknowledge that they *should* be talking with their kids about sex, but they just can't quite manage getting started. A recent journal article concludes that parents—whether they realize it or not—are *always* providing sex education, either by what they say or by what they communicate nonverbally to their children. In *What's Love Got to Do with It*, Dr. John Chirban helps parents to present a deliberate, focused education on sexual issues.

"The sex-education books currently out there have all the accurate information, but they don't do very well addressing how parents can feel OK about raising the whole issue of sexuality with their kids. Dr. Chirban does an excellent job at this daunting task, giving parents specific information about how to talk with their kids about love, intimacy, and sex."

— JOSEPH LOPICCOLO, PHD,
University of Missouri,
Department of Psychology

"In today's world, whether or not children should know about sex isn't the issue. It is plastered all over in advertisements, songs, and even on the Internet. But knowing about sex as a vital part of an intimate and loving relationship is something that isn't well known. *What's Love Got to Do with It* helps parents to dialog with their children about this gift that can last a lifetime."

— SANDRA R. LEIBLUM, PHD,
UMDNJ–Robert Wood Johnson Medical
School, Director of the Center for Sexual
and Relationship Health; and Author of
*Getting the Sex You Want: A Woman's
Guide to Becoming Proud, Passionate, and
Pleased in Bed*

"*What's Love Got to Do with It* takes a very progressive and highly enlightening look at the provocative field of sexuality and children. Dr. Chirban makes it easy to not only talk about a subject that tends to be difficult to approach but also gives real-life examples to prepare parents for a healthy and ongoing conversation that will equip their kids to own their own sexuality. His insights are essential for professionals as well as parents."

— CAROLINE MYSS,
Author of *Entering the Castle*
and *Anatomy of the Spirit*

WHAT'S LOVE
GOT TO DO WITH
IT

WHAT'S LOVE
GOT TO DO WITH
IT

Talking with Your Kids about Sex

JOHN T. CHIRBAN, PhD, ThD

THOMAS NELSON
Since 1798

NASHVILLE   DALLAS   MEXICO CITY   RIO DE JANEIRO   BEIJING

Published in Nashville, Tennessee, by Thomas Nelson. Thomas Nelson is a trademark of Thomas Nelson, Inc.

Thomas Nelson, Inc. titles may be purchased in bulk for educational, business, fund-raising, or sales promotional use. For information, please e-mail SpecialMarkets@ThomasNelson.com.

Illustrations by Aurora Andrews.

Library of Congress Cataloging-in-Publication Data

Chirban, John T.
    What's love got to do with it : talking with your kids about sex / John T. Chirban.
      p. cm.
    Includes bibliographical references and index.
    ISBN 978-1-4016-0339-7 (hardcover)
    1. Sex instruction. 2. Teenagers—Sexual behavior. 3. Sexual ethics. 4. Parenting.
  I. Title.
  HQ57.C574 2007
  649'.65—dc22   2007018042

Printed in the United States of America

07 08 09 10 11 QW 5 4 3 2 1

For my wonderful daughter

Alexis Georgia

who introduced me to many of the
challenges and joys this book presents

"Heart, out, and around."

Contents

Foreword

I would like to be the first to thank and congratulate my friend and colleague, psychologist John T. Chirban of Harvard University, for writing this important and much needed book. As anyone who watches *The Dr. Phil Show* knows, I am a big believer in open communication between parents and children, especially on matters as important as sex, intimacy, and love.

As a member of the show's advisory board, John has helped us pass that advice on to our guests, and now with this informative, intelligent, and important book, he offers his expert advice to you.

Since parents are not the only influence in their children's lives, they absolutely must be the biggest, and quite simply that takes some planning. But as John points out with the use of some very compelling stories, parents all too often shrink from their responsibility to educate their children about sex. We know it can be a tough thing to look into the eyes of your children and talk about this delicate subject. But it is the parents' responsibility. If you don't do it, the other kids on the bus or, worse, some yahoo on the Internet will provide misinformation that could potentially hurt your children or, at least, corrupt their understanding of what should be one of life's blessings.

It is evident in John's approach in this book that he totally gets that—from the standpoint of being both a parent himself and a professional psychologist. He recognizes the challenges that many parents have to face in talking with their children about sex, and he offers solid advice on how to overcome those challenges. Most of all, he stresses—as do I—that parents have to work from day one to keep an active dialogue going with their children. You must talk about the small stuff that doesn't matter so that the lines of communication are established and open when something big and important—such as questions about sex—does come along. John's book makes sure you are ready when, not *if* but *when*, that first moment arises.

Getting started is the hardest thing in talking with your child about sex, but if those lines of communication have been running both ways and are connected with trust at both ends, that first talk and every subsequent conversation will be much easier.

As John says, it doesn't hurt to let your child know that everyone has both questions and shy feelings about this subject. Humor can make it easier, too, as long as you don't mock or tease your child. I've found that kids really like it when we make fun of ourselves. (Mine might enjoy it a little too much!)

In the title and throughout the pages of this book, John also stresses the very important point that after you have discussed the mechanics of the body with your child, you need to talk about sex as a normal, healthy experience within the context of a loving and mature relationship—something you do after you've grown up. He puts the *cart* back behind the *horse* by emphasizing the importance of relationship and maturity first and sexual connection second.

I have had so many people to ask me over the years how they can know when it is appropriate to discuss specifics about sex with their children—how much is too much, too soon, too graphic, too infantile. So I know you will find it especially helpful that John has included advice on what information should be imparted at each stage of a child's development—and by which parent.

At a time when sexually transmitted diseases are a real and serious threat to teens and even preteens, this book also provides invaluable information that can help parents spare their teens from lifelong, chronic health problems.

John, thanks again for writing this important book.

—DR. PHIL MCGRAW

PREFACE

Before We Begin: A Personal Note to Parents

An outraged Courtney walked up to her second grade teacher to complain: "Marty was trying to look up my skirt and see my china."
"Your china?" her teacher asked.
"You know," Courtney insisted, "my china. My mommy says girls have chinas and boys have peanuts."

It's easy to laugh about the miscommunications that occur when we try to talk about sex, especially with our children. However, when parents and children don't communicate clearly and thoughtfully about sex, the impact isn't funny: it can be serious and long lasting. Nevertheless, I realize that the last thing you might want is some doctor telling you what your child needs to know about "the facts of life." Who am I to talk to *you* about what to say to *your* child?

It is true that no one knows your children better than you—you are the one who loves your children most and is most committed to them, and that gives you a unique and crucial role in reaching out to them. So who, then, is better positioned to talk about sex, intimacy, and love with your children than you? That's right—nobody! But how will you do it? What will you say?

Sex is a difficult, complex topic, and talking about it is challenging for everyone. In fact, most of us don't even talk honestly to ourselves about sex—much less to our spouses and kids. Why is something that is so natural, so pleasurable, and such an important part of life so difficult to talk about with those we love the most? Even though sex is a universal human experience, it also taps into our anxiety, vulnerability, and even fear.

The fact is, sex is one of the most important but least talked about subjects in parenting. So please allow me to walk with you through this subject. You may not need any new pointers at all. In that case, feel free to review this material as a confirmation of what you already know. But whatever you do, don't miss the opportunity to engage in conversations about sex with your child. When done well, talking about sexuality can be one of the most important and positive experiences in the relationship that you share with your child.

"Do you think we're helping our kids develop a healthy sense of their sexuality?"

We need to give our children good information and, most importantly, we need to help them understand that sex is not like a Nike slogan—we don't "just do it." Rather, sex is a vital part of intimate and loving relationships.

I find that most kids know the basics of sex. They understand the plumbing and get the nitty-gritty of the "bump and grind," so to speak. But very few understand how sex affects their relationships. Who will help them make the important connections between sex, intimacy, and love? Who will help them confidently integrate their sexuality into how they relate to the world? Learning the plumbing is one thing, but our children also need to know how to make sex a safe, healthy, and sacred part of their lives.

Children grow up seeing images of sex plastered around them as mindless acts of lust. Sex is portrayed as an idealized thrill instead of one of life's great gifts. Sex is in our faces just about every waking hour: from the bosoms popping out of the Victoria's Secret catalog to gyrating youth strutting alluringly in MTV music videos—we can run but we cannot hide. Without parental guidance, our children are left trying to make sense of their emerging sexuality by taking their cues from a culture that relentlessly promotes sexual gratification, aggression, and provocation. Have you considered the message sent to your kids by the purveyors of Viagra pills and Jessica Simpson's "Deliciously Kissable Body Frosting"? Would you rather they learn about sex from you or from television shows such as *Grey's Anatomy* or *Desperate Housewives*? Or how about the Internet, where who knows what sexual behaviors are just a click away? If we as parents don't help our children develop a balanced outlook on sex and sexuality, we risk seeing our kids' views of sexuality twisted and warped by those who do not care about their welfare.

What's Love Got to Do with It is a call to action for parents to get a dialogue going with their kids on this vital aspect of life. The effort you put into this subject will also give you great rewards as a parent. You will talk with your children about some of the most sensitive and critical aspects of their lives. You will witness your children's fulfillment in making strong connections between sex, intimacy, and love—and in developing honest and meaningful relationships. By helping your children to feel comfortable with this topic and to connect sexuality to everyday thoughts and emotions, you can give them an invaluable lesson that will last a lifetime.

But before you can discuss sex confidently with your kids, you need to get a handle on how you yourself feel about it. With the help of this book, you will clarify your thoughts and learn how to guide your children in developing the confidence, integrity, and honesty necessary for dealing with the challenge of sex with a healthy perspective.

So, who is this man who's about to guide you along the path to explaining the "facts of life" to your child? While you are the expert on *your* child, I have worked with thousands of patients and students to help them overcome their personal struggles with sex, intimacy, and love. I'm also in your shoes. As a parent, I have confronted firsthand the challenges that kids meet today, confirming our critical and unique roles in our kids' lives to coach them as they embrace their own budding sexuality.

The truth is that today's kids talk about sex incessantly with each other. It's the parents who avoid the subject like it's wired with dynamite. I've found that just breaking the ice and uttering the word *sex* is a major challenge for many parents. Even the most caring and attentive mothers and fathers can become tongue-tied when trying to provide guidance on sex, and those who are willing to give it a try sometimes fail because they don't know how to approach their children. We need to determine what children need to know and when they are ready to hear it. This book will help you assist your children in developing healthy and confident approaches to sexuality based on practical, scientific, and proven advice.

Our children—from infancy to adulthood—need to know that they can always come to us with questions and concerns. They need to know that we are willing to share information and provide meaningful guidance even if we are uncertain ourselves.

So, are you with me? I hope so. And I hope that you will embrace this most meaningful task as your child's trusted counselor in sex, intimacy, and love.

Acknowledgments

Writing this book has been a deeply meaningful, passionate, and enjoyable experience. In working on *What's Love Got to Do with It,* I drew on professional research and case studies, but this material also evoked many memories of important people who shaped my life and my understanding of sex, intimacy, and love.

As a dad, I have learned so much from my own kids. I've dedicated this book to my firstborn, Alexis Georgia (age 13), who first introduced me to many of the issues you'll find in these pages and whose genuine heart of gold, natural warmth, and cheerful kindness speak to what lies at the core of this book—love. This dedication could never detract from the significance and guidance of my other two stars, Anthony Thomas (age 12) and Ariana Maria (age 9). I am particularly indebted to all my children for providing contributions that helped me to address age-appropriate issues and for sharing, in a spirit of good-humored collaboration, interesting stories from their even more interesting lives and, of course, to their mom.

This book ultimately took on its form through the guidance and intuitive genius of my agent and dear friend Jan Miller. Jan placed this book in the competent and thoughtful hands of Thomas Nelson's exceptional publisher, Pamela Clements, and editor Jennifer Greenstein, whose seasoned abilities, solid skills, and balanced judgment guided this book's final presentation. It has been a joy to work with this team!

Topics like sex, intimacy, and love can only be addressed successfully through attention to multiple perspectives and standpoints. Blessed by a research and editorial team of brilliant student-scholars, I take pleasure in acknowledging their substantial labor and assistance. I thank my editorial and research staff: Zoe Savitsky, Laura Maludzinski, Andrew Russell Varyu, Lisa San Pascual, and Sanden Avarett. I also thank my research staff: Anamika Marianne Broomes, Kate Henley Long, Sohrob Nabatian, Kip Richardson, and Danika Brook Swanson.

In addition, it was a pleasure to engage the artistic talents of Aurora Andrews, who creatively captured in her delightful and humorous drawings the thoughts that came to mind as we tackled this material.

Special gratitude goes to my respected colleagues and friends who offered their professional guidance: Frank Lawlis, PhD; Maria Pantelia, PhD; Derek Polansky, MD; Yula Ponticas, PhD; and Wes Smith.

I am particularly thankful to Bette Davis and her son, Michael Merrill; Tom Hanks; and Archbishop Desmond Tutu for releasing segments of our interviews for sidebars in this book. Their involvement and trust enhance the significance of this endeavor.

Finally, I am deeply grateful to Dr. Phil McGraw, who hosted my Survey on Sex Education on his Web site, as well as to the Institute of Medicine, Psychology, and Religion in Cambridge, Massachusetts, which also distributed my survey; together they gathered more than twenty-thousand respondents who shared their experiences in sex education.

INTRODUCTION

In the Age of Sexual Un-Innocence

Welcome to the age of un-innocence, where no one has breakfast at Tiffany's and no one has affairs to remember. Instead, we have breakfast at 7 a.m. and affairs we try to forget as quickly as possible.

—Sarah Jessica Parker as Carrie Bradshaw in *Sex and the City*

Abby: What's It All About?

Abby was a seventh grader who went to visit her school counselor after she started dating Bobby, her middle school's star basketball player. She had had a crush on Bobby for more than a year and was ecstatic about being able to date. She regarded her parents as conservative because many of her classmates had been dating since the fifth grade. Abby hadn't talked much about sexuality with anyone in her family; it was one of those subjects in "don't go there" territory. Despite her early excitement about going out with Bobby, Abby quickly grew uncomfortable with the direction the relationship was taking.

At first, Abby's dates with Bobby involved going to a movie or taking a walk through the mall, but soon Bobby suggested they move the dates to more secluded areas. He said he wanted "to talk." After a little conversation, Abby found Bobby's hands slipping beneath her undergarments. Then Bobby had her perform oral sex on him. On each date, Bobby's expectations and demands escalated. Although Bobby appeared steadily attached to Abby, she wondered if his attraction to her had more to do with what they were doing than with who she was. When Bobby asked Abby to shave her pubic hair in front of him, he laughed at her hesitation and insisted that all couples did those kinds of things.

Abby felt both confused and uneasy. She didn't know exactly where this sexual activity was leading, if it was right, or even if she wanted to go along with it. Sometimes what they did was pleasurable, but other times it was painful and humiliating.

Abby's counselor was very upset by Abby's story. Without breaking confidentiality, she went to the school's principal, arguing that not having a sex education program in place was archaic—the school needed to inform students about sexual behavior and help them prevent problems like Abby's from occurring with other students.

Do you think that sex education programs could help students avoid situations such as Abby's? Do you know if your daughter is prepared to handle a boy like Bobby? If you were Abby or Bobby's parent, do you feel you would know how to intervene? Providing you with answers in such predicaments is one of several important goals of this book.

Unlike what we may remember from our own childhoods, sex is not a taboo topic for kids today. While systems (schools, churches, and homes) and authorities (parents, teachers, and clergy) often operate as if sex is a foreign word to kids, youth today are bombarded by—and actually becoming anesthetized to—thoughts and images of sex. They're not only familiar with sex, they're comfortable with it, and many are actually having sex. According to the Kaiser Family Foundation, seven out of ten television programs that teens like to watch include, at least, one scene with sexual content.[1] Sex as an act is a norm for teenagers in America, and the subject of sex is common on elementary school playgrounds. Knowing this, does it make sense to act as if we can keep sex hush-hush?

While it's true that teen pregnancies have recently dropped for the first time ever, thanks to widespread information about birth control, the rate at which high school girls are engaging in casual sexual encounters is now equal to that of boys. According to the National Center of Health Statistics, more than half of America's teenagers are sexually active and most of them describe their experiences as "casual" or "not meaning anything."[2] Statistics don't lie: our kids' generation is far more sexually active than generations before.

Yes, this is the age of sexual un-innocence. Kids today, like never before, are propelled into a highly combustible sexual culture that creates the potential for explosive results—not only because of how sex may entangle them but also because of how it can distort their understanding of intimacy and love. What makes it more complicated—and the reason this book has been written—is the fact that most children do not have lines of open communication for discussing these topics with their parents. Too often they are forced to face these issues alone.

Furthermore, parents most often deal with sexuality by suppressing information or by ignoring the impact of the sexualized culture our kids face every day. Some parents deflect the problem by blaming the media and pop culture:

"My daughter wants to dress just like that half-naked singer!"

"Those rappers use filthy language!"

"Now they're showing sex on the nightly news!"

Regardless of the source, we are still left asking: Who is going to be responsible for making the connections between sex, intimacy, and love for our kids? How can we take hold of the situation and harness these powerful forces?

We could act like ostriches. We could stick our heads into the sand to avoid the realities that our children meet, or we could do what we do in every other area of their life—educational, economic, vocational, and social—and give them our all.

It's time to roll up our sleeves, regardless of whether or not we think we have the answers, to show our love through our presence and our willingness to talk and listen as our children determine their course on these topics: Be with them as they make sense of what they're experiencing and feeling. Help them sort out the sexual influences of mass media, the advice of their peers, the impact of pornographic images in print and television media, and other disturbing influences.

Sex Education and Family Values

To begin getting acquainted with the subject of sex education and family values, let's check with a parent who is in the midst of addressing these issues.

Jim and Marcie: Holding Your Tongue

Marcie is in fifth grade and attends a private school, where her dad, Jim, teaches. Jim came to see me because of unexplained "anxiety." In our initial conversation we discussed his relationships with his family members and his sexual satisfaction. Jim said that his home life was happy and that he enjoyed a warm and sexually fulfilling relationship with his wife.

At first, it was hard to zero in on the cause of Jim's anxiety. While nervously laughing, though, he disclosed that Marcie was attending a sex education course at school where students were being taught how to place condoms on dildos. Although Jim did not fully express his shock, as a parent of a fifth-grade daughter as well, I echoed his discomfort, "A 10-year-old being shown how to put a condom on a dildo?!"

As we talked about it more openly, Jim admitted how helpless he felt to do anything about the school's sex-ed program. He and his wife had taken the step of signing a waiver to excuse their daughter from the program.

Marcie was excluded from the regular class meeting with the health education teacher and given extra assignments. However, the instructor had announced to the student body that only three students in the entire school were not participating in the sexuality curriculum, "which," she said, "was for every-one's well-being." In the end, Marcie suffered from being publicly identified and reprimanded.

After that, Jim wanted to stay out of it to save his daughter from any more humiliation. Yet he, his wife, and Marcie were all uncomfortable with the class. Jim still felt the program "put the cart before the horse," encouraging a sexual standard for 10-year-olds rather than simply providing age-appropriate infor-mation. Unfortunately, the backlash created by the family's decision to remove Marcie from the program left him feeling disempowered within the school. Besides the program's inappropriateness for fifth graders, Jim felt that it did not do justice to promoting the context of loving relationships in which he felt sex-uality should be placed.

What do you think about Jim and his wife's situation? What about Marcie's? How would you manage it if you were in Jim's position? Should your child participate in a sex education program when it runs counter to your family's values? Is sex education value-free and simply informative even when it seems to be directing kids toward certain behaviors? Is it *possible* for school systems to align general sex education programs with each family's values? Can any such program adequately and openly consider everyone's values?

Sex, Intimacy, and Love: A Whole Package

Jim's story leads us to consider some big questions. If, like Jim, you find your-self looking for an approach to sex ed that combines biological facts with sen-sitivity to your values, I hope to lead you to some answers.

All too often, our children grow up seeing sex represented merely as an act of physical gratification; they do not learn to equate sexual pleasure with love and fulfillment. I believe that sexual thoughts and feelings are natural gifts that serve as gateways to building loving, intimate relationships. By giving our chil-dren a greater perspective on sexuality, one that incorporates sexuality into the fullness of a holistic, whole-life experience, we not only help them to under-stand how sexuality relates positively to their entire life but also establish a warm, loving, lifelong connection with our children that in itself demonstrates the intimate and loving experience we want to encourage.

In *What's Love Got to Do with It* you will learn about the connection of sexuality to the various spheres of life—biological, emotional, relational, social, and spiritual—that you may not have linked to sexuality. You will learn how these areas of life can inform your child about sexuality and build the foundation for relating sex to intimacy and love, which is necessary to develop fulfilling sexual relationships.

Our society churns out endless images promising sexual fulfillment, but it doesn't adequately make the connections between sex and intimacy and love. Our kids need to learn to integrate their sexual, emotional, and spiritual feelings and values with their real-life experiences in relationships. There is no one more appropriate than you to launch and guide your child in this journey. We must figure out how to model positive approaches to sexuality while responsibly guiding our children through the confusing and often negative sexual images and messages that they constantly receive.

The Parents' Role in an Ongoing Dialogue

While most of us do everything in our power to meet all of the needs (and most of the desires) of our children, dramatic avoidance and denial often set in when faced with the task of helping them understand their sexuality. The first step to help kids is for parents to admit that kids (including their own) of all ages have sexual needs. No matter how hard we may try to pretend otherwise, children don't magically turn into sexual beings at age 16, 18, or 21— or when they get married. Children are sexual from the womb. As their parents, we are entrusted to guide them in creating a healthy sexuality. What messages do you give to them regarding your role as their guide?

Do these comments sound like you or someone you know?

"No matter what I say, kids learn all they need to know about sex from their friends—if not from the TV."

"They teach sex ed at my kids' school. I say leave it to the experts!"

"No one ever talked to me about sex, and I figured things out all right."

Ring any bells? Might that be you, allowing somebody else to do what should be your job? If we stop to think about how our sexuality is connected to the core of our personality, our self-esteem, and our ability to love and relate to other human beings, then how could we neglect to support our children on this crucial subject?

I know the task seems daunting because, let me assure you, most parents feel the same way! Everyone has feelings of uncertainty. You shouldn't worry about giving inadequate information about sex. No one knows all the answers. Sexuality is so different for everyone. Given that sex ed in schools tends to focus on factual information *without* a context of values, parents are in the unique and important position to interpret sex ed in the framework of their family's particular emotional needs and values. This means that what *you* say to your children *will* make a huge difference. They will realize that there's a lot more to sex beyond what goes where.

But remember, learning doesn't just come through what you say. Kids learn by watching. They learn especially through the examples we set in the home—both verbal and nonverbal. That means they are constantly gathering information, even at times when you don't think you're talking about sex at all.

How to Use This Book

What's Love Got to Do with It is designed to be engaging, enlightening, and inspiring as it provides practical and effective ways to teach your children how to make crucial connections between sex, intimacy, and love. With the goal of helping you to establish an ongoing relationship with your child, this book will help you make the connections between sex and its biological, emotional, relational, social, and spiritual roots as well as help you address your relationship with your children and their sexuality from infancy to adulthood.

This book offers tools and information to free you from inhibitions and help you tune in to your child by strengthening your relationship in the following ways:

- Opening lines of communication for the long term
- Mentoring your child on sexual matters

- Defining your values and modeling how your child can determine his or her own understanding about the connections between sex, intimacy, and love, thus connecting the dots regarding the relationship between body, mind, heart, and soul

This book will help you make these connections so that your children can themselves replace the shallow picture of sex presented by pop culture with an integrated and healthy outlook that allows them to celebrate their bodies with honesty and a deeper appreciation for sexuality within loving relationships.

What's Love Got to Do with It provides exercises to help you clarify your own feelings about sexuality, to become aware of and take responsibility for the conscious and unconscious messages you send to your kids, to improve your listening skills, and to learn how to explore the pressures your children confront daily about sex. The book also provides guidelines on what to say, when to say it, and who should say it, and offers troubleshooting tips on some tricky topics that might have left you floundering.

Most of the anecdotes and examples in this book are drawn from my professional experience and from my own efforts to talk about sex with my son and two daughters. The book also includes up-to-date information on issues that parents need to know about, from controversies in sex education to studies about how sex in the media affects our kids. I've also drawn on the results from the Survey on Sex Education that I conducted in cooperation with Dr. Phil McGraw; this survey attracted more than twenty-thousand respondents, and I've highlighted their insights throughout the book. Additionally, drawn from my personal interviews with them, I've included valuable insights from celebrities on relationships and sexuality.

What's Love Got to Do with It is a guidebook for parents to help them develop their relationship and an ongoing conversation with their kids. While it is not intended to be read aloud to your children, as you discuss sexuality with them, you may find several of the stories useful in your discussions. This book is designed to help you participate actively in your children's sexual education or, at least, carve out your role in conjunction with programs in which your children participate. This book includes several exercises and models for dialogues to discuss sexuality and directs you to outside resources to guide you in your efforts to address these issues in greater depth.

As you read this book and determine the ways you can guide your children through sexuality, I think you will also realize how your own sexual upbringing, by your parents and others, has affected your life today. In the end, you will be able to use your own experiences to bolster your message to your children. While some may find the challenge of looking at their own sexuality uncomfortable or unrelated to their objective, I strongly encourage you to go though the exercises of self-examination and reflection that will deepen your understanding of sexuality, intimacy, and love and empower you in your genuine parental role as you speak about sexuality with your kids.

PART I

Sex Defined

ONE

Cleaning Up
the Dirty Little Secret

We do not even in the least know the final cause of
sexuality. The whole subject is in darkness.

—CHARLES DARWIN

*First-grader Johnny wanders into the living room, where his father
intently reads a business magazine.*

"Daddy, where did I come from?" the boy asks.

*The anxious father—caught off guard, not expecting such a
question for years—hastily answers, "Uhh . . . Bloomingdale's."*

"Then where did you come from, Daddy?"

*The father, taken aback yet again, remembers a childhood fable.
"From a stork!" he says.*

*Johnny, still fixed on his inquiry, continues, "How about Grandpa?
Where did he come from?"*

*Johnny's father now desperately tries to think back to the stories he
was told as a kid and, as if he has landed on the perfect answer, blurts
out, "From under a cabbage patch!"*

*Johnny's father breathes a sigh of relief as Johnny wanders off to the
kitchen.*

*The next day Johnny returns to school, armed with his completed
homework assignment.*

"Where did you say I come from?"

"Well, Johnny, did you find out how your life began?" the teacher asks.

"Not really, but I figured out why I've been so confused," he says. "I don't think my family's had sex in three generations!"

If you want to talk with your kids about sex, you'll need a sense of humor. When we're anxious about something, humor can help us through an uncomfortable silence. But be careful. Don't let humor become a way of avoiding some of the most complex and serious issues regarding sex. Dealing only or mainly in jokes can give our kids the impression that we've adequately addressed something when really we haven't.

Imagine a parent telling a funny joke about sex to his or her child—no harm done, right? But, just like with Johnny, questions will keep coming from your child. We need to consider who really answers our kids' questions. Did Johnny's dad feel he had answered his son's questions adequately—or was he just relieved to be done talking about it? More importantly, which path will you follow when *your* kid comes asking the tough questions?

Sex and Humor

Kids find everything related to sex to be either funny or gross. They giggle with their friends in the schoolyard about "doing *it*," whatever the mysterious "it" may be, and don't even get them started with the words *penis* and *vagina*—those are beyond hilarious. We would be fooling ourselves if we thought that people grow out of finding sex humorous: many media, from television sitcoms to humor columns in the newspaper, depend on sex as a reliable source for jokes. Whether it's a reference to strange animalistic sexual behaviors or a joke about a celebrity's sexual escapades, we seem to be fascinated and titillated by sex.

Is it wrong or immature to find sex humorous? Yes and no. Sigmund Freud viewed humor as a mature defense to alleviate tension and to deal effectively with such an important and uncomfortable topic. Yet humor about sex can also be used to denigrate or dismiss a person and his beliefs or behavior or to cover up ignorance and discomfort. It's important to know when and where to use humor to talk about sex and when it's important to be serious. Being able to use humor as a tool to help your child feel comfortable talking with you is a vital skill!

Sometimes our kids know a lot more about sex than we think they do. With this in mind, we as parents need to prepare to answer questions like Johnny's both accurately and completely while avoiding turning them off with what kids often call "TMI"—too much information. So some joking is fine. It can help keep things comfortable and buy us some time to get our bearings. But in the end, we should take our children's questions seriously. Every exchange is important for building a trusting relationship with them. We'll get into how to strengthen the relationship with our kids in more detail later on in this book, but for now let's look at some basic pointers.

Answering Unexpected Questions

If you're reading this book, you're preparing yourself for good conversations with your kids about sex. But that doesn't mean they'll wait till you're ready; kids always have surprises in store, and maybe they've already sprung a sex talk on you. When you get hit with the unexpected from your kid, it's always best to put as many cards on the table as possible. A good starting place for a parent would be to reassure "Johnny" that you're interested and will help him find answers.

To help you move forward, you may want to ask your child a few questions. Start by asking what led him to the question. Ask him if he has any ideas about the answer. You want to avoid answering a question that's not actually being asked, thereby overwhelming or misleading your child as Johnny's dad did. Even if it means having to explain your initial reaction to the questions—maybe surprise or discomfort—your child will benefit from the message that even if you seem taken aback at first, deep down you're ready to help and really glad he asked.

Now, on to the most basic question: what *is* sex?

Ask kids, and you'll hear everything!

- "It's about privates!" (a 5-year-old girl)

- "It has to do with making babies and grown-up stuff."
  (a 7-year-old boy)

- "It's wild." (a 16-year-old boy)

So how about you? What is sex to you?

Sex means so many things to different people that it can be hard to nail it down, especially for someone a fifth your age. You may recall President Clinton telling the press, "I did not have sex with that woman," then admitting to having had *oral* sex with her. People have become insistent about defining sex in their own ways.[1] This book presents the broadest definition of sex: all that concerns sexual health and activity and their wider implications for well-being.

Being (Naturally) Sexy

Chimpanzees mate every few years when females signal their fertility—by revealing bright red genitalia. But for humans, sending the "open door" message is not so clear, perhaps shedding some light on why sex can often be a daily preoccupation for us.

Have you noticed that human women are the only females in the animal kingdom to have enlarged breasts even when they're not breast-feeding? Some scientists think that because women in protohuman societies didn't give distinct signs to indicate their readiness, men were motivated to hang around the cave, so to speak, waiting for sex at any time. It has been suggested that human females thus evolved to display attractive qualities men would equate with fertility—such as curvaceous breasts—to keep men interested all the time.

Additionally, evolutionary psychologists have found that certain adaptations that we retain today have taken on sexual significance: some men apparently are attracted to ballerinas because a well-arched foot used to indicate a talent at tree-climbing, and both women and men are attracted to more symmetrical faces because symmetry indicates healthy genes. These are just a few examples of the ways in which sexuality is naturally built into the body.

What Is Sex?

The World Health Organization defines *sexual health* as involving the integration of "physical, emotional, mental, and social well-being." Sexual health is not just the absence of disease or sexual problems but also requires "a positive and respectful approach to sexuality and sexual relationships as well as the possibility of having pleasurable and safe sexual experiences, free of coercion, discrimination, and violence."[2]

That's a valuable and meaningful definition for parents because it can help us talk about a whole range of factors that bear on sexual health—not just the sex act itself. Sex, then, is far more than body parts and raging hormones—it is also an emotional act that requires proper understanding in order to become part of a healthy expression of love and intimacy.

In other words, sexuality is an outgrowth of our whole being and encompasses many spheres of our life. This is what I mean by taking a "holistic" approach to talking about sex. You may find it helpful to consider these aspects of life when you address your child's questions. She may be asking what part goes where, but your job is to help her integrate her sexuality into a healthy understanding of her life, as far as she's able. Let's look at those different pieces of the puzzle: the five aspects of our sexuality.

Physical. These are our physical drives, needs, and actions—the physical part of the sexual act that we can visualize and feel when we hear or see the word *sex*.

Emotional. This encompasses our inner feelings and their connections to intimacy and love. For example, powerful feelings such as tenderness, vulnerability, excitement, and love as well as hurt, shame, and fear can be stirred when we talk about sexuality.

Relational. Sex never takes place in a vacuum. Relationships with specific people, especially the person with whom you're having a sexually active relationship, are crucial. All relationships, including sexual ones, are characterized by a variety of factors, such as power, control, communication, and dependency. When these and other factors are in good balance, a healthy, respectful, and loving sexual relationship becomes possible.

Bette Davis: Defining Gender Roles

Fiery, frank, and unconventionally beautiful, actress Bette Davis was the quintessential woman of strength. Her striking features and even more striking demeanor inspired film critic E. Arnot Robertson to write, "She gives the curious feeling of being charged with power which can find no ordinary outlet." Bette Davis forged a career based on roles that defied the fragile "delicate doll" template of the day. I spoke with Davis on several occasions about her private life, and she had deeply heartfelt things to say about the role of women in relation to men. Davis said the following about the changing attitudes toward gender roles:

> The tragic thing is that men have interpreted the women's movement today to mean that we don't like men. Let me tell you something, the stronger the woman, the more she needs a man. She needs a strong man! . . . I think that women who work out a successful marriage are very fortunate as they get older. The only other thing I will add about that is that a famous wife is not easy for any man . . . I personally believe that men in all sincerity think they can cope with it, but they can't . . . Any enormously accomplished career woman is going to run into this, no question about it!

Davis cuts to the root of the difficulty for both men and women. Even today both men and women may feel the need to live up to prescribed expectations. The potential danger is reinforcing gender stereotypes that are possibly inappropriate for your child. For example, it's important that we reexamine our definition of "strength." Traditionally, we equate "masculinity" with strength, both physical and emotional, and silence. A masculine man is supposed to be aloof and emotionally inaccessible, someone who "sucks it up" instead of talking it out. But strength can also mean being kind (even when you don't feel like it), forgiving others, and providing for the household in ways other than financial. By helping your child to see his or her qualities in terms of strengths and weaknesses, instead of "masculine" or "feminine," you're equipping your child to let his or her true self shine through.

Though on the surface it may seem that Davis reinforced stereotypes about strength and weakness, her point may go deeper than that: "strength" doesn't mean we have to travel solo! A relationship is a partnership, where each partner can grow and challenge the other to grow as well. Partners can work together to build each other up, to sharpen and support one another. Instilling this notion of teamwork in your children will help them develop a healthy and full perspective on relationships.

Social. Culture influences our attitudes about sex as well as our behaviors. Culture gives to us, for example, our definitions of masculinity, femininity, and gender roles, through everything from our family upbringing and education to movies, music, TV, and the Internet.

Spiritual. Our faith and spirituality can have both positive and negative effects on how we view sexuality: on the one hand, religious teachings can create guilt, fear, and even the denial of sexuality; on the other hand, spirituality and religion can direct us to values that support a healthy understanding of how to relate sex and love. Sex can also take on spiritual aspects that are very personal and not tied to particular religious traditions.

Talking about sex requires sensitivity to all these aspects because sexuality comes from and affects our whole being. So talking about sex shouldn't stop at discussing pleasure and reproduction; we need to take into account all our attitudes, feelings, and behaviors.

What makes us different from the rest of the animal kingdom? In sex, it's our unique ability to integrate these five aspects or spheres into one grand experience of sexual health. But that's easier said than done—we humans sometimes let one or more of those spheres fall by the wayside. You can help your kids move toward overall sexual health by always thinking of their questions and your advice in this broad context. The key is to not let the questions get disconnected from the big picture. And remember, also: sex is different for each person. Each of us makes these connections in unique ways.

It can be helpful to imagine the aspects of sexuality as spheres in our life (see Figure 1.1). Each of us integrates the physical, emotional, relational, social, and spiritual spheres in our own ways. They may be overlapping or disconnected, and some spheres may be larger than others or totally absent.

The interplay among these five spheres affects how we think about our sexuality. For example, if our spiritual sphere is small or neglected, spiritual concerns will not weigh into our sexual thoughts, feelings, and behaviors. Or if the social sphere is largest, social expectations and attitudes will largely direct our sexuality while other spheres won't weigh in as much. Understanding our own big picture—the size and connections of our spheres—is important if we are to guide our children in putting their own pictures together.

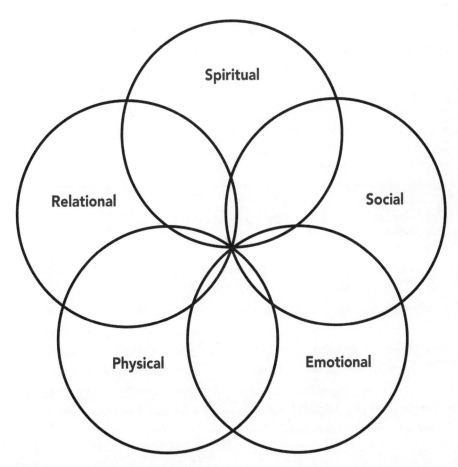

Figure 1.1 The Spheres of Sexuality

Purposes of Sex

If your child asks what sex is, the question "what's it for?" will probably not be far behind. You should be thinking of how to explain the various functions of sex in addition to explaining what it is. Sex serves several purposes: pleasure, stress relief, formation of our identity, intimate connection, and (of course) procreation.

But the goal of sex can be defined in one word: fulfillment (*finally*, you might be thinking, *one word and not a list!*). Certainly, orgasm is one of life's most pleasurable experiences, but true fulfillment in sex comes when such physical pleasure occurs within the context of an intimate and loving relationship. Fulfilling sex transforms what could be a pleasurable but merely mechanical event into an expression of intimacy and love that engages us emotionally, relationally, socially, spiritually, and also physically. It feels good because it connects with our core values and character.

Helping your kids understand sex will be infinitely easier when you are clearer in your own mind about what you expect from sex and what you're getting from it—in the terms of these five connected spheres. Complete Exercise 1.1 to see how you're doing.

Exercise 1.1: Expressing Sexuality in Life

First, on the following page, draw each of the spheres of sexual wholeness in different sizes, according to the degree of emphasis each sphere receives in your life and the degree to which they overlap. Second, on the blank lines provided, give specific examples of behaviors and activities that illustrate how the sphere appears in your life. For example, if you find that cultural norms greatly influence your sexuality, you might write for the social sphere: "I define my level of sexual attractiveness by society's standards." Or if you find that your spirituality plays a large role in your sexuality, you might write for the spiritual sphere: "I feel most sexually satisfied when my partner and I share a spiritual connection."

Spiritual

_____

_____

_____

_____

Relational

_____

_____

_____

_____

Social

_____

_____

_____

_____

Physical

_____

_____

_____

_____

Emotional

_____

_____

_____

_____

Figure 1.2 presents a model of how a 29-year-old man might draw and describe the spheres of sexuality for Exercise 1.1. Note that the relative size of your spheres should reflect the significance of these aspects (physical, emotional, relational, social, and spiritual) as they factor in your sexuality. The spheres may be connected (if they connect in your life), disconnected, or absent. Identifying actual behaviors and activities will ground your responses.

How does your sexual wholeness look to you, now that you look at the big picture you've drawn? Is one area limited? Does another command all of your energy? This honest self-assessment is the first step in presenting to your kids your thoughts about something you've considered deeply, in all its aspects.

If you found that for you, one or two spheres is all that sex is, you're not alone—many of us experience sex this way. But this never does justice to the holistic nature of sex. A lack of balance in our approach to sex can destroy the fibers that connect sex with intimacy and love. So much of how we view sex is implicit in our language. Consider the expression, "I got a piece." This expression reveals a lot. When a partner is just an object for sexual pleasure, we have treated that person not only as a "piece" or object but also have experienced only a piece of what sex can be. In this kind of sex, the wholeness of both partners' sexuality has been shattered because the emotional, relational, social, and spiritual dimensions of sexuality have been diminished or even eliminated.

We may choose to approach sex by compartmentalizing it rather than appreciating its whole reality because we can (and often do) learn about sex in physical terms, either for pleasure or procreation, disconnected from the other spheres. Ironically, when some religious authorities insist that the purpose of sex is procreation alone, they further fragment the character of sexuality. By implying that pleasure in sex is bad, they may overemphasize their understanding of the spiritual sphere. Though such faith-based positions are intended to preserve the sanctity of sex, they actually create a disjunction between body and spirit, blurring the importance of healthy emotions and relationships—all equally important to sexual health.

As you explore and explain what sexual fulfillment means to you personally, you will be helping your kids understand the connections between sex, intimacy, and love. Then you can impart to them your family's values, rather than letting them accept what society hands them. Understanding how you want to

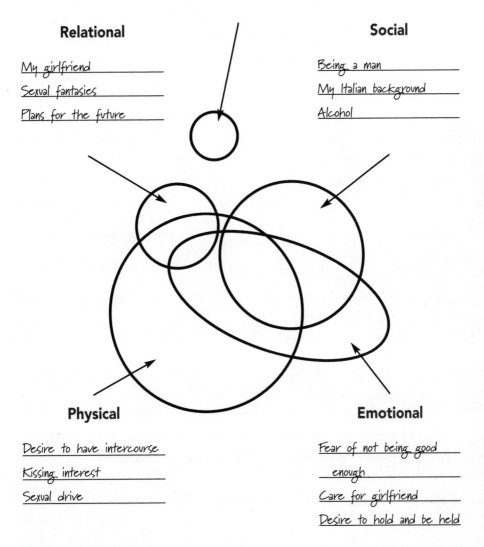

Spiritual

No sex until marriage

Not really a factor for me

Relational

My girlfriend

Sexual fantasies

Plans for the future

Social

Being a man

My Italian background

Alcohol

Physical

Desire to have intercourse

Kissing interest

Sexual drive

Emotional

Fear of not being good

enough

Care for girlfriend

Desire to hold and be held

Figure 1.2 Model for Completing Exercise 1.1

define the sentence "Sex is fulfilling" is the key to making the ongoing talk with your kids about sex totally rewarding, and helps them to start building the bridge between sex and intimacy and love.

The A-B-Cs of Sex: Knowing What You're Talking About

It's amazing that we spend so much time thinking, dreaming, and fantasizing about (and even sometimes having!) sex. Yet when it comes to talking about it, we get tongue-tied. Getting the facts straight is a big step toward feeling confident about opening up that box of tightly guarded secrets with your child. So let's take an inventory to see where we're coming from. What do we know? How did we learn about sex? What values do we hold about it? And what kind of messages do we broadcast about sex?

Parents have several reasons for feeling uncomfortable talking with their kids about sex, but the biggest fear of all is being unsure of what is true. Exercise 1.2 will help you assess how much you need to get up to speed about the facts of sex.

Exercise 1.2: General Information Quiz on Sexuality

Answer the following questions T (true) or F (false).

_____ 1. Sperm and semen are different substances.

_____ 2. Women experience nocturnal orgasms.

_____ 3. It is possible for women to ejaculate.

_____ 4. If a woman's hymen is broken, it means she is not a virgin.

_____ 5. Sexual desire naturally decreases a lot after 40 or 50.

_____ 6. Imbalance in sexual hormones is the main cause of homosexuality.

_____ 7. Infants experience vaginal lubrication and erection.

_____ 8. Masturbation can be harmful if it occurs more than twice a week.

_____ 9. Genital herpes can be cured.

_____ 10. A female cannot become pregnant the first time she has sexual intercourse.

_____ 11. A person may infect someone with the HIV virus even if he or she has not tested positive for HIV.

_____ 12. Approximately 25 percent of males have a homosexual experience in their teen or adult years.

_____ 13. A woman will not get pregnant if a man withdraws his penis before he ejaculates.

_____ 14. To screen for cancer, teenage boys and men should examine their testicles for bumps as often as girls and women examine their breasts.

_____ 15. The average length of a man's erect penis is 7 inches.

_____ 16. Athletic performance is not affected negatively by sex before a game.

_____ 17. As a result of AIDS, the term STI is preferred over the term STD.

_____ 18. Alcohol does not inhibit sex drives.

_____ 19. Urination after a woman has sex prevents pregnancy.

_____ 20. Sexually provocative material causes people to commit sex crimes.

_____ 21. Doctors are professionally trained to deal with sexual problems.

_____ 22. It is normal behavior for boys to measure their erect penis.

_____ 23. The age of the onset of puberty has remained constant.

_____ 24. Teenage girls have easier and healthier pregnancies than older women.

_____ 25. Fertilization of the ovum occurs in the vagina.

Check the answers at the end of this chapter (pages 35–36). What was your score?

> 23 to 25 correct—You are well informed.
> 17 to 22 correct—You're fairly up to date.
> Fewer than 17 correct—We'll help you brush up!

If the results of Exercise 1.2 show that you need to catch up on a few details, don't worry! The most important ingredients for helping your child develop a positive understanding of sex are your motivation and care. These will lead you not to just talk about sex with your kids but to want to get the facts straight. Your natural desire to help your child will motivate you to do the research you need.

Your Sexual History

To help you get comfortable talking about sex, one additional important step is reconnecting with your own sexual history. The situations in your life that you found useful, as well as those that could have gone better, can all help you talk with your child about sex. It's good to bring our experiences to the forefront of our minds so they don't distract us from being present when we talk with our kids.

Discussing your sexual history with your spouse, partner, or a friend may help you recall struggles, uncertainties, and the sources of your underlying attitudes and values regarding sex. As you understand how your history guided the development of your sexuality, you will appreciate the significance of effective guidance regarding sex, intimacy, and love and "flesh out" (excuse the pun) issues and approaches for talking about them.

Hypocrisy and Being Judgmental

Because of how loaded the subject of "values" can get, it's no wonder that parents often shy away from talking about sex. The fact is that very little sex conforms perfectly with specific ideologies, whether conservative, liberal, or other. While some people talk about sex as something that should *always and only* reflect a connection of self, others, and God (a good description of the sex act in marriage), that position falls short when you consider something like masturbation. Where do we draw the line? How do we manage the gray areas?

Because parents know their own sexual activity doesn't always conform to their beliefs about sex, it's natural to feel like a hypocrite if you impose strict standards on your children. The unease about hypocrisy may be one of the main reasons we don't want to talk about sex. It's the old "Do as I say, don't do as I do." However, you can work it out if you see your role as someone who must weigh in with your children on all the various purposes of sex, not just lay down the law about behaviors they may not even be ready to learn about yet. Helping your children understand the various spheres of fulfilling sex takes time and care. Time and care are critical elements of love that this topic and your child require. You'll need many opportunities to get it right—which is why you have to start early with the ongoing discussion, not a one-time "talk."

Ongoing Discussions

Sex is not a one-time discussion. Drawing the big picture at a pace your child can handle takes a lot of time and dialogue. It isn't a sermon, though you may be tempted to launch into one. Here are some points to consider as you start down this rewarding path of communication.

Sex is a reflection of our self. It is organic—a process. It is not like walking a tightrope—there is no straight line from here to there, or only one way to do it. It involves taking honest responsibility for ourselves in our developmental

"Are we making our kid walk a sexual tightrope?"

processes. Our sexual self is not mature when we're 10 years old, or once we've hit puberty, just as we are not mature as people at that age, either. Rather, sexuality is dynamic—growing, living, and evolving, just like us. As parents, we have to keep this natural evolution in mind as we address sexuality with our children. By relating and talking with your children from a young age about the connections between mind, body, and spirit that exist within a healthy under-standing of sex, you can lead them toward a self-discovery of their own chang-ing emotions and attitudes about sexuality.

No one can tell someone else how to *be* sexually—because sexuality is unique to each person. Nor can we expect that one's sexual self is fixed and unchang-ing. What we find sexually attractive and fulfilling at 20 might be quite dif-ferent from what we find sexually attractive and fulfilling when we are 45. While certain parts of our biology are set, our sexuality, like our personality, can develop and change. You want to instill confidence in your children so that they can embrace and express themselves in their sexuality—and, just as impor-tantly, feel good about themselves in doing so.

Creating the Sexual Self

In a world where few parents take on a proactive role in discussing sexuality with their kids, it is not surprising that so many children *and* adults are confused about sex and love. Often people use the words *love* and *sex* interchangeably, and we are left to our imagination to figure out how this really works. One of the goals of this book is to help parents and their kids clarify the meanings of these terms for themselves.

Living Words: Our Values about Sex

Our own feelings about sexual behaviors affect how we discuss issues of sexuality. Exercise 1.3 is designed to help you recognize your feelings about various sexual topics and clarify your position on them. It covers a range of potential subjects you may encounter throughout the years with your child, especially sensitive topics on which you are sure to have your own particular opinions. As I said before, sexuality is not like walking a tightrope; it's more like navigating a beautiful, expansive sea. Your ability to be an empathetic communicator will require at least a tolerance for thoughts, ideas, and even behaviors you may not fully understand or like. Your ease in managing and discussing the issues your child brings into your life will have a big impact on the confidence and ease your son and daughter will feel in speaking with you. This doesn't mean you have to change or hide your views, but that you communicate them gently and comprehensively.

Exercise 1.3: Sexual Values

Consider the following list of sexual topics and check off your position on these issues.

	Absolutely Do Not Support	Somewhat Do Not Support	Neutral	Somewhat Support	Support
Masturbation					
Sex education in schools					
Condoms distributed in junior high school					

	Absolutely Do Not Support	Somewhat Do Not Support	Neutral	Somewhat Support	Support
Homosexuality					
Bisexuality					
Premarital sexual intercourse					
Sex with someone you do not love					
Women initiating sex					
Abortions to terminate pregnancy					
Prostitution					
Pornography					
Rights of father during pregnancy (to participate and bond)					
Oral sex					
Anal sex					
Deep kissing (French kissing)					
Premarital necking or petting					
Masturbating each other as a couple					
Sexual fantasy					
Sexual toys					
Sexual exploration or experimentation by oneself or with a partner					

After you complete the exercise, think about your consistency regarding your values and how it affects the messages you send out about sex. For example, you might belong to a religious faith that advocates virginity, sexual abstinence, and purity, yet you may find yourself laughing during a sitcom where adolescents are "hooking up." This confuses kids. When our actions aren't consistent with the values we claim, they don't know what to think. They probably won't ask, either. Our kids are faced with many different values about sex. It's when they don't know the basis of these values that they become confused when confronted by alternative points of view. That is why we must work to link our practices to our beliefs, and our beliefs to our formative experiences.

Communication about sex, intimacy, and love does not happen only during focused chats with our children when we directly advocate our opinions and values. It is also embedded in the daily verbal and nonverbal messages we send in our home. We're constantly sending messages about sex, whether directly by saying, "Tia, your skirt's too short!" or indirectly by leaving out an X-rated movie or magazine where it can easily be found or by frowning during news reports about the government's support of abstinence-only sex education programs or ban on gay marriages. Regardless of how the messages are conveyed, it is important they are consistent. Exercise 1.4 will help you compare the messages you send and see if they are consistent. Continue to write down (and analyze) messages you send your children as you keep reading this book! Chapter 2 will offer more guidance on communicating with your kids; we'll focus on tuning into our kids and creating an environment that fosters healthy, meaningful exchanges about sexuality and values.

Exercise 1.4: Your Sexual Messages

Answer the following questions regarding the messages you currently send to your children and those you hope to send in the future.

	Currently	Hope for the Future
What are your explicit messages (what you tell your children) about sexuality?		
What messages do you send when watching a love scene on TV with your kids?		

	Currently	Hope for the Future
When holding your spouse's hand?		
When kissing and embracing your child?		
When talking about sex?		
What messages do you think your kids learn from you about sex?		
Are these messages consistent?		

Review the answers you wrote above. How do your explicit messages (what you said to your child) compare with your actions around the home? How do your explicit messages compare with messages conveyed nonverbally (with your eyes or facial expressions and your enjoyment or avoidance of a topic)?

_____

_____

_____

_____

_____

Exercise 1.2 Answers

1. **True.** Sperm contains the male's half of the contribution to offspring; semen contains about 2 to 5 percent sperm and a white, milky substance from the male reproductive organ.

2. **True.** Both men and women experience orgasms during sleep.

3. **False.** Though a few women have some emission of fluid at orgasm, they do not experience the spurting of ejaculate in orgasm as men do.

4. **False.** The hymen may stretch out of place by an injury or even with the insertion of fingers or tampons.

5. **False.** Though sexual frequency often decreases with age, desire does not decrease.

6. **False.** The jury is not in regarding the causes of sexual orientation, yet hormonal levels seem to be a significant factor.

7. **True.** Both vaginal lubrication and erections are normal experiences of infant girls and boys.

8. **False.** Masturbation rarely has harmful effects. Such effects are usually confined to ritualistically driven and uncontrollable repetition.

9. **False.** Drugs may reduce the symptoms of pain and swelling, but the virus remains in the body throughout the person's lifetime.

10. **False.** Pregnancy may occur any time when intercourse occurs—from the first time until menopause is complete.

11. **False.** A person cannot contract HIV from sex unless his or her partner is HIV positive.

12. **True.** While approximately 3 to 4 percent of men and half that number of women identify themselves as homosexual, 25 percent of men have had one or more homosexual experiences.

13. **False.** Ejaculate containing semen is usually released before a man's orgasm.

14. **True.** While in recent years great strides have been made to fight testicular cancer, teenage boys and men should screen for lumps in their testicles monthly, and should consult a doctor if a lump is found, especially if it is only on one side.

15. **False.** The average length of an erect penis is 6.5 inches.

16. **True.** While individual athletes report differences, athletic performance is not weakened.

17. **False.** STIs are sexually transmitted infections that can be transmitted from one person to another through intimate sexual contact and are not limited to HIV or AIDS.

18. **False.** Alcohol, as with most drugs, deadens nerve endings and affects sexual performance. However, for some people, a small amount of alcohol may decrease inhibition and increase sexual comfort.

19. **False.** The urinary system is separate from the reproductive system and its normal functions do not affect pregnancy. (However, urinating after intercourse can help prevent a woman having bladder infections.)

20. **False.** Violent material may lead to increased aggressive acts, but criminal behavior is not correlated with sexually provocative materials.

21. **False.** Though some medical schools provide instruction regarding sexuality for their students, many do not.

22. **True.** It is well within the norm and part of sexual self-awareness for boys to measure the size of their erect penis.

23. **False.** Puberty has gradually occurred at younger and younger ages over time. For females today the onset of puberty occurs between 8 and 13 years of age and for males between 9½ and 14.

24. **False.** Teens have higher-risk pregnancies and more health problems with pregnancy than older women.

25. **False.** Fertilization normally occurs in the fallopian tubes.

TWO

Setting the Sexual Tone

The best sex education for kids is when Daddy pats
Mommy on the fanny when he comes home from work.

—WILLIAM H. MASTERS

Let's consider two sets of parents who each think they have clearly addressed sexual values with their children following very different approaches. Let's meet them to see what can be learned from their stories.

John and Mary: Monitoring Her Moves

John and Mary decided the subject of sex would lead to too many questions or sexual behaviors. Therefore, they monitored and censored their daughter Kathy's social activity from infancy through adolescence, keeping her out of contact with anything having to do with sex. From age 3 she was in carefully structured gymnastics and dance programs and was not allowed to watch TV without a parent, but she kept busy with school, family events, and sports.

When I met Kathy in therapy at age 16, she was very self-conscious and had a number of physical symptoms that doctors diagnosed as emotional rather than physical in origin. Kathy said her parents were "terrified" of her developing sexuality and of the fact that she was "growing up." She felt especially sad that she hadn't been asked to the junior prom. But she had had limited contact with boys, as she had attended an all-girls religious school and hadn't interacted with boys her own age since elementary school. Kathy's disappointment over not being asked to the prom was compounded by the fact that she had never experienced an actual crush on a "real guy" but had only fantasized about boys.

Kathy had been essentially quarantined from sex because her parents were afraid of the pain that Kathy (or perhaps they themselves?) might feel in confronting sexual issues. They intentionally tried to shut off her sexual energy and, in the end, shut down what Freud properly called her "life force."

Paula and Martin: Sex Is Natural

In contrast, Paula and Martin anticipated "normal" sexual issues with their daughters, so they attempted to head off the subject with a very different approach.

Ellen was their third daughter. Both parents were academics and boasted that they were solidly realistic about sex. They regularly stated that "sex is nothing to be afraid of" and talked about it a lot at home, so Ellen got the message early on that sex was okay. However, though she understood that "healthy" sex was a "fact of life," Ellen never actually *talked* with her parents about what healthy sex really meant. Sex was so silently accepted, in fact, that when Ellen was 16 years old, her mom brought her to her doctor, ordered the Pill, and didn't say anything else about it. Following this cue, Ellen had sex with several boys during high school. She even remembers accompanying her older sister to an abortion. At the time, her mom commented, "These things happen." Ellen felt that "going for the abortion was no different than going to the dentist." While she appeared sexually uninhibited, Ellen admitted what she had was "fake sophistication." She was confused and unhappy about her sexual freedom and felt she was missing dignity, honor, and self-respect in her sexual relationships.

In both stories, we see how powerfully parents' attitudes affect the sexual development of their children, even when they don't address it directly. Messages were sent, received, and absorbed based on the parents' conscious and unconscious beliefs and fears. The parents were shaping their kids without taking time to check on the kids' actual needs and experiences. Though these sets of parents had parental styles on opposite ends of the sexual spectrum, the results were similar: both girls grew up disconnected from their own feelings and were left confused and uncertain about their sexuality. What we can see is that in addition to sex involving many spheres of life, it also involves a special relationship—the genuine connection of parents with their children. An obvious point, maybe, but one commonly missed. Sometimes, the messages are loud and clear, but that doesn't mean the people are communicating.

While both these couples dealt with sexuality for their kids, we don't get a sense that either of them really communicated *with* their kids. So how do we talk *with* our kids about sex? What do we actually say?

Do you think these parents were attuned to the experiences, feelings, and needs of their daughters? Did they listen and convey that they cared about what

Cover Up

It was very hard for my mom to talk with me about basic body changes, much less discuss sex. When I first got my period, I remember being frightened and tearfully holding out my underwear, and asking her, "What's wrong with me?" She limited her comments to the basic essentials.

After my honeymoon, my mom asked me, uncomfortably, "Do we need to talk?"

I couldn't understand why she had such a hard time dealing with the private matters of life. When I eventually asked her, she explained that as she was growing up in Argentina, the body was seen as evil and dirty—and that when she took showers, she had to wear her underpants and a bra!

This story related by a participant in my Survey on Sex Education unearths a serious challenge many parents face when having "the talk." When parents are the product of an unhealthy sexual education, it can be uncomfortable or even scary to try to broach the topic with their own kids. But rather than being part of the domino effect, parents need to get the facts, address their anxiety, and establish healthy rapport with their kids. Ignorance about sex is the single most destructive cause for sexual mistakes, problems, and a lack of self-confidence.

their kids were feeling? In these cases we don't get a sense of how the kids' thoughts and emotions figured into the discussion about sexuality. And when a discussion is one-way, it can't really be called a discussion. Neither set of parents were attuned to their kids and neither involved their kids in the discussion; both attunement and involvement are necessary to ensure that the vital issue of sexuality is thoroughly addressed.

Attunement: Deeper Understanding

"Attuning" means gaining understanding *with* your child—not just *of* him or her. Attuning is "tuning in," empathizing, resonating, caring, and "getting" how your child puts together the world around him. Attuning means being there to help.

While most parents acknowledge sex as a reality of life, their approaches to talking about it run the gamut. Many parents provide too little information, leaving out whole spheres of concern—they may get through the physical details but neglect to ask how their children feel about what is being said or lead them to say what the parents want to hear, by asking questions such as "You feel okay with this, right?" Sharing facts is certainly important, but attuning to your children's experience of what's being shared and what's going on in their minds during your conversations is the critical part of talking about sex. Often, our children will have questions that are different from the ones we think we are answering. Thus when talking with our kids, we can't just recite facts; we must make sure we're talking about the same thing. Asking open-ended questions instead of leading questions is the key. For example, you might follow a conversation on puberty with "How do you think puberty will affect you?" or "How do you make sense of what we just talked about?" That kind of questioning also helps you assess how much they're taking away from the conversation.

The information we impart is important. But even more important is the relationship we establish with our children in such exchanges—a two-way, open relationship based on attuning to and listening to our kids. What we hear should establish the agenda for the conversation. After all, this conversation is really about them and their needs—not ours.

Listening in a manner that shows you understand what your child feels will draw the two of you closer together. Ask how your child feels and respond to the reply. Try to put your child's thoughts accurately into words; then ask your child, "Is this what you mean?" This approach will assure him or her that you get it.

What Are You Saying?

When it comes to talking with kids about sex, the majority of parents fall somewhere between the extremes of the two families we just discussed—with most erring toward the side of Kathy's reticent parents, John and Mary. In most cases, parents and kids both know information about sex, but neither is necessarily clear about the meaning and significance of that information for the other. Kids often think that their parents "don't have a clue" and are way out of touch, whereas parents begin with the assumption, "I've seen everything—and even if I haven't done it *all*, I know all about it." This, they presume, prepares them for all possible exchanges because their kids must surely recognize what a wealth of information their parents possess and will come seeking answers. Such assumptions often lead to what I call "telegraphic exchanges." Telegraphic exchanges are what happen when bits of unclear information are passed between parents and their kids and no real heartfelt attempts are made to create open communication.

Avoiding Telegraphic Exchanges

Because we're sometimes uncomfortable with what we think and feel, we often communicate as if by telegraph, using short words and symbols or avoiding sexual terms—essentially leaving children to fill in the blanks. For example, we may have "conversations" without using words like *sex, penis,* or *intercourse,* and we may smile or literally use the word *blank* as we leave out the sexual term or example, thus conveying anxiety. The single most common characteristic among the patients I see for sexual dysfunction—men and women alike—is a lack of good, clear communication about sex during their childhood and adolescence. This communication gap often becomes a trend that continues through adulthood. Because they never received clear guidance as children about how to attune to their own feelings and develop the confidence needed for asking real questions about their sexuality, they are unsure about themselves and continue to engage negatively with their partners. The ambiguity that resulted from murky communication in childhood can lead to anxiety, which sets the stage for a whole host of problems later on.

"Dad, what's Vi-a-gra?"

You have probably experienced telegraphic exchanges. For instance, there you are at a baseball game with your daughter or son, and staring you in the face from behind left field is a huge billboard with the letters V-I-A-G-R-A next to a picture of a man smiling. Your child asks, "What's Va-gra? Vi-a-gra? What does that mean?" to which you probably can't come up with a better response than, "Let's just watch the game!"—ignoring the fact that it is between innings. Though it may seem minor at the time, this communication essentially sends a telegram to your child that reads something like this:

DEAR CHILD—I'M UNCOMFORTABLE WITH TOPIC (STOP)
PRETEND NOTHING HAPPENED (STOP)
DON'T ASK IN FUTURE (STOP)
SUPPRESS CURIOSITY (STOP)
XO—PARENT

What beneficial information might your child possibly take away from this verbal exchange? He or she gets the sense that whatever Viagra is, it must be either very controversial or very problematic, neither of which is the message you ultimately want to communicate. You can imagine how hard it must be for our kids to understand such exchanges, especially since they're looking for clear, simple answers, and these interactions don't produce any. They're effectively being told to be quiet, but they don't have the tools to figure out why. The real message of the telegram is, "Don't ask!" and that's just what your child learns to do!

You're probably wondering what I might say to my daughter or son about that Viagra sign at the baseball stadium. It would depend primarily on his or her age. I might have said to my youngest daughter, when she was 7, "It's for a medical problem that some men have when they get older." If it seemed like the child wanted to pursue this discussion and was near puberty, I would say that we would talk more about it when we got home. And then, of course, we would.

One of the primary challenges of childhood, and particularly adolescence, is clarifying identity. Our children question all sorts of things about themselves— their likes and dislikes, their desires, their wishes and hopes for the future, their budding sexual selves. To understand who they are, they begin to construct and internalize an identity based on how others see them, all the while trying to comprehend the actual messages brought before them both internally (such as their feelings) and externally (such as what people say about their attractiveness or competence). Their confidence is developed based on the information they receive and how successfully that information is communicated to them. Thus, as parents, we must do everything we can to provide them access to good, clear information. If my younger daughter had further questions about Viagra, I might say, "Viagra helps men to deal with problems that they have with their privates."

As parents, we are the translators for our children: we are in an excellent position to decode telegrams sent by outsiders. And we have to be careful not to further complicate matters by sending telegrams ourselves. When our kids come to us, they are looking for honest information that will help them better understand themselves and the world. If they receive secretive, inauthentic, or confusing telegrams from us, they will learn that we are not the ones they should be asking and will interpret messages based on unclear information. They will also try to find their answers by themselves or from other, often less reliable, sources—which is precisely what we've indirectly suggested that they do.

Talking indirectly about sex or avoiding it altogether during our kids' childhood often evolves into more fully developed and unhealthy telegraphic exchanges between our kids and us as they get older. In addition to conveying that although sex exists, we don't talk about it, such advanced telegraphic exchanges create doubts, anxiety, and confusion about sex. Here's an example of an "advanced" telegraphic conversation:

(Connie comes down the stairs, looking beautiful in a floral summer dress, hair and makeup in place, to go out on a date.)

MOM: Just be careful.

DAD *(chiming in from the living room)*: You know how we raised you. Don't make any mistakes!

CONNIE *(running toward the door)*: Yup, Dad. Of course.

MOM *(teary-eyed, whispering to her daughter in the corridor as she exits)*: You know, in case you decide to share yourself, I love you.

CONNIE: Okay. I love you, too.

This is an awkward moment for everyone. While Connie's parents are worried that she will do something that's sexual, Connie just wants to get out of the house as quickly as possible!

Beneath the surface of this half-hearted exchange, Connie's parents are genuinely concerned for their daughter's welfare; they just don't know how to express it clearly and openly. As a result, Connie receives many rapidly sent telegrams containing numerous mixed messages: "You know what you're supposed to do," "Don't make any mistakes," "You'll possibly do something other than what we're suggesting," and "We love you." But were the concerns of Connie or her parents really shared?

Connie's date was probably an important, exciting occasion for her. And if her parents had fears and anticipations regarding sex, Connie would have genuinely benefited from a loving conversation with her parents—rather than this lightning attack ten seconds before she ran out the door! Supportive encouragement before her date is replaced by a pseudo-connection wrought with guilt, anxiety, and expectations. Undoubtedly the exchange was based on many previous ones, and during each the parents may have thought their point was somehow getting across. By now the family is in advanced telegram mode—it seems too late to have the frank discussion of values that's needed.

Although many parents would tell you that their kids can talk with them about anything, the degree to which this actually happens greatly depends on the way the parents have handled previous exchanges. In general, parental approaches to conversations with their kids about sex fall into three categories.

1. Limited exchange. Questions on the topic get raised and quickly dismissed. In such a scenario, telegraphic messages are sent and communications remain unclear, as in the case of Connie. (Parents in this category may say it's best to let sleeping dogs lie when it comes to sex and blindly trust that their kids will be proactive and persistent, somehow obtaining answers to their questions from somewhere.)

2. Basic talk. Discussion occurs, but it is limited to specific, predetermined issues, and the exchange feels unnatural and constrained for everyone involved. While facts get out there, it's clear to the children that from then on they should fend for themselves. (This category includes parents who prepare for the One Big Talk on the Birds and the Bees.)

3. Ongoing conversation. Rather than approaching topics as if they can be covered in a single conversation, the ongoing conversation invites a living and loving dynamic in which the child is free to communicate spontaneously his or her questions and concerns. In such a scenario, parents realize that they don't necessarily have all of the answers, but they are still willing to help their children find the answers they're seeking and to openly initiate conversations.

By now you realize that you're aiming for category three!

The Ongoing Conversation

Though such openness may seem daunting at first, this "ongoing conversation" is ultimately easier than the "limited exchange" and "basic talk." In an ongoing conversation, you don't find yourself tied up with questions and feelings that make you twitchy and uncertain ("Did I say enough?" "Is it over?") as you inevitably do after a limited exchange. You don't have to go crazy trying to remember to cover all the points for that overrated, often dreaded (by parents and kids alike), one-and-only opportunity that is the basic talk. The ongoing conversation removes the temptation to put yourself, as the adult, in the position of Great Sexual Expert, and instead keeps you in your place as a loving parent committed to mutual dialogue. Thus, you're not pressured to model what's "perfect" or "always right," but rather, you can be a reliable, honest resource—someone who has experienced some of life's challenges, has made some mistakes, and because of all this, can provide special perspective.

The Three V's

Parents and kids don't innately have the perfect vocabulary with which to discuss sex. Finding the right words involves uncovering layers of privacy, concerns, uncertainties, and aspects of ourselves that we haven't always consciously confronted, much less developed the proper means of sharing with others. Therefore, as we begin to build the conversation about sex with our children, we must develop ways of expressing ourselves while also being sensitive to the three V's. The three V's are problems that often characterize both parents' and children's initial difficulties in talking about sex, or any thorny subject, with one another:

Vagueness. We tend to speak *around* the subject, avoiding specific words, often because we are embarrassed to say them. In the example of the Viagra billboard at the baseball game, not only is the dad vague, but he doesn't even acknowledge the word or the billboard. In the Connie story, both of the parents seem to reference sexual behavior but never actually mention the word *sex.*

Vulnerability. Sex is a highly personal issue and, especially when it is first brought up, a new territory in discussions between parents and kids. The lack of familiarity with this territory can lead to fear for both parties, and kids are often afraid to talk about sex with their parents because they don't know if it's safe. At the baseball game, the kid doesn't say another word after his father's telegraphic message about Viagra—he is shut down. Connie probably has a very good idea about what her parents are getting at, but wouldn't dare engage with them. Instead, she gives her folks quick replies and darts out of the house!

Volatility. Kids are often a little unstable to begin with. Add on the uneasiness of talking about sex to the other adolescent burdens of hormones, stress, and social pressure, and you shouldn't be surprised if the result involves strong verbal reactions and "acting out." Without any guidance, kids do not know how to relate their physical sexual impulses to the cultural messages (both positive and negative) that they receive about values—they haven't yet made those connections. Their inability to productively express what they're feeling often leads to rash action that can be a source of sadness and guilt later. Think of Ellen, who interpreted her parents' messages to mean that sex was a purely physical act, devoid of any emotional meaning. She thus resorted to a "fake sophistication" that left her feeling a lack of dignity, honor, and self-respect. Parents are also subject to volatility; when pressed to respond on sexual matters, they may react strongly or harshly because they feel uncomfortable and uncertain.

Of course, you're concerned with what your kids learn about sex and how they learn it. You want to guide them—but how do you start the conversation?

While many of the lessons we learn about sex come in indirect ways—through attitudes observed in others, by the ways in which we display affection, by how we respond to sexual topics—to prompt more meaningful, focused discussions with our kids, we need to initiate conversations. In the following pages, we will consider how to approach this first, often daunting step, and what makes this kind of meaningful communication possible.

Setting the Tone

It's important to establish a positive, constructive, and open tone if you want to develop a reciprocal dialogue. The spirit that you convey when discussing sex will affect how comfortable your children will feel in return. Although initiating a conversation with your young children about sex might seem awkward, if you've been attuning to their daily behaviors and events and answering their questions honestly and fully, you will realize that you already know where to begin. Kids start wondering where babies come from at a young age and, because they have not learned to have inhibitions with regard to sexuality, they will spontaneously ask all sorts of questions. Contrary to popular opinion that this is a parent's worst nightmare, these questions are *great!* These early moments provide excellent opportunities to begin your *ongoing* exchange, and I'll be reviewing several ways to comfortably engage your children in conversation in the chapters ahead.

Being open to your child's curiosity and questions creates a natural rhythm for your communication. Not all sensitive conversations will take place where and when you expect them to—so be prepared to be honest, open, and loving, whether you're in a grocery store, at a baseball game, or kissing your child good night. And if you don't know the answers to his questions—no problem! These are perfect opportunities for you to be honest with your child about your own lack of knowledge and to state the need to research the subject and get it right. (Actually, one of the nicest benefits of parenting is that when you're in a teaching role, you get another chance to sharpen up on what you didn't get down solid the first time around.) By working to make things clear, you also show that sex is an important issue and that you're still learning, too, while engaging in an honest relationship with your growing child. In the following chapters, I'll offer clear advice concerning your body language, the setting, and useful materials that "set the scene." First, let's talk about the details of your relationship with your child.

Developing the Relationship

As the conversation develops with age, you'll obviously need to confront issues of increasing difficulty. If you felt self-conscious about some of your responses during the exercise about your Sexual Values or just the General Information Quiz, then it's useful to recognize your discomfort sooner rather than later and understand that if left unresolved, these feelings may affect how you talk with your child about sex. If you convey discomfort, embarrassment, or anxiety, your child will learn that the subject (whether it's menstruation or homosexuality) is uncomfortable, and may avoid sharing concerns with you.

Of course, bonds don't grow overnight. Nor do they multiply exponentially. Learning how to talk openly about sensitive material requires time and attention, but doing so secures and strengthens these parent-child bonds.

It's the little one-on-one things that make your child feel close to you—things that become special traditions, creating powerful connections that let your child know that you care. It could be a Saturday run to the donut shop, a regular walk at the neighborhood pond or park, or a drive—just the two of you. These times that you spend one-on-one with your child are incredibly valuable for maintaining communication.

Tom Hanks: The Importance of Parents' Involvement in a Kid's Life

I've interviewed Tom Hanks on several occasions. One of the most surprising facts about one of Hollywood's nicest guys is the lack of parental support he had while growing up.

From a very early age, my parents never really communicated to me what was going on in the dynamic between them . . . My mother moved away from our home when I was 4 years old . . . My father, through all of his marriages, never, ever sat me down and told me how much he either loved or did not love the women he was married to, or shared with me the problems that he was going through. So I was just constantly attempting to cope before I really learned how to cope. I would go through some brand of self-medicating process: becoming very involved in something like going to church or making sure that my calendar was filled with something that I was doing every minute.

Some of you may relate to Tom Hanks's past. Alienation from parents can happen to any of us, including our kids. It's important to remember that people all respond differently to situations. Some, like Hanks, overcome a childhood in which they feel unloved to find success in life; for others, the effects of feeling unloved can manifest as diseases or disorders. That's why it's important to be in touch with our kids and find out from *them* if their emotional needs are being met.

When our children were very young, my wife and I began developing rituals to assure that both of us bonded with our children as individuals. Here are a few examples from my experience to help you envision what you could do with your son or daughter.

A night out on the town. Spending a night out alone with each child a few times a year has been a regular activity since my kids were toddlers. This allows me to share in the particular adventures that bring smiles to their faces, and it also gives us a chance to hear each other's stories and just "hang out." Sometimes I plan a special event, based on their interests, thinking up something that would be fun and new. One particularly special night my 6-year-old daughter dressed up for a "princess evening," for which I was her date. We went out to a museum, had a nice dinner, then attended a ballet. In contrast, catching a college hockey game is often first choice on my son's wish list. The combination of front row seats, hot dogs and ice cream, and rooting and hollering for our team makes his special night complete. No matter what we do—and we try to make it different each time—what really matters is making genuine contact and enjoying time together.

A "Daddy Night." This means regularly setting aside time for each child following family dinner, time where we either throw around the football, go biking, or "check out" the mall and talk. Afterward, we may watch a film together—just the two of us—with special consideration given to a fun and artery-clogging dessert. We talk about the film and its message, but usually end up having a conversation that gives me an idea of how my kid is making sense of life.

Like most parents, every day I ask my kids about their day's experiences—their schoolwork, homework, updates, and activities. However, getting to the recesses of deeper feelings requires sharing quality time. I recall that when one of my daughters was 7, she would usually give favorable reports about her day, but on our long walks around the pond she'd share her more vulnerable feelings, telling me about times when she may have felt hurt or disappointed by others. On one occasion she was initially quite chipper and upbeat, but when I asked about the boys in her class, she disclosed her sadness with large tears, describing how she no longer wanted to play with a boy whose company she had enjoyed in previous years because he was "saying bad things and not being as nice as he had been before." This was a story about a relationship and people in her life that she really needed to share and understand. Without quality time together, that wouldn't have been easy.

Special weekend. In addition to family vacations, each year I plan a weekend trip, one for each child. The purpose of these times, again, is to attune to their heart and soul—to pay more attention to my children as individuals. Because it's the two of us far away from the full clan, personal reflections invariably come up, whether it's a problem at school, reminiscing over funny old stories, or just plain old gossip. Once when I had to go to Philadelphia for business, I brought my fifth-grade daughter so that we could enjoy a weekend in that historical city and have some personal time. By spending time with her in a setting different from our hometown, I got to see her in a new light. How does she manage difficult people or situations? And how does she respond to people who see the world differently from us?

Special moments. I also carry out general "special moments." Sometimes I build these around school or sports activities, but other times I and one of my children do something just for the two of us when shopping or catching a film that we like together. However, it's not about the event, it's about the connection. How and when do you make space for your special moments?

Such relationship-building events are ways for both dads and moms to create intimate time with their kids and to ensure that kids have space, time, and the comfort level for the spontaneous conversations that are often the most important.

It's important to remember, however, that special events do not replace or trump the precious daily interactions that we have with our children. Ultimately, it's our everyday behavior that will remind our kids that we're there for them. Some of the best day-to-day things we can do include family dinners, bedtime stories, bedtime chats, and hugs throughout the day. What's most important is the eye-to-eye contact that confirms for our kids that they are 110 percent worthy of our unwavering attention.

So let's say you're a single parent with limited time and money. Certainly time and quality of time are the most important factors. The connection is the priority, not the event. It's not about being able to afford special events; the experience occurs through being *with* our kids and making the time to find out who they are. Placing emphasis on your connection is the issue in question: do your kids know that they have access to you and that they are the priority—not only when a rule or limit is broken, but because they are the lights of your life?

Such intimate moments of connection confirm to your children that they are some of the most important people in your universe. You know they've developed this particular confidence when you see the love and affection that they reciprocate. By establishing such deep roots, your children feel a strong sense of security that will pay off in big ways throughout life—including feeling comfortable speaking to you about the most intimate matters they encounter. It's thus your own experience of general intimacy with your kids that leads to good, comfortable talks about sex.

Each of my children, much like your own, I'm sure, communicates in an individual way. As a result, each one has an individual way of handling my trust and openness about all topics, including sex. While my son will introduce any topic to me out of the clear blue sky in the middle of the day, my older daughter often chooses to write down her wishes, fears, dreams, and uncertainties in notes that she shares with me—regardless of whether or not these thoughts conform to mine. And then there's my youngest, who treasures our private moments, which she calls "our juiciest/goosiest time," to tell me her insights, anxieties, joys, and sorrows—moving from crocodile tears to broad smiles as if flipping through channels on the TV set. Whatever their way of expression, what matters is that the foundation has been laid so that they can tell me what's on their minds, allowing us to deal with whatever it is *together*.

Now, how about you? What have you done to lay a strong foundation for your relationship with your child? What else can you do to strengthen this vital bond?

Parents express care in their own ways; each lets their children know that they love them according to their own style. Whether it is through certain events, activities, or perhaps special gifts, parents attune to their children in unique ways. Since every parent-child relationship is distinct, take a moment now to complete Exercise 2.1. In this exercise you will reflect on *your* relationship with *your* child, noting the ways that you have established, built, and nurtured this relationship, and the ways in which you can continue to improve.

Exercise 2.1: Strengthening Your Bonds and Connections

If you have established a special connection with your child, list below the methods you have used.

Special words or phrases: _____

Special activities: _____

Special events: _____

How can you build onto these connections to develop what you've established? List connecting events (special times for heart-to-heart sharing, activities that support your sharing and connection) that you plan, taking into consideration how these might evolve over time.

1. _____

2. _____

3. _____

How can you nurture activities that support your closer engagement with one another, to ensure that your bond is kindled and maintained?

1. _____

2. _____

3. _____

How do you know that you are making progress in your relationship? (How can you tell? What are the signs? What are your measures?)

1. _____

2. _____

3. _____

Unfortunately, it sometimes feels as if there's not enough time for what's most important in life; we get bogged down by 101 other things that seem to require our immediate attention. Beneath it all, however, we know that nothing is more important than our children. Like anything else, it takes time and commitment to stay close to our kids. Check in with yourself after completing Exercise 2.1—maybe it's time to get out your calendar to schedule your next date with your child.

Getting Down to Business: Some Conversation Pointers

Whether you're talking to your child about school, outer space, or a recent crush, to pursue meaningful conversations you need to have a genuine relationship. Establishing a solid connection is the basis for really talking about sex. Here are some ways to make both you and your child feel more comfortable, and to ensure a positive, two-way conversation.

Start on their level. Before initiating a conversation, think about how you might engage your child's interest. What's on his or her mind? How does sexual information apply to his or her life now? Try to think of whether your child is interested in a magazine/book/movie/TV show that's relevant to what you want to talk about.

Avoid preaching/teaching. Be *with* your son or daughter. Don't lecture. The more they talk and share, the more they are involved. Attune; listen actively.

Avoid judgments; emphasize understanding. Your criticisms of others may be experienced as actually being indictments of your child. If you feel judgmental, talk about the reasons for your position.

Talk about the two of you. Stay with how you feel and how your child feels. Try to stay on topic while listening and following the train of his or her thoughts— and don't talk about others who aren't in the room (whether it's your child's teacher or friends, or even your spouse).

Attune to feelings over ideas. For example, while trying to understand why your son or daughter wants to wear pants that expose their rear ends (a hint: social rewards for wearing "in" clothes), you may need to take time out and return to the unresolved topic later, rather than arguing with them as they try to leave the house looking half-dressed. Don't create a standoff. Rather than making a final policy decision right then and there, simply agree that you'll discuss the issue later but for now, as you have concerns, he or she will have to find something else to wear. There's always another day to sort out the issue. Remember, we don't want to win the battle but lose the war.

Read body language. Establish patterns for mutually respectful interactions, like eye contact and speaking respectfully. If your kids' bodies look like they are walking out of the room while their mouths are talking, open up a conversation about their feelings during the discussion and try to address those first. If your child looks like he wants to escape and a controversy's brewing, it's important to go beyond the words and get to the feelings that are fueling the fire.

Put into words what you are hearing, and ask if you got it right. It's communication; it's setting up signposts for your conversation and making sure that they are accurate.

Communication requires that we express what we want and that the other person understand this. It's actually quite a complicated process—and its failure is the root of all kinds of family battles. As parents, we are responsible for checking that our intentions are having the anticipated impact. For example, if we dissect a conversation between you and your child regarding choice of clothes, we find that there are many feelings, issues, and messages at stake. Rather than turning these complex and important interactions into an all-or-nothing situation, you and your child each need to take time to sort out the pieces—from your love for each other to the other issues that may make the two of you sound like you're not family members but opponents in a war.

As you are reading this, you may be wondering if you'll be successful in these conversations with your kids. It seems like so much to deal with! While we've begun to address these issues, don't worry if you don't feel fully prepared quite yet because there are still many more tips to come. What's in store will help you effectively communicate your positive intentions and strengthen your bond with your child. In Chapter 3, we take the concept of attuning a step further, and offer practical suggestions for how to deal with unexpected questions. We'll also practice getting calm and centered before talking to kids about sex.

THREE

Going Public with Privates

There is hardly anyone whose sexual life, if it were
broadcast, could not fill the world at large with
surprise and horror.

—W. SOMERSET MAUGHAM

Danny: Getting Honest Answers

Twelve-year-old Danny came home from school one day and, upon seeing
his mother in the kitchen, asked, "Mom, what's '69'?" Shocked by the question, she anxiously replied, "What did you say?"

"69! Do you know what it is?"

"Where did you hear that?" she asked, visibly distressed. Like many parents of her generation, Danny's mother did not view sex as an acceptable topic
of conversation. Her son's question roused deeply ingrained anxieties.

Getting the message that his question wasn't acceptable and that his mother
wasn't going to answer it, Danny said, "That's okay" and walked away.

Later that evening, Danny went to his older sister's room and asked if she
could tell him what 69 meant. Her eyes grew big as she exclaimed, "What?!"
Seeing how uneasy his question made her, Danny decided not to ask again and
instead retreated to his room to contemplate the question alone.

That evening, when Danny's friend Steve came over, they speculated on the
meaning of "the numbers" that they heard tossed around on the playground but

didn't understand. Danny remembered that his older brother, Dominick, was coming home from college the next morning. Danny knew that his brother would tell him.

After the excitement over Dominick's return had died down, Danny wandered into his brother's room. Following some small talk, he at last posed his burning question: "Dominick, what does 69 mean?"

"Wow! Where did you hear about that?" Dominick said.

"From a friend. What does it mean? No one will tell me. Is it bad?" Danny replied.

"Bad? No, not necessarily. Hey, why don't we look it up in the dictionary?" Dominick pulled out a dictionary and flipped to the word, then read definitions aloud to Danny. Following explanations of the number, he read, "Slang (vulgar)—simultaneous oral-genital sexual activity between two partners."

"Oh, now I get it. Whoa!" Danny said, though he still felt a bit perplexed. He responded, "I could see why Mom wigged out . . ."

"Well, bud, it's kind of adult sexual stuff. Don't worry, it'll make sense as you get older," Dominick calmly replied. As Danny started to leave the room, Dominick called after him, "Hey, Danny, if you come across any other questions like that, just let me know, okay?" Danny turned around and nodded, smiling. Finally, he felt like he had found a clear answer.

As a parent, how would you have responded to Danny? Would you have reacted like his mother did—shocked and unwilling to respond? Does his mother sound like *your* mother or father?

We can respond in many different ways to almost any question, and we often respond nervously when those questions have to do with sex. As we've seen, parents sometimes reply to their child's questions in a black-and-white manner, responding with whatever the parent thinks the child should know rather than attuning to what the child is actually asking. Whatever you do, as a parent you don't want to shut down communication with your child, especially about such important matters. Your child will inevitably find the answers from someone else, so instead of giving a hurried, flippant, careless, or reactionary answer, use the question as an opportunity to better understand your child and make an honest connection.

Responding in a Balanced Way

In this section, we'll review a chart that I call the Balance of Attunement. This chart can be helpful in gauging how you have responded in the past to questions from your children about sex as well as in helping you move toward more useful responses in the future.

Think back to Danny's story. His mother offered no answer to his question, missing out on an opportunity to connect with her child and impart knowledge to him from a safe source. Of course, sex education is not just about flooding kids with information. One appropriate response might have been telling Danny that 69 refers to adult sexuality, which might have satisfied his curiosity for the moment. His mother also could have asked if he wanted or needed more information. Communicating openly and honestly about these issues requires attuned responses to your child's questions so that the child can make sense of potentially confusing and difficult information.

It's reasonable to say that many answers would have been appropriate for Danny, depending on how far his curiosity or interest reached. This is where the parent plays a vital role. No one knows better than you what your kids respond

"Dad, can we talk about sex?"

to best or how they uniquely process information. You want to respond to their questions with accurate information while allowing them to feel comfortable talking with you. The Balance of Attunement chart below can help you craft a loving, informative response that is appropriate for your child. It groups types of responses around core qualities of listening that will nurture your connection with your child. Developing this sense of attunement will strengthen your communications about sex and improve your overall connection with your child.

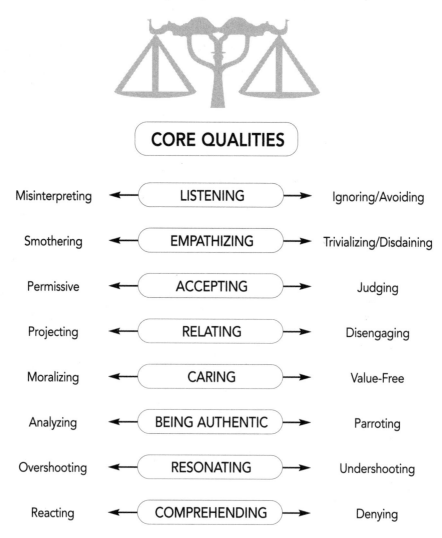

Misinterpreting	←	LISTENING	→	Ignoring/Avoiding
Smothering	←	EMPATHIZING	→	Trivializing/Disdaining
Permissive	←	ACCEPTING	→	Judging
Projecting	←	RELATING	→	Disengaging
Moralizing	←	CARING	→	Value-Free
Analyzing	←	BEING AUTHENTIC	→	Parroting
Overshooting	←	RESONATING	→	Undershooting
Reacting	←	COMPREHENDING	→	Denying

Figure 3.1 Balance of Attunement

The Balance of Attunement shows that the closer your response is to the core qualities in the middle—avoiding either extreme—the closer you are to attuning to your child. You can use this model to guide yourself in answering your child's questions about sex, or any complex subject, with an open and fair response.

Parents like to think that their kids can talk with them about anything. But the depth of those conversations depends in large part on how parents respond to the questions their kids pose. Let's take a look at some ways of initially responding to the sample question, "What's 69?"

On the scale between misinterpreting the question and just ignoring or avoiding it:

1.

	Negative Extremes	
MISINTERPRETING		IGNORING/AVOIDING
A. "So now you want to be cool and talk about sex, huh?"		A. "Why don't you go play with your friends?"
B. "You mean, the number after 68?"		B. "Go ask your father."

Positive Responses

LISTENING

A. "Can you tell me what you think it means?"

B. "What have you heard about that word?"

On the scale between smothering your child with "TMI"—too much informa-tion—and trivializing the question as insignificant or disdaining it:

2.

	Negative	
SMOTHERING	Extremes	TRIVIALIZING/DISDAINING

SMOTHERING

A. "Let me tell you about the first time I discovered 69."

B. "It's one of the most amazing things to experience!"

Negative Extremes

TRIVIALIZING/ DISDAINING

A. "It's nothing."

B. "Shut your mouth! What a horrible thing to say to your mother."

Positive Responses

EMPATHIZING

A. "Now, there's an interesting number. It sounds like that's sparked your curiosity."

B. "Sit down for a bit, and let's talk about it."

On the scale between being inappropriately permissive and repressively judg-mental:

3.

Negative Extremes

PERMISSIVE

A. "It's great that you're learning things like that. Soon you'll be a real man!"

B. "Sounds like you're ready for the facts of life. Let me show you this video I have."

JUDGING

A. "Now, *that's* the wrong question for a nice person like you to be asking."

B. "Why would a son of mine ask a question like that?"

Positive Responses

ACCEPTING

A. "I'm really glad you came to me with that question."

B. "It makes sense that you might begin wondering about words like that."

On the scale between projecting your own fantasies or fears onto your child, or disengaging completely from the question:

4.

	Negative	
PROJECTING	Extremes	DISENGAGING

PROJECTING

A. "You know, when I went to school my friends talked about that too. In fact, I remember . . ."

B. "I figured you were thinking about that kind of thing."

DISENGAGING

A. "Yes, that's an interesting question, isn't it? But not one we're going to talk about."

B. "That's funny you'd be asking about that. You'll find out someday."

Positive Responses

RELATING

A. "I'm glad you thought to ask me. I'd be happy to talk with you about it."

B. "Let's check it out in some books together."

On the scale between making the question immoral or totally mundane:

5.

Negative Extremes

MORALIZING

A. "That's not a very proper thing to discuss."

B. "We don't talk about that kind of thing in our religion."

VALUE-FREE

A. "It's just a sexual behavior."

B. "With time it will all make sense."

Positive Responses

CARING

A. "Let's figure out what this means together and figure out why it's getting so much attention on the playground."

B. "Now that's a question we'll want to spend time making some sense of."

On the scale between being overly analytical and just echoing the question back without answering:

6.

Negative Extremes

ANALYZING

A. "Hmm . . . what must be going on for you to be asking that question?"

B. "Well, that's a complicated part of human sexuality that helps bring adults to orgasm."

PARROTING

A. "Well, what is sex?"

B. "Ooh, Danny wants to know what 69 is."

Positive Responses

BEING AUTHENTIC

A. "Wow. I wasn't prepared for that question just now, but I want to see if I can help you understand it."

B. "Remember when we talked about the differences between girls and boys and how we all mature into adults? This is one of the details about adults and sexual pleasure."

On the scale between giving too much information and not enough information:

7.

OVERSHOOTING	Negative Extremes	UNDERSHOOTING
A. "69 is a practice that gives adults pleasure and is a big part of sex for adults."		A. "It's a number for adults."
B. "Well, it sounds like you're really ready to know everything about sex."		B. "It's a detail you don't have to worry about yet."

Positive Responses

RESONATING

A. "I see that this has captured your attention, and it sounds like we should figure it out together."

B. "It sounds like the boys at school are investigating new territory about sex. Why don't we try to make sense of this together?"

On the scale between overreacting to the question and denying the question:

8.

REACTING

Negative Extremes

DENYING

A. An emotional reaction like the response of the mother in this story: "What did you say?" "Where did you hear that number?"

B. "Who told you to say that?!"

A. "It doesn't mean anything."

B. "I'm gonna pretend I never heard that word come out of your mouth."

Positive Responses

COMPREHENDING

A. "I know that this is a time when you're starting to ask about sex. Do you have any ideas about how to start us on this one?"

B. "This is difficult for someone your age to understand. But let's give it our best shot to make sense of it for you."

I hope these examples give you some ideas about how to begin to construct centered, clear, and appropriate responses to your children's questions. Although we used the example of Danny's question about 69, the Balance of Attunement can be used to frame responses to any questions about sex. You may want to try practicing positive, balanced responses. Write down some questions that make you a little nervous, then practice what your responses might be. That way, when you get an unexpected question, you're not scrambling to figure out what to say or how to say it in an open and loving manner.

In light of all the sample responses I've just presented for responding to Danny, you're probably wondering how to know which is the most appropriate at any given time. Since your response is part of a dialogue, its shape and content will depend on the direction and tone of Danny's question. Danny's brother's response is sensitive and attuned: most importantly, he accepts Danny's question as serious and legitimate and accepts Danny's right to be curious about this topic. Dominick offers assistance for finding the correct answer in an open and accepting way. If I were posed the same question by my own 12-year-old son, I'd probably explain that adult sexuality involves sex for pleasure and 69 refers to a way in which some adults give each other pleasure—and check his reaction to see how interested he is to pursue the topic further.

The key question here is: how much does Danny *want* to know? As this type of question comes at a transitional place in a kid's development, it may be a legitimate query that requires either a detailed discussion *or* just a general framework: that 69 involves sex. Flooding him with information may be overwhelming and counterproductive. Kids on the playground often make flip comments to demonstrate their power and make an impact on others. Thus, responding to your child's confusion over those words requires classifying the extent of his interest and not forcing too much or the wrong kind of information on him.

While questions like Danny's pop up out of nowhere, your response may initiate a whole talk. Practicing attuned responses by using the Balance of Attunement can help you center yourself in preparation and avoid letting your emotions be stirred toward responses that are anxious or critical rather than calm and effective.

Exercise 3.1 offers a simple way to review your responsiveness to complex questions about sex based on the various core areas of listening. Imagine your child asking a difficult question, even one more complicated than "What's 69?" In this exercise, you will write down your responses and then rate them on different scales (corresponding to the Balance of Attunement in Figure 3.1) to see what your responses resemble most. Which approach are you most likely to take? An extreme response on either end of the scale? A centered response? Something in between? Take a minute and find out.

Exercise 3.1: Balance of Attunement

Write down your actual or imagined responses to difficult questions about sex, such as "Is sex ever okay before marriage?" or "Do you and Dad ever do 69?"

_____

_____

_____

Now plot where your responses fall in these eight categories of the core qualities of attunement.

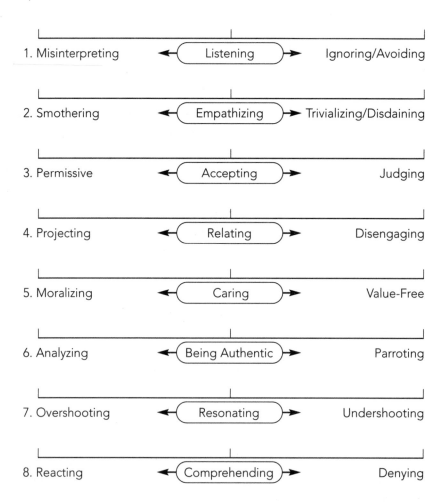

1. Misinterpreting   ← Listening →   Ignoring/Avoiding

2. Smothering   ← Empathizing → Trivializing/Disdaining

3. Permissive   ← Accepting →   Judging

4. Projecting   ← Relating →   Disengaging

5. Moralizing   ← Caring →   Value-Free

6. Analyzing   ← Being Authentic →   Parroting

7. Overshooting   ← Resonating →   Undershooting

8. Reacting   ← Comprehending →   Denying

If you find your responses in Exercise 3.1 are on the far right or far left of center more than one-third of the time, think about why you've chosen those particular responses and how you could provide more centered, attuned comments. Discuss this exercise with your spouse or partner: Are your responses similar? Do you find that you take the same approach, or do you come from different—even opposite—perspectives? Does your spouse or partner agree with the rating you gave yourself for your responses?

Exercise 3.1 provides an opportunity to consider which areas can use a little extra attention in your parenting. Practicing with hypothetical questions will keep you from totally being caught off guard when your child approaches you with a tough question out of the blue one day.

After locating your parenting style in this exercise, see if you can recognize what's going on with the adults in the following story. Think about which elements of the Balance of Attunement are at play in the story. What would you do in the same situation?

Lana and Billy: Just Curious

Six-year-old Lana and 5-year-old Billy were visiting their grandparents' house for the weekend. Following lunch, their grandmother brought them to the spare bedroom and nestled each into one of the twin beds in the room for an afternoon nap.

While the youngsters were settling down, they started to talk about their "pee pees." They knew that each other's were different but didn't really know how or why this was so. Lana asked Billy if he wanted to come see hers, so Billy went over to her bed, and they got ready to show each other their privates. Just then their grandmother walked into the room, and seeing Billy in Lana's bed, asked accusingly, "What are you two doing?"

Before the children could explain, she continued, "You should never look at someone else's privates." Lana and Billy were mortified—not only had she caught them, but she knew exactly what they were doing. Seeing their normally gentle grandmother so distraught, Billy asked, "Are you going to call the police?"

"No," their grandmother answered, and as she turned to leave the room she said sternly, "No one should ever hear about this."

The next day, Lana and Billy's mother came to pick them up. After getting back to their house, she called them into the kitchen, sat them down at the table, and told them that she was aware of what they had done and that they should never do "such a thing" again.

Like their grandmother had done the day before, their mother also avoided going into detail about what she knew they had done or why it was bad. Instead, she simply portrayed the whole incident—and, by extension, the kids them-selves—as wrong and bad.

When the children's father got home from work, both Lana and Billy were summoned to the living room for yet another reprimand. Shaking from dread about what would happen, they listened as their father told them that what they had done "was very wrong," and that "this must not happen again." Lana and Billy nodded, wishing that the whole situation would just go away.

I think you'll agree that all three of the adults' responses were far from cen-tered. Not one of these adults was attuned to the feelings of the children. The adults were probably responding to a situation that was only really occurring in their imagination! Lana and Billy weren't acting out sexually—they were merely exploring their bodies and their differences, which is appropriate for their ages.

Children are fascinated by discovery—and discovery about their body parts should not fall into a category of taboo because of our own misplaced moralizing. What was actually an opportunity for teaching and attuning to their children's interests became a lesson for Lana and Billy about how bad it is to try to under-stand the differences between a boy's body and a girl's body. The adults' anxieties about how to manage the scenario caused them to shut down the subject for their children. Now Lana and Billy have received a powerful message about their bodies and their sexuality: that they are shameful, wrong, and better kept a secret. Unless such a message is reversed through positive experience, just imagine how difficult it will be for these children to feel at ease sexually and to develop healthy relationships with others or with their parents when it comes to sex.

Thou Shalt, Not "Thou Shalt Not"

Associating sex with sin or being bad sends a confusing and unhealthy mes-sage for kids. Danny gets the sense from his parents that 69 is bad, and Lana and Billy get the same message about their bodies and sexuality.

"Thou shalt not" is the wrong way for a parent to begin a conversation about sex. The Ten Commandments conjure up feelings of strict authority—this is not the tone you want to set as a parent as you begin the delicate conversation on sex, which is a central part of life.

The Powerful Impact of Early Experiences Involving Sex

An elderly gentleman told me a poignant, amusing story about his early introduction to sexuality. Ironically, it happened through the church. When he was 11, his mother made him go to confession. Though he was young and innocent, a stern priest suspiciously asked him whether he'd ever touched himself "down there," looking toward the boy's groin. The little boy was shaken and insisted that he hadn't. The priest told him, with a grim look, never to do anything like that. The boy left the church overwhelmed with guilt about what he hadn't understood. Childish curiosity led him to go home and start to experiment with the behavior the priest had warned him about. Having discovered how much he enjoyed exactly what the priest had condemned, he continued it and never returned to confession. After the man shared his story with me, I asked how he made sense of the incident. His answer showed that he had thought long and hard about the encounter:

> While religion pretty much controls the market on giving answers to life's big questions, religion's rules about sexuality are just an attempt to control a physical drive that supposedly competes with a spiritual, religious drive. I think a lot of times, religion doesn't win.

What can we learn from this story? When we shut doors through our imposing manners and words, we close ourselves off from discussion with our kids, but that doesn't mean the doors to the behavior we're addressing are completely shut. Sometimes we actually create more curiosity and confusion because of our own anxiety. In this particular case, the admonished boy ignored the strictures of the priest and ultimately created his own philosophy about religion's fear of sexuality. Whether or not he correctly interpreted the motives of the priest, the point is that the boy became disengaged from both the clergyman and the larger system. To keep our own kids engaged, we need to take a deep breath before talking to them and make sure that we're tuning in to their concerns, rather than speaking to our own anxieties.

Of course, this is not to say that personal, moral, and ethical values should be left out of discussions about sexual behavior. But our conversations should start by increasing understanding and encouraging dialogue about positive values, not by limiting our children's understanding to conclusions based on our values. Commandments, rigid rules, and harsh punishments tend to inspire rebellion, creating anxieties in children regarding sexuality and their parents' willingness to hear their concerns in a loving and open way. The "Thou Shalt Not" attitude does not help build self-esteem or encourage positive attitudes about sexuality in our children.

As an alternative, consider approaches that strengthen your child's self-esteem by giving clear guidance. The purpose of personal values is not to restrict experience, but to give children a framework for making decisions that guide them toward reaching their goals. In the following chapters, we will consider specific examples of how to offer loving guidance so that your children develop sexual behavior that relates their values to their experiences and actions in meaningful ways.

The Question of Boundaries

At this point, it is necessary to raise the subject of boundaries. Boundaries involve respecting the privacy of others—including your children!—and recognizing that privates are also, for the most part, private. Privacy is an important aspect of sexuality through all human development, and as parents, we need to allow our children to have that safe space.

Sex and Privacy: Drawing the Line

Is there anything more private—and yet more public—than sex? People talk about sex all the time: in the news, in advertisements, in casual conversation. Yet what people actually do behind closed doors or between the sheets is often shrouded in mystery.

Is it wrong to want privacy when it comes to issues of sex? Many people might jump to the conclusion that anyone who keeps their sex life private must have something to hide. But privacy and secrecy shouldn't be confused—a desire for privacy isn't necessarily indicative of skeletons (or worse!) in the closet. It's important to see a desire for privacy as a desire for respect: respect for every individual's boundaries.

Imagine the following scene: while cleaning her 14-year-old daughter Sandy's room, Janet finds a hidden diary. Curiosity wins out over conscience, and Janet leafs through the little book. Janet is shocked to learn that Sandy has been writing about her crushes on both boys and girls, and she is disappointed that Sandy has never come to her to express these feelings. While Janet is reading the diary, Sandy walks in and bursts into angry sobs when she realizes what her mom is reading. This is undeniably a tense situation.

Janet could react in a number of positive ways. She could simply apologize for disrespecting her daughter's privacy. She also could acknowledge her daughter's feelings of hurt and betrayal and make a stronger effort to reopen lines of communication in the future. But instead, Janet reacts like many of us might in this situation: she becomes defensive and begins arguing with Sandy, only deepening the divide between mother and daughter.

As a parent, it's important to treat your kids' desire for privacy in their developing sexuality with the same respect that you'd want them to have for your sex life. That said, it's also vital to make sure your kids know that your respect for their privacy isn't a mark of disinterest in their lives. Rather, it's essential that your kids feel comfortable talking to you about sex if and when they want to.

This is not to say that, upon finding your children "playing doctor," you should simply close the door and declare "children at play." But you don't want to frighten them either, as happened for poor Lana and Billy. Instead, try to help them to make sense of the things they are exploring through their normal, healthy curiosity. Such support will go miles toward helping them not to be ashamed of sex. An incident like Lana and Billy's would, in fact, be a fitting moment for gently explaining some basic anatomy. The bottom line is, although sexuality involves privacy, we need to help our children understand appropriate boundaries for respecting each other's privacy and avoid making sexuality taboo.

Secrecy versus Privacy

To many, it makes sense that sex is kept as a deep secret. Because the topic of sex is physically and emotionally sensitive, people of all ages are cautious when discussing it. Many people feel uncomfortable discussing such intimate subjects, preferring to keep their thoughts and feelings about sex to themselves. This logic may be what contributed to the overreaction of Billy and Lana's family—because they saw sexuality as deeply sensitive, they did not want their children to be delving into it before they could understand it.

However, the adults' reactions introduce an important difference between secrecy and privacy. A secret is something that we can't share, even if we want to. Privacy, however, is a natural and dynamic boundary established between people based on respect. When the lines between secrecy and privacy are blurred, kids end up thinking sex is something they should never talk about, rather than realizing that it is something that *should* be talked about and explored privately with those they trust. Sex does not need to be secretive, but it is, naturally, private. We can help our children learn this boundary by establishing it and respecting it in our relationships with them.

Thinking about secrecy versus privacy helps us clarify some other possible responses to kids like Lana and Billy. After discovering the children engaged in exploring their bodies, an appropriate context should be found for explaining to the preschoolers about their body parts, perhaps with the help of some books or pictures. Boundaries can also be discussed here. You might say, "These are private parts, and there are rules about privacy to protect us. No one else should touch your privates; that's why we call them privates!" You might go on to add that it's not appropriate to show your privates to others, unless there's a special reason, such as during a medical exam—when a parent is also in the room.

Yet let's not forget that little kids have sexual interests. They find pleasure in touching their privates. Yet these are their privates—not publics! Therefore we can explain to our kids that when we touch our privates we need privacy—like when we're washing ourselves in the bathroom or dressing ourselves in our bedrooms. We need to be clear and open about how sexuality develops over time. We can damage normal, healthy growth by being unclear and too secretive about sexuality and body exploration.

Boundaries Between Ourselves and Our Children

Just as we don't want to reveal all the private details of our sexual lives, neither should our children have to reveal all of theirs. Parenting is not about controlling your children's every move.

On the other end of the spectrum, appropriate boundaries can be crossed by giving too much information. When too much information is given, we push our children into a level of sexual understanding for which they're just not ready. Answering the question "What's 69?" with a detailed explanation appropriate for a high school student—oral sex play, intercourse, and orgasm—is way more than a 12-year-old needs to know. When this happens, often the adult's needs or issues are being unfairly imposed on the child. Boundary issues can sometimes come up when parents are unaware of their own secret interest to live through their children. Unconscious behaviors like these may harm our children.

Maintaining Appropriate Boundaries

Exposure to sexual materials such as books, videos, or props used by their parents can distort kids' natural learning process about sex. Children are not equipped to handle all of the truths of their parents' sexual behavior, as shown in a story told by Ned, one of the participants in the Survey on Sex Education:

The most difficult aspect was finding my parents' stash of porn, watching it, getting very excited by it, but also becoming very confused by the emotions and feelings I was having . . . To this day I have problems with knowing what is true intimacy and love. When

> *I watch porn now it makes me very comfortable . . . It is something that I probably could have an addiction problem with, not a sex addiction, but an addiction to fill a void, a space of loneliness because that is what I did when I was 8 years old.*
>
> Because Ned discovered sex alone, without guidance or real meaning, he grew up with tough, conflicted emotions and ideas about sex. Now, as an adult, Ned has problems connecting sex and love, as pornography is more comforting to him than genuine intimacy.
>
> This doesn't mean that parents should hide sexual feelings or displays of physical affection. But parents need to keep some aspects of their sex life (particularly magazines, movies, and other paraphernalia) carefully guarded to allow their children to learn about sex at their own pace.
>
> We should be vigilant about giving our kids the chance to learn about sex in the context of open, honest, and loving dialogues, rather than through a medium that may distort the healthy messages that we want to convey.

If you're wondering how much is too much information, don't worry. We'll cover normal development of sexuality in the next chapter. For now, let's look more at what can happen when parents violate a boundary by projecting their needs onto their children.

Parents Living Vicariously through Children

Children are particularly susceptible to tuning in to the unconscious, unfulfilled desires of parents who live them out through a vision of how *they* want their kids to be in life. Kiddie beauty contests, for example, can significantly dramatize adult aspirations as children play out the competitive needs of their parents. Here we find pint-sized toddlers flaunting makeup more than a decade before their friends will. Pageants and modeling can become a disturbing masquerade including hair extensions, false teeth, and even plastic surgery. Teen models get Botox injections, and even little boys act out with male machismo. What can we expect of these children who are not only prematurely pushed into adolescence but introduced to sexualized behaviors they can't possibly understand? And what can a parent who has broken these boundaries with their children say when the child acts out sexually?

I've observed moms during figure skating competitions coaching their young daughters with earphones, telling them when to turn, how to jump, and when to smile as they approach the judge's booth. And I've seen fathers obsessively coaching their young children to achieve levels of athleticism that they themselves have never met, degrading and berating their sons at hockey and football games. My son told me that some of his teammates get paid for doing well in athletics, and others get hit when things don't go well. These vignettes highlight a spectrum of inappropriate parental expectations and demands that each of us needs to keep in check as we guide our children to live *their* lives.

This is not to say that every parent of a child model or athlete is in error—they may be supporting their child's interests. However, we have to be aware of our own motives, which can range from living out our parental fantasies to the expectation that modeling or sports will pay for college. We must manage our motives to permit our kids to live their own lives.

Our job as parents is to act as guiding lights for our children. We must model appropriate actions and support our children as they follow *their* paths—whatever those may be and not our own. We must protect and guide them in the best way we know so that they choose to thrive in their individual, authentic ways. This is especially important when it comes to sexuality. In the following example, a mother lives out a sexual issue vicariously through her child and fails to help her daughter balance independence and dependence in her relationships.

Sylvia and Laurie: Living Vicariously

Sylvia could not have children of her own, so she and her husband adopted a 3-year-old girl named Laurie. Because Laurie was adopted, Sylvia worried that she might not be one of "the popular kids." To counter this fear, Sylvia began dressing Laurie a couple years ahead of her age and worked hard to ensure that she never felt lonely or left out. Sylvia did her best to make sure that Laurie was always in the "in group" and "in the know."

Sylvia had grown up with parents who were prudish and overly modest when it came to sex; she had felt left out of what the "cool" kids did and blamed her parents. Therefore, she made decisions in parenting Laurie that were "progressive" regarding sexuality. She even walked around the house naked and encouraged her husband to lounge around in his underwear. Later in life, Laurie would remember that her parents had explained, "Nakedness is a sign that we're comfortable enough with ourselves to be in our natural state," and "Sexuality is nothing to be ashamed of." This had a definite impact on Laurie's understanding of boundaries.

When Laurie was in third grade, Sylvia arranged for her eighth birthday party to be a dance. She explained to the other parents that this would be "cute" and would "kind of get them going." However, she didn't understand why no boys actually showed up for the party (as dances are usually the furthest things from the interests of 8-year-old-boys).

By the time Laurie was in fifth grade, she took pride in leading all-girl discussions about her kissing fantasies and experiences. She once criticized a seventh-grade boy she was "seeing" for not knowing how to kiss, saying, "Instead of kissing me on the lips, the idiot stuck his tongue in my mouth!"

"Everyone knows you kiss with your lips, not your tongue!"

Although Laurie thought she was the progressive member in her pack, she had never been introduced to French-kissing. Because she was acting out the fantasy her mom had for her, Laurie did not know she was in over her head when it came to sexual involvement.

Sylvia was living vicariously through Laurie. She felt that she had failed socially as a child because of the restrictiveness of her parents, so she was retracing her steps, trying to get it right through her daughter. Paradoxically, instead of resolving the problem of her childhood, she was repeating it. Her parents had failed to tune in to her as a child and had acted out their fears in guiding her. In the same way, Sylvia was guiding Laurie, driven by her own fears, and not attuning to Laurie's needs.

By trying to live vicariously, Sylvia did not honor Laurie's natural development. Crossing the parental boundary and imposing her issues on her daughter had harmful consequences. Rather than finding her own understanding of sexuality, Laurie had been trained to accept her mother's. Encouraging kids to be sexual at a young age can lead to immature and inappropriate sexual behavior, setting them up for more pain by not knowing what's appropriate and what's not. Billy and Lana's elders also violated a boundary by disrespecting their children's natural sexuality. By not knowing how to deal with their own anxieties, they swept the whole issue of sex under the carpet for their children.

These examples show how important it is to attune to your children in a calm and centered way. The Balance of Attunement is a helpful tool for understanding the appropriate answers to your kids' questions. The opening lines we reviewed and practiced in this chapter can help you make it over that bridge between being caught off guard and beginning a conversation as part of an ongoing, authentic exchange with your child.

Of course, there are many shades of gray between the black and white examples I've been giving. But by understanding how to attune to your child, and by getting comfortable with both your and your child's boundaries, you'll be able to maintain an ongoing conversation about sexuality that allows your children to grow into healthy sexual beings. When parents have been actively and appropriately involved from the start, they provide a foundation that helps their children develop healthy, intimate connections of their own.

Part II

Sex on the Table

FOUR

Are They Normal?

If there is anything the nonconformist hates worse than a conformist, it's another nonconformist who doesn't conform to the prevailing standard of nonconformity.

—BILL VAUGHAN

Sometimes it's hard to know what our kids are up to or what to expect from them next. One day we're changing diapers, and the next they're threatening to elope. How do they grow up so fast? What are they really doing when we imagine them still playing with Barbie dolls or Hot Wheels? We tend to think our kids are younger than they actually are. Wishful thinking, perhaps.

This point was driven home for me a few years ago when I picked up my 9-year-old son from a summer ice hockey camp in Canada, his first week away from home. As I approached the camp, my concerns were: Did he get enough sleep? Was he eating well? Had he been homesick?

I soon discovered that his ice buddies had been measuring their flaccid penises and ridiculing the less endowed in the group. Far from innocently missing their mommies, these kids were acting out a machismo well beyond their years—or so I thought.

Their exaggerated, playful posturing gave a 9-year-old spin to something they may have overheard from a big brother or adult as they said things like, "My penis is so big I can hit a hockey puck with it," or "My penis is so big I'll help you out by whacking yours, so yours swells and doesn't look like a Tweety Bird anymore!" My son and I burst into laughter as he told his war stories on

83

the car ride home; we also made the time to flesh out his feelings and discuss the impact of the peer pressure on his privacy. However, this was a wake-up call for me—it was time for me to realize my son was entering a new phase of sexual awareness.

This chapter will help prepare you for what to expect from your children at certain ages: what they probably know about sex and how much you should tell them. Because talking about sex in age-appropriate ways can be tricky, I'll give you an idea of what kinds of questions and actions regarding sexuality you should expect from your children at different ages and how to answer them in a manner that conveys a clear message.

When a young child asks where babies come from, you might simply say, "A baby comes from a mommy and a daddy. When a mommy and a daddy want a baby, they get together and have one." If your child is 4 or 5, that may be enough. If she's 7 or 8, however, she'll need more information. You might say something like, "Both mom and dad help make a new baby. The dad's sperm goes inside to meet the mom's egg, and they make a tiny baby that begins to grow in a special baby-room inside the mommy." Taking into account the limited span of knowledge in most young kids, it's important to keep the answer short and clear. Young kids can't recall lots of facts in a row, so they're not asking for specific details—they just want a reassuringly calm and simple answer that gives them the basics.

As their bodies start developing, most kids have questions about what is normal, why all of these changes are taking place, what they should expect, and the time frame when certain things "should" occur. As your children's body and mind develop, their questions will change—therefore, your answers should change too. As with any subject, you want to respond to your child's questions in a thorough manner.

Some kids will approach their sexual development quite bluntly by asking questions like, "Dad, will my voice ever change?" or "Mom, will my boobs *ever* start growing?"

Some children, on the other hand, will be afraid or too embarrassed to bring anything up with their parents. Some may just feel "too weird." The same is true for parents. Some parents may be attuned and ready to open up a dialogue about sexuality with their children, but others may feel uncomfortable addressing the subject. It's important to develop comfort both for your kids *and* you around this subject as this will help facilitate the open conversation that will help your children understand the changes that are occurring in their bodies.

When Does Sex Education Begin?

Some people say sexuality begins in the womb because it starts with touch, and infants touch themselves while still in the womb. After birth, being held and caressed marks the earliest connection that infants have with intimacy and love. These connections come directly from you, the parent.

The way that you relate to your child's body—through both body language and words—shows your level of comfort with your child and with the private topic of sex. This will set the foundation for your child's sex education. As we've discussed, both direct and indirect communication have an impact. Let's go over what we've covered about the many ways children pick up messages from us: kids are like sponges—they learn about our feelings toward sexuality through all of our words, actions, and interactions.

Think first about the seemingly insignificant things: How do you handle children's jokes about going to the bathroom? What's your reaction to your toddler seeing you naked? How do you respond when other adults bring up sex in the presence of your child? Such early parent-child interactions start your child's understanding of what is appropriate with regard to sex, even before you know they are interested. These messages set your children's comfort level for talking to you about sexual issues. Kids develop (or fail to develop) comfort about their sexuality through exploration, play, interactions, and relationships. By developing these avenues in your relationships with your children and helping them understand their experiences, you let them form a confident and healthy understanding of both sexuality and themselves.

One of the most natural springboards for starting a conversation with your kids about sexuality comes from the practical task of developing good hygiene. Helping your children understand their bodies through the process of caring for them provides an excellent starting point for teaching ownership and awareness of their bodies and sexuality. Cleaning privates is an important topic in its own right, and these conversations can lead naturally to related discussions about normal growth (sexual development) and abnormal growth (such as a tumor), and the functions of your child's sexual characteristics.

Hygiene, Touch, and Sexuality

Some of the most important early sexual contact in your child's life involves things we don't usually think of as sexual. But sex isn't just an experience of physical gratification; it involves many spheres, as we've already noted, that begin in the womb. Throughout childhood, children learn to take responsibility for cleaning themselves and, in doing so, are in a natural situation for connecting with and communicating about their bodies, their parts, and their functions. When infants are touched in a loving and appropriate way, they learn to touch their own bodies in ways that are healthful and pleasurable; this wholesome model continues throughout their development.

We all seek touch. Studies confirm that we are healthier when we are touched, hugged, tickled, and massaged.[1] If ever there was an easy and welcome opportunity to pursue touch, it's through the many tickling and hugging opportunities that arise during childhood. Permit yourself to be involved, and celebrate these wonderful moments with your kids. On the tickling topic, there is a cautionary note: sometimes adults may not be "in touch" with the impact of their tickling or their own impulses. What they intend as joyful play may lead to the child's discomfort. Therefore, it's important to be vigilant about what your kid's actually feeling.

You should talk to your child as early as you can about proper and improper touch and explain that her or his body is under *her* or *his* control. Explain the absolute necessity of telling a responsible adult (you or a teacher or counselor) if they ever feel uncomfortable about the way someone else touches them. (There will be more on this topic in Chapters 8.)

Helping your children become comfortable with their whole body includes encouraging them to be comfortable with its natural functions. Communication with small children includes pointing out where privates are and why they are considered private. While you're on the topic, let them know how their privates work: how to use the toilet, and that it's something normal everybody does. ("Yes," tell them, "even teachers, doctors, and the president of the United States.") Talking directly to kids as you show them how to do these things is an important first step in conveying that talking about sensitive issues and areas is okay.

Sex, Gender, and Play

It's okay for boys to play with dolls. Really. Likewise, it's fine for little girls to make truck noises just as loud as their brothers. Children will not always follow stereotypes, particularly when they're younger and less discriminating—nor should they have to follow outdated gender roles or separation of boys from girls. While most children will be attracted to things consistent with their gender's stereotypical norms, it's important for you to know that little kids who do not follow these patterns are not necessarily confused about their gender, nor is their attraction to activities not identified with their gender any prediction of future gender identity or sexual orientation.

Young children often say they'd like to be the opposite sex. So don't get freaked out if your boy says he wants to be a girl, or your girl expresses a desire to be a boy. Comments like these often are spurred by a close friendship with another child of the opposite sex—or by a child hearing that a girl or boy can or cannot do certain things. The gender roles we adopt in society evolve over time—they don't come naturally from birth. In a similar vein, when you talk with your adolescents about crushes (which we'll cover further in Chapter 6), don't be surprised if they reveal a crush on a person of their own sex. This youthful crush is often not related to sexual attraction but is rather a part of sorting out personal heroes and deciding whom they want to be like.

Responding to Children's Sexual Behaviors

Now let's look at key aspects of sexuality our children will explore at different stages of their development, organized according to the five spheres of sexuality we looked at in Chapter 1: physical, emotional, social, relational, and spiritual. By understanding your children's sexuality as it is experienced at different ages, you will be better prepared to understand, guide, and reassure them in what they are going through.

Infants and Toddlers (Ages 0–3)

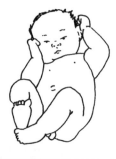 

Expected Behavior	Appropriate Parental Response
Touching genitals	*Recognize and acknowledge:* "That's called your vagina"; "Do you know what the real name for your pee-pee is? It's your penis."
Bodily self-exploration	*Affirm and support:* "Sometimes it feels good to find parts of your body and touch them, doesn't it?"
Desire for relational connectedness	*Provide loving, caring interactions:* Tell your child that you love him, both verbally and through hugging, kissing, and gentle tickling.
Nongender-specific play	*Attune and engage:* "Let's play ball," with both girls and boys. Regardless of the type of play, join them in their chosen activity.

Holistic Responses to Sexuality

Physical: Self-Touching

The innocence of children is clearly expressed in their sexual behavior. Infants and toddlers will quite naturally touch their genitals. Little boys have erections and little girls often experience vaginal lubrication. As children explore their bodies, they find pleasure in touching their genitals.[2]

Embracing and celebrating a child's natural spontaneity is the responsibility of every parent. Enjoying your children's openness and curiosity about all their body parts sends positive messages about themselves and their bodies. If this infantile sexuality—an awareness of excretions coming from body parts and the positive feelings that result from self-touch—is ignored, denied, or denigrated, the child will develop the idea that something is wrong with his or her body.

As soon as your young child can connect words with meanings, talking openly about nudity, male and female body parts, and appropriate levels of modesty sets the stage for your ongoing conversation as the child grows older and more complicated issues arise. Responding positively to your child's pleasurable experiences supports a positive sense of self and builds confidence for your child about first sexual experiences. Recognizing a child's pleasure without judging it while also offering instruction about which behaviors are appropriate expressions will help your child develop positive confidence and mastery of his or her sexuality while growing up. If your child is touching his or her genitals, you might acknowledge that this feels good while also pointing out that this is private touching and should be done *only* in private. It's important to let your young child know that while this kind of touching feels good to do by yourself, other people should not participate in touching you.

All parents have different values and expectations concerning sexual behaviors, so couples should clarify their views and positions ahead of time so they can give unified guidance. This can avoid unnecessary confusion for your child and show that sex is not a point of conflict between parents.

Emotional: Understanding "Love" and Identity

While our temperaments are essentially wired at birth, personality or sense of self is deeply affected by interactions with others. Kids know when we're happy to see them. Embracing your children with a joyful "I love you!" first thing in the morning is quite different from greeting them with a gruff "What's going on with you?" or ignoring them. Our words and emotions have a powerful impact, especially at early ages. Even before they are old enough to remember particular events, the general sense they get of their importance in your life will stay with them for their entire lives.

Setting reasonable and consistent messages about boundaries—what is their space and what is another's space—strengthens a toddler's sense of self and place within his or her world. Our children's self-concept is continuously developing, as can be seen in how a 3-year-old will tell you (with attitude, particularly if you pretend to disagree with him or her), "I am a boy!" or "I am a girl!" Creating respect in your children for self and others—while establishing and enforcing limits—provides both security and order while they form their identity. This foundation establishes a basis for fair play, relating, negotiating, and effectively interacting with others.

Toddlers are not too young to learn the difference between kid and adult expressions of love. Just as little kids will often touch themselves everywhere and anywhere, they also tend to use the L-word without restraint. There are many times when your kids can warm your heart with three simple words— "I love you" (which might make you momentarily wonder why you didn't have a dozen of them). Sometimes kids can take the wind out of your sail, though, by blurting out destabilizing remarks such as "I hate you" when something isn't going their way. After the dust settles, you'll certainly want to talk about love and hate and the proper use of the terms, and you should explain to your kids that it's hurtful to use the word *hate* against people for angry, selfish reasons. In clarifying this, you won't be inducing guilt but guiding your child, stating how even when they do something wrong, you'll always love them. (Loving their behavior may be another story!)

Relational: Learning about Others and Making Friends

As infants and toddlers, kids already learn to differentiate the kinds of affection they receive from different people. Children are clearly aware of who their mother and father are, and even before they can recognize a person by name, they remember voices and faces. Their ability to trust—a key quality for future relational success—is tied to the success of their earliest relational encounters with the people around them.

As children develop from infants to toddlers, their world stretches outside the borders of home. By setting reasonable expectations for relationships and expressing the qualities that are valued in friendships, your child will have the skills to successfully interact with peers and other adults. Developing the qualities that make for "good friends" begins with toddlers; your assistance with this challenge will prove invaluable.

Social: Learning to Play

Some children have shy temperaments while others are outgoing; some are quiet and pensive, while others are loud and smile a lot. As parents, our responses to their individual personalities influence how they learn to interact with others as they get older. If we fawn over our children to show our love for them, they may expect others to similarly express love. Since parental behavior is the measure of all things, what we permit at home will be repeated at preschool or in the shopping mall, as kids test their impact on different audiences.

Due to the gender norms in our society, as toddlers begin interacting with other children more often, you will notice their play with others beginning to take on gender-based differences: little boys will often choose to play with trucks and rockets while girls may gravitate toward dolls and playing house. Though this sort of self-differentiation is typical, parents should allow their toddlers to play with whatever makes them happy even if what they choose is not what you'd expect for their gender. When socially determined expectations are strictly maintained at home by the parents, it limits a child's imagination and may lead to self-doubt.

Many scientists today claim that excessive television exposure at young ages has negative effects on children's development. But even if you restrict television viewing, it is likely that your toddler will come in contact with daytime television while visiting friends or relatives or while being watched by a nanny. Indiscreet ads appear even during daytime TV, adding to rather detailed sex scenes that characterize the afternoon soaps. You should be aware of the sexual messages your child is exposed to through television. Though your child may not understand exactly what is going on, he or she is at an age where everything is unconsciously internalized. The preschool age daughter of a friend of mine was found at daycare pinning a younger boy to the couch, both of their shirts off, repeating words and sounds from the movie *Dirty Dancing.* Too much exposure to sexualized content and advertising may lead to situations or questions about things that children are not ready to understand.

Cartoons are not necessarily safe either. An entire genre of adult cartoons has cropped up on television, from *Family Guy* to *Aqua Teen Hunger Force,* including content that you should be aware of before letting your children view them. Even seemingly benign cartoons often feature excessive displays of violence that children must learn to understand is not acceptable in reality. Though cartoons may not appear potentially harmful to your child's development, without proper explanation of the actions the cartoons depict and the difference between television and reality, your child will likely face confusion and learn to act in ways that are not acceptable.

Spiritual: The Roots of Morality

Though spiritual development is obviously limited in infancy and in young toddlers, you will notice that by age 3 your child has begun actively imitating your behavior in developing a sense of self. This shows that children have naturally started looking for evidence of the difference between right and wrong, good and bad. However, you should not just set an example—you must reinforce their understanding of these concepts through clear guidance.

For many parents, their own religious beliefs are the basis for teaching children these important moral lessons. For Christians, Jesus Christ embodies what is good, and teachings from Jesus or the Old Testament guide people away from what is bad. This is just one example of how a religious tradition can help to explain right and wrong; many faiths and practices across cultures and traditions can provide excellent guidance for children's development.

More commonly, however, at this age many children are taught to believe in the power of prayers and saints as well as in Santa Claus. Parents use these kinds of models to teach children the benefits associated with being good as well as how to give and love through actions. Given the rewards of such belief systems, kids will begin to learn that a certain set of behaviors generates positive consequences. Young children are ripe for learning the virtues of right and wrong. It's therefore important to encourage virtuous behaviors, such as giving and caring as expressions of love, because these experiences develop personality traits and promote activities that will enrich their lives and nurture their relationships later on.

Now that we've gone through the different aspects of your toddler's development, let's do a short recap of what you should expect and what you should avoid when dealing with your young child.

What can I expect of my toddler?

- Masters use of the toilet.
- Becomes aware of genitals—both their general purpose and how to clean them.
- Identifies body parts by their proper names.

- Pleasures through touching his or her own genitals.
- Develops relational skills; expresses love and affection.

With infants and toddlers, do not:

- Say that some part of the body is bad or shameful.
- Shame your child because of something she or he says or does.
- State to others, particularly in your child's presence, things that he did or said that were "bad" or even "funny." (Such statements can be embarrassing and can cause further embarrassment if repeated.)
- Project onto your child advanced sexual actions or interests beyond his stage of development. For example, if a boy embraces his mother and inadvertently touches her breasts, do not joke about his sexual fascination.
- Criticize your child—or others in your child's presence—because of how they appear.
- Assign limits based on gender.

It's a good idea to avoid these six areas not just at this early stage but through-out your child's life to help him or her avoid developing self-doubt or low self-esteem.

Recommended activities:

- Hold, tickle, and embrace your child—though not all at the same time.
- Guide your child's self-care and discuss body parts and their function as you clean them.
- Exhibit and guide positive social skills. Show your child how a simple smile makes people comfortable and want to play. Teach your child to say hello to people when entering a room.

Preschoolers and Kindergartners (Ages 4–5)

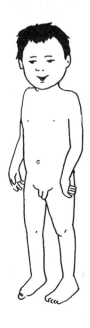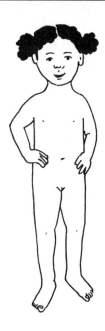

Expected Behavior	Appropriate Parental Response
Awareness of male/female differences	*Confirm and discuss:* "What are the differences between boys and girls?"
Masturbatory play	*Provide positive guidance:* Redirect when kids touch themselves in public; explain privacy again.
Sexual investigation, playing doctor, exploration	*Confirm and discuss appropriate behavior:* "We do not touch others' privates, and they don't touch ours."
Gender identification as male or female	*Support and provide opportunities for activities:* "Would you like to have a 'girls only' party, where we invite your girl friends, their moms, and their dolls, and even play with trains?" "How about a father and son game of catch? We can even make dinner together—and, of course, dessert—for the family." (Include whatever toys or activities appeal to your child.)

Expected Behavior	Appropriate Parental Response
Enjoying toilet humor	Provide positive guidance, and support play with limits: "You call it a pee-pee and your brother calls it a winkie, but it's also a penis!"
Recognizing curse words	*Provide positive models and set limits:* Explain that certain words should not be said, and implement "time outs" for use of inappropriate language.
Inquiries about childbirth	*Discuss basic anatomy and explain the life process:* Explain about the special house for a baby called a "uterus," and how the baby begins from a mommy and a daddy.

Holistic Responses to Sexuality

Physical: Hygiene and Exploration

At preschool age, kids start understanding slightly more sophisticated concepts of how their bodies work. You can introduce them to the difference between the reproductive system and the digestive system (which includes waste elimination), while also showing them how these systems overlap. You might explain how the body is a special machine that takes its fuel from food and discards the waste. Again, toilet training and bathing provide excellent opportunities to talk about body parts—the opposite of "out of sight, out of mind" mode. When things are right in front of you, it's a good opportunity to refer to them by real names and discuss them. One way to help your child increase his or her awareness of body parts is bathing with your child (bathing with the same-sex parent is ideal). This modeling opportunity allows you to remind children of good hygiene habits and also helps them become comfortable with their bodies and the body of the adult that they will one day become.

Communicating in a positive, caring, loving, and natural way about these issues lets children's curiosity develop into self-awareness and confidence. If you're feeling a bit uncomfortable with the idea of this talk, remember that you can always be playful with this subject: try to laugh about bathroom stuff. Kids, for some reason, never cease to find the words *poop* and *pee* hilarious.

How children are exposed to touch and hygiene have important effects later in life. A senior executive in a national firm came to see me because he had problems urinating in the presence of others in public restrooms. He said he could not use a urinal in a public restroom if other men were there, which had caused him anxiety and embarrassment for years. If others were present when he entered the restroom or if someone entered the bathroom while he was standing at the urinal, he would not be able to relax enough to release urine. He attributed his anxiety to early childhood when he was frightened about his "pee-pee" being seen, recalling how his parents would anxiously laugh when he had exposed himself as a young child. This man grew up with parents who were very uncomfortable dealing with anything sexual and had told him to "deal with those things in private." He had taken their words literally and absolutely and grew into a man afraid of being seen when using a urinal.

If you catch your child playing doctor, don't be alarmed—this is normal for this age. Children see each other as perfect opportunities for satisfying some of their curiosities about bodies. However, you will want to set clear limits regarding privacy, boundaries, and appropriate play. Although their curiosity is natural, touching another person's genitals is not a good idea because it invades that person's privacy and can set up habits of touching others that will get them into trouble. If such an imaginative situation occurs between your child and someone else's, you will want to call the child's parents to inform them. It would not be fair or wise to startle, frighten, or scare children who are exploring, but you should talk with your child soon afterward to make it clear that they shouldn't be touching anyone's genitals but their own.

Emotional: Naming Needs and Exploring Boundaries

As children grow, they learn to identify their feelings and needs. A preschool child may approach you to be hugged or say, "I love you!" They gain freedom as they are exposed to a larger range of social opportunities with family and peers. Preschool and kindergarten kids are purposeful, comparing themselves with others and going for what they desire. Managing their exciting "self" and sharing with others is a major challenge. Preschoolers and kindergartners tend to refuel on a parent's affection as they begin to extend the boundaries of their world. They take breaks to sit on your lap, hug, and embrace; once they are satiated, they exit, explore, and return again. Your kids will feel more secure at this age moving away from home base—but not too far. We have to be sensitive to their attachments and neither smother them nor presume that they don't need an embrace just because they don't ask for one. In fact, sometimes your 4- or 5-year-old will say that they are "in love" with you and "want to marry" you. They glow in your presence or when you arrive. While these are well-deserved kudos for good parenting, we have to keep in mind that our kids need to find a balance between dependency and independency.

Relational: Noticing Differences

From the ages of 4 to 5, a child's primary contact remains with his or her family. Some time may be spent at preschool, but in general this age group doesn't usually ask to visit friends or invite friends over as often as in future years. Instead, the child's outside interaction is primarily organized by his or her parents. Your child's activities with others provide opportunities for broadening his or her understanding of different family structures and traditions. Your child may ask you about things that are different from home, and you should explain that these differences should be respected and reemphasize what is expected in your home. For example, families have different bedtime rituals, such as prayers or reading; different mealtime rituals, such as holding hands for prayers; and a variety of individual and cultural customs that are rather unique.

By 4 to 5 years of age, children tend to become engaged in gender-specific play. Parents should support, however, a child's wishes to play, whether or not it conforms to normal patterns, and also display openness about the choices of others. Some play differences that you may observe between boys and girls include the following:[3]

Girls	Boys
Play in groups of two or three	Play in large groups
Prefer to play inside	Prefer to play outside
Cooperative	Physical, independent
Empathetic toward others	Competitive
In conflict, use social distancing	In conflict, use aggression
Play near adults	Play away from adults

While your child's behavior may not conform exactly to these patterns, it is helpful to recognize the patterns in your own child's behavior so you know what to expect and can plan activities appropriate for your individual child.

Social: Practicing What They've Learned

By modeling positive and open engagement with people who have different traditions, abilities, and skills, we can increase our children's ability to establish friendships in broader circles and support them in developing the values of freedom, justice, equity, cooperation, and fairness.

By this age, most children will have formed a sense of what is expected and what is inappropriate behavior, and most will begin to initiate kind and loving actions toward others. At the same time, you'll observe that things don't always unfold the way children intend. For example, children may know that it's not appropriate to touch their privates in public, but may do so, unconsciously.

As children get older, you will notice that they begin asking more sophisticated questions about their own and others' sexuality. In addition, you may notice that they have begun forming their own words for their body parts, or using the words of others, as they learn new words from their peers. A positive, supportive conversation using both "their" words for body parts and the correct terms conveys acceptance of this development while also providing guidance.

Spiritual: Bodies as Part of the Bigger Picture

When they are 4 and 5 years old, children will begin asking questions about religious beliefs they have heard in religious school or from friends. Depending on your belief system, you may encourage your child's awareness of his or her healthy body as being a product of "God's design." The idea of a godly design to the body helps a child understand that people join *with* God in the miracle of creating life—an idea that will build over time, joining the spiritual realm with the very concrete and mechanical interests of children at this age. Though many hold that God creates out of nothing, we join in creation even though we depend on material or thoughts that we can build on. Even if you're not religious, you can still help your children connect their bodies with something greater than themselves—nature, history, the stars, or whatever helps them feel important and good about their bodies. We explain creation to our children religiously, scientifically, historically, or through personal belief systems. Additionally, helping children realize that they are creators who build things using good words and actions is a powerful way of helping them apply their faith and take responsibility for building positive relationships.

What can I expect of my preschooler and kindergartner?

- Interested in the functions of her or his body parts.
- Not embarrassed about sexual topics.
- May self-stimulate genitals.
- May grasp genitals for comfort when upset.
- Requires boundaries.
- Requires privacy and respect.
- Falls "in love" with both parents; may express the desire to marry you!

With preschoolers and kindergartners, do **not***:*

- Criticize curious behavior when you want to establish that an act is inappropriate. For example, if your child touches his or her genitals in public, give clear directions or a previously agreed upon signal rather than criticizing or scolding.
- Limit children's play to gender-specific choices.
- Judge people whose values and lifestyles are different—whether they are in single-parent families, divorced, or of a different religion or sexual orientation.
- Allow free access to unsupervised television or the Internet.

Recommended activities:

- Discuss birth, taking out your child's baby pictures and looking at ultrasound images to review pregnancy and development in the womb.
- Encourage qualities that strengthen friendships: guide relationships by discussing what makes good friends and act as a role model so that your kids develop behaviors that build healthy relationships.

- Identify different traditions and types of family structures so that your child recognizes that families have many variations, yet are all valuable. For example, help your child understand that there are different religions and beliefs about the world and that each of the traditions teach important lessons about life and relationships—and that each value family and nurturing love.

Primary School Kids (Grades 1–3 / Ages 6–8)

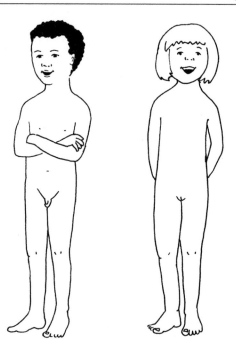

Expected Behavior	Appropriate Parental Response
Development of a sense of modesty	*Discuss discretion:* Talk about privacy and establish rules to support the child's comfort.
Questions about birth	*Discuss growth and how school presents information:* Encourage discussion about human reproduction and feelings about human sexual design.

Expected Behavior	Appropriate Parental Response
Development of friendships	*Support positive, healthy friendships:* Discuss their choice of friends and what they like about their friends, and invite friends over to play.
Development of gender-specific activities	*Affirm their interests and discuss activities:* Sleepovers, for example, should be supervised in a careful yet loving manner.
Sexual identification through activities and involvements	*Encourage activities that support self-esteem:* Recognize that interest in same-sex activities supports identity formation.
Name-calling	*Set limits and respond to negative behavior:* Establish rules about appropriate and inappropriate language, and establish consequences for violations of rules.

Holistic Responses to Sexuality

Physical: Developing Bodies and Sex Ed

In primary grades, kids learn to follow rules and develop discipline, especially through sports. Their growing bodies allow them for the first time to demonstrate strength and grace. They are already developing physical models of masculinity and femininity, and you will notice that they identify with particular styles as they develop their personalities.

Though somewhat uncommon, it is not unheard of for 7- or 8-year-olds to develop secondary sexual characteristics (such as budding breasts and pubic hair), so it is important that you begin talking earlier rather than later about the changes that happen to our bodies as we grow up. Kids at this age also start to take more responsibility for their own hygiene, so you'll need to initiate conversations that keep up with their physical development so they are prepared to take more care of themselves as their bodies change.

During primary school, children are often introduced to rudimentary sex education or science classes that give specific information about differences between male and female anatomy and the stages of human reproduction. It's important to be aware of the content of material covered regarding sexuality so that you can direct your conversations to blend what your kids learn at school with your family's values. For example, in later primary school, kids will start to put together, either from what they've heard in classroom instruction or on the playground, that sexual intercourse occurs when a man inserts his penis into a woman's vagina. You want to make a link between this information and your own talks about sexuality—particularly because sexual information may be taken by kids as secretive if it is not also addressed at home. You want to show that you understand sexuality as natural and support them so they feel comfortable with it.

What Are Our Kids Learning in School?

In April 2006, a Lexington, Massachusetts, teacher used the children's book *King & King* as part of a lesson plan on the subject of marriage. *King & King* is a fairy tale in which a prince falls in love and lives happily ever after—with another prince.

Parents' reactions mainly fell into two camps. Some argued the school was indoctrinating children to accept gay marriage as healthy and normal—and in response to this curriculum they demanded a broader parental notification law in the state. Others maintained that the school's job is to teach children about the world they live in—and Massachusetts, after all, was the only state in the nation to sanction same-sex marriages.

How would you react if your children were in this classroom?

Realize that you could use it as an important teaching opportunity to introduce your children to families and viewpoints different from your own. Think about how your reactions to this children's book would send messages—both verbal and nonverbal—to your children.

Remember that teaching your kids about sex is an ongoing conversation, and part of your job is to help your kids make sense of what they learn in school. So open up the lines for any questions your kid may have about stuff at school—there are likely to be at least a few!

Emotional: "Kissing is Gross!"

Children at this age begin to develop stronger friendships in primary school, and often develop best friends. These friendships become more and more important as they get older. With their friends, children in primary grades may partake in games in which they "play house," taking on identities as "mommies" or "daddies." These games often recreate perceived gender stereotypes—the man goes to work while the woman stays home with the children or cooks the dinner. You may want to observe this play and use it as an opportunity to point out that many women also go to work, and men can take care of children and cook too. In primary school, children begin to be aware of sexual activity, and their reaction tends to be mild aversion: things like kissing are considered "gross" (with the exception of parents—we hope). Jokes begin to develop around sexual humor, and kids will laugh (and sing songs) about who likes whom. As kids express a full range of emotions and develop the capacity to think for themselves, parents have an obligation to pay attention to their growing child's feelings, whether of joy or sorrow, pleasure or embarrassment.

And You Thought They Were Just Playing . . .

Ice cream soda, Delaware punch,
What is the name of your honeybunch?

So goes the jump-roping rhyme of prepubescent girls. Another common childhood rhyme follows:

[Girl's name] and [boy's name] sitting in a tree
K–i–s–s–i–n–g.
First comes love, then comes marriage,
Then comes baby in the baby carriage.

Such rhymes, sung out during playground games, show that children start wondering about and piecing together connections between love, sex, and their consequences even before puberty.

This wasn't always thought to be the case. Sigmund Freud proposed a theory that between age 6 and puberty, children have no sexual feelings. This theory of "latency" is still accepted by many parents, possibly because it puts their minds at ease.

It took Freud's daughter, Anna Freud, to prove that her father's theory was not entirely accurate. By conducting extensive analyses of data on children's games, sports, entertainment, and interactions, her research team found plenty of evidence for sexual curiosity and budding awareness of sex—including the rhymes above!

While your children may not be as blunt in asking about "private" things after age 6, don't think their curiosity has disappeared. Rather, your children have started to learn that sex is a somewhat "private" topic at the same time as they start to develop more social self-awareness and monitoring skills.

Instead of worrying—or feeling relief—that those questions have passed, it may be time to tune your parental radar and start to admire the creativity our children have in finding ways to satisfy their curiosity through games, rhymes, and other socially acceptable forms of exploration. We need to be aware of how sexually charged life is, even for kids still young enough to be playing playground games.

Relational: Different Expressions and Feelings of Love

School, friends, and activities take children out of the home more and more. At this age they learn that there are different kinds of love (for family, friends, and parents, also the idea of being "in love"). As they expand their definitions of love, you will notice that they begin to initiate caring gestures—from bonding gestures in sports events (such as patting a teammate on the back) to embracing a friend after a long summer vacation.

Though kids at this age primarily gravitate toward friends of the same sex, the opposite sex is beginning to be increasingly noticeable. Conversation about girlfriends and boyfriends stirs at school, and boys start to catch up with girls and include the opposite sex in their network of awareness—though admittedly they're usually well behind girls in social consciousness.

Social: Basics of Relationships and Peer Acceptance

Primary school children begin to understand different circumstances that lead to marriage or divorce. They observe that relationships often evolve from friendship to courting, then dating, then falling in love, and finally, marriage, and they also may learn that having kids does not mean that people are necessarily married. Primary school kids begin to learn how to manage conflicts and develop long-term relationships with others, identifying qualities that they admire and desire in friends. At this time, children become aware of differences in communication and interaction styles between homes and individuals. This is an appropriate time to help your child deal with and understand why he or she is valued or not by peers. By taking the time to discuss friendships and qualities that nurture healthy relationships (such as kindness, fair play, generosity, and understanding), you help your child to develop practices that will serve him or her throughout life.

Beyond the Three Rs

When we drop our kids off at the school's front gates or wave good-bye to them at the bus stop, we hope that the main event is the three Rs, but we know that reading, writing, and arithmetic are not the only kinds of education kids get at school. As Ralph Waldo Emerson observed long ago, "I pay the schoolmaster, but 'tis the schoolboys that educate my son." Teachers, like parents, are caught in the middle of the maelstrom—preadolescents just coming into their own sexuality may practice kissing on the playground, hold hands in the halls, and play "games" to experiment with different kinds of intimate expression. How do we make sure our kids are managing these games, such as "Truth or Dare" or "Seven Minutes in Heaven," in a way that is safe and healthy, but that also allows them to test the waters of their developing sexuality?

One teacher's clear-sighted way of handling the situation can offer insights to us as parents. In response to rumors about kids kissing, this teacher took the time to hold an "open circle session." In an environment where they felt safe, the kids were able to honestly share their concerns and discuss the ways they were trying to explore their sexuality. The teacher's basic messages were: "Listen to your inner voice—and don't engage in dares that make you go against your *inner* voice," "Boys and girls can be friends," "Kids should not be kissing anybody but family members," and "Talk to an adult if you ever feel scared, nervous, or uncomfortable."

We can learn a lot from the way the teacher handled this situation. We have to recognize that our kids face challenges and pressures at school that we may find difficult to imagine. But our response can still be comforting: although we cannot be present on the playground or in the hallways to guide our children along, we can provide them with a set of pointers, similar to the ones offered by this teacher, to remember when they're in a situation of pressure. The more we stay aware of the pressures our children face from their peers, the more we can equip them with the tools to explore their sexuality in a healthy and values-rich way.

Spiritual: Connecting Values to Choices and Effects

Through exposure to religious traditions other than their own, primary school kids learn how different religions or belief systems can have different values. This age is a ripe time for discussing the values that are important in *your* family as they relate to lifestyle choices and current events. Part of understanding values is accepting that individuals' choices may have broad consequences. Value systems are important in helping kids understand why sex is appropriate at some ages while not at others. As they come to understand and accept these values, they can see how values determine whether sexuality is seen as positive or negative, that it may be abused or used improperly, and that it is something to be handled with care.

By this age children are better able to conceptualize the different types of love that people experience. Children learn that marriage in our society is based on spiritual and religious principles of love, and they begin to explore these ideas by looking at the relationships that surround them.

If you make the effort to engage in an open dialogue with your children about your values and your perception of God, they will be equipped to develop a spiritual life, providing them with yet another resource (besides parents!) for seeking counsel in trying times, as their connection with God becomes personal.

What can I expect from my primary schooler?

- Aware of physical differences between sexes.
- Identifies gender stereotypes.
- Expresses desire for privacy.
- Uses playful words for sexual behavior.
- Openly shares observations of sexuality with parents and peers.

With primary school kids, do **not:**

- Avoid discussions about sex.
- Miss what kids try to communicate verbally and nonverbally.
- Present poor models of relating and interacting with others.
- Permit your child to bully or be bullied.
- Speak above your child's head about sexual topics and miss a genuine connection.
- Let children interact with those whose values you do not endorse.
- Permit children unmonitored media or Internet access.

Recommended activities:

- Discuss positive models of healthy relating and behavior. Talk about their satisfaction in their friendships and how they may improve their relationships with others.
- Build a positive environment where your children may share concerns and grievances with you.
- Establish a two-way respectful dialogue and make time to talk.
- Discuss news events or school situations to get your children's perspective and help them make sense of the world.
- Practice responses to life situations they may confront on the school bus, playground, or in the locker room.
- Listen to your children so you can understand the trends and forces that shape their lives in the school community and greater culture.
- Come up with role-playing situations together or discuss various scenarios that require them to use judgment and make decisions (such as responding to an inappropriate gesture from a friend or bully).
- Talk to them and always love them.

Preadolescents (Grades 4–6 / Ages 9–11)

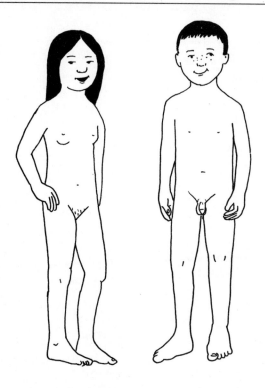

Freud named the period from 6 to 11 years old *latency,* believing that there were few, if any, sexually charged issues generated at this time in children's lives. However, kids at this age exhibit vibrant sexual interest. Though it would be nice to think of latency as the calm before the storm, it really isn't. Instead, it may be more useful to remember actress Bette Davis's words when she descended the staircase to the party in the movie *All About Eve:* "Fasten your seat belts, it's going to be a bumpy night."

Some girls in grades 4 to 6 have begun batting their eyelashes at certain special boys, and whispering about cute guys and potential boyfriends. Boys, on average, lag a little bit behind and don't start tuning into girls as people—much less as anything very special—until a few years later. Paying attention to the opposite sex tends to start in middle school for girls, often spurred by cultural suggestions to develop this interest. Boys are generally focused on their play, usually with other boys (and on some form of dirt). Most boys presume that all girls "suck" at football, basketball, and other physical measures of prowess—which, at this point, makes them not worthy of their interest.

Expected Behavior	Appropriate Parental Response
Recognizes gender as a constant, regardless of behavior	Support development of personal understandings of masculinity and femininity: Avoid gender stereotypes in words and actions.
Establishes and maintains firm boundaries of privacy and individuality	Respect integrity of their developing personalities: Discuss elements of healthy and positive relationships.
Negotiates relationships with peers	Empathize with social challenges they confront: Help them strategize to navigate social challenges.
May experience onset of puberty	Inform child of developmental changes: Discuss child's experiences, questions, and adjustments.
Develops concepts of relationships and feelings, particularly intimacy and love	Recognize that "first" crushes begin: Support them and accept their feelings (usually earlier for girls and later for boys).
Realizes that sex is not only about procreating	Explain various purposes of sex: Help them identify values that guide their sexual behavior.

Holistic Responses to Sexuality

Physical: Time to Go into Detail

Though ideally you will have already been discussing the changes that happen to your children's bodies as they get older, this is a particularly important time to bring up the subject again. Since they are now approaching the age at which big changes begin, they will need a more detailed and concrete understanding of what to expect and how to deal with it, and the next chapter provides guidelines for these discissions.

Here are some of the most important topics to review:

Maturation of male and female bodies. Remind your child of the changes that occur in the body as a result of hormone changes during puberty. They will notice differences in their genitals, and also experience secondary changes (new body hair growth, voice changes). Remind them that these changes occur at different ages for different people, so they don't worry if puberty comes faster or slower for them than for their friends.

Menstruation. This is a particularly important subject to discuss with your daughter. A girl's period and the changes that come with it can create a very intense time for her. Since everyone reacts differently to this rite of passage, you want to be sure your daughter knows she can talk to you about any questions or concerns she might have.

Erections and wet dreams (involuntary ejaculations during sleep). You've probably already discussed erections with your son. At this time, you may want to discuss the cause of erections that get prompted by touch during sleep because of hormones as well as sexual excitement while awake when sexually attracted to someone. You may also want to explain how to manage wet dreams. (See page 223 for a helpful guide to discussing wet dreams.)

Masturbation. This stage can be a good time to distinguish masturbation for sexual pleasure and orgasm in intercourse. Your own values and thoughts should be brought into this discussion. Chapter 8 provides several insights for approaching this talk in view of your values.

Sexual intercourse. Sexual intercourse as a requirement for reproduction will have inevitably been brought to your child's attention. Now you may want to discuss sexual intercourse in view of pleasure—answering a bit of what's the "big deal" or "secret" about sex. Children will usually express their degree of comfort and need for detail, either verbally or nonverbally through body language and gesture. Keeping the doors open for any of these and related themes is key. Having introduced the topic, let your kid know you're game to speak about it.

Some parents think it is only helpful or necessary to speak about changes affecting their son or daughter. However, it's also very helpful to demystify the sexual changes affecting your child's peers or siblings of the opposite sex.

Emotional: Hormones and Identity

One of the most difficult aspects of puberty (for both you and your child) involves the emotional changes that occur as a result of fluctuating hormone levels. Hormones have a powerful impact on mood, so be sure to warn your child how these changes affect how he or she feels. In addition to the emotional impact of physical and hormonal changes, kids also experience emotional swings over how they feel about themselves personally and socially. Riding a rollercoaster of highs and lows, at one moment they feel on top of the world for no extraordinary reason, and moments later, they feel genuine despair over something seemingly trivial.

Another great life challenge that begins in preadolescence is figuring out identity. As kids search to uncover their *real* selves, it helps to remind your children to make time to delve deeper into thinking about who they are and who they want to be.

Relational: Increased Exposure

At this age, kids start hearing more about sexual intercourse and encounter stories about kids who are already either "doing it" or at least experimenting sexually. Even if you wish you could shield your child from exposure to the realities of sex at this young age, the truth is they have access to so many outside outlets that protecting them entirely is impossible. Television, movies, the Internet, magazines, music, and the mouths of their schoolmates are all filled with sexual connotations and imagery, from seemingly innocuous ads for soft drinks to the innuendo that pervades evening sitcoms. This exposure is nothing to be afraid of, however, if you have already begun teaching them about sexual intercourse, the importance of safe sex, the threat of AIDS and other STIs, and sexual abuse.

Though kids at this age are old enough to understand the physical aspects of sexual intercourse, chances are they aren't feeling ready to pursue or act out any curiosity that they might feel. Because our culture is so saturated in sex, you want to remind your child that sex is something for adults, and it's okay if they're not ready to think about it for themselves. The bottom line is that your 9- to 11-year-old child has the intellectual and relational capability to understand sex and needs your guidance to place it in perspective.

Social: Guidance in Expanding Activities

By preadolescence, kids are ready to expand their friendships and activities to include both girls and boys. Often this is because they feel a physical interest in another person. The same feelings produce urges and desires that get directed into crushes on celebrities and inevitably crushes on friends. Talking about these feelings and offering guidelines for dating, dancing, and other age-appropriate activities is an important part of your role in this stage of their life. In this period of transition into adolescence, it's essential to establish rules that protect your child yet also demonstrate your trust in his or her judgment.

Deciphering Kid Codes

One day my 11-year-old son came home from school and asked if I had heard this question one of his classmates had asked him: "Are you a 0, a 1, an 8, a 10, or an 11?" Totally confused, I asked, "What does that mean?"

He explained to me: "A 0 is a vagina, a 1 is a penis, an 8 is two women doing 'you know what' together, a 10 is a man having sex with a woman, and an 11 is two men . . . you know."

I wasn't ready for all of that detail but chose to laugh with him and then move on to a little conversation about sex and taking responsibility for what information we share—and with whom. Kids have a knack for coming up with new ways to talk about sex, and it's very helpful if they can share with you as they test the adult world to figure out how their parents might respond. Humor, in such situations, can be a child's way to test the waters, to figure out what's acceptable, to gain mastery over new concepts, or maybe to just be silly.

How do you help your kids decide to invite you into their worlds? First, demonstrate by your responses that there are no unacceptable questions. You can respond with gentle, open-ended questions such as "What do you think that means?" and "How does that question make you feel?"

Chaperoned activities or outings such as bowling, picnics, or school dances provide an excellent stepping-stone during this stage as they allow for expanded social involvement while stopping short of dating or private situations, which most kids at this age are not yet prepared to manage.

Spiritual: Other Sources of Guidance

As preadolescents develop an understanding for interpersonal relationships, their capacity for empathy and love increases. Their spiritual resources become more personal and relational. An engagement with one's own spiritual tradition and its values that improve life—such as fair play, respect, and responsibility—can be meaningfully applied to sexuality. Children look for consistency and principles that support well-being, trust, and integrity.

Supporting your preadolescent's relationship with God through religious programs affirms your child's personal desire for directions from a higher, spiritual authority. Religious youth groups provide a great opportunity for children to develop spiritually and socially. Even nonreligious youth groups, such as scouting and civic organizations, provide community and fellowship and are an invaluable resource for managing the challenges of sexual issues and relationships for preadolescents.

What can I expect of my preadolescent?

- Understands changes brought on by puberty.
- Develops decision-making skills regarding sexual actions.
- Gains awareness of budding emotional and sexual feelings in relationships.
- Realizes that sexuality can be a source of pleasure.
- Understands family values to guide sexuality.

With preadolescents, do not:

- Dismiss romantic feelings as insignificant or neglect to express empathy as tender feelings for others develop.
- React to emotional changes. Instead, stay above the emotional swings and offer stability.

- Criticize those whose sexual values are different from your own.
- Demean others on the basis of prejudice and stereotypes.
- Ignore the strength of peer pressure and its influence on your child.

Recommended activities:

- Develop strategies for decision-making: role play and talk through scenarios that could create sexual dilemmas for your child.
- Discuss peer pressure and how your child negotiates with peers.
- Talk about your child's feelings for others or how he or she manages the romantic interests of others.
- Spend private time with your children and set up other ways for them to talk to you about things they want to share.

Be it known that Mark Knight is 12 years old and has officially entered puberty.

Adolescents (Grades 7–College / Ages 12–21)

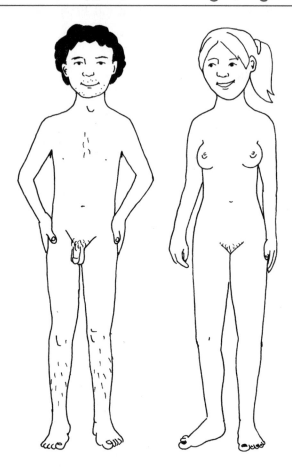

While the middle or latency years may not really be the calm before the storm that Freud perceived them to be, adolescence is unquestionably "the storm." Don't let it catch you unprepared!

Spanning almost a decade in modern society, adolescence is a course of self-discovery that includes excitement, possibility, and endless challenges, not to mention moods that can be irrational, impulsive, and self-centered. Because physical changes are happening faster than emotions can keep up, this is a tumultuous time, packed with demands and questions. Thus, this is the time when more help is needed than ever before.

With increased access to and emphasis on college, 18-year-olds are no longer entering the workforce in such high numbers as in years past. This has led to what some call an "extended adolescence." I characterize adolescence as having three major periods (early, middle, and late), beginning at age 12 and extending through age 21. Let's consider these periods with particular emphasis on the sexual changes that characterize each of them.

Early Adolescence (Ages 12–14)

Though the vast majority of kids at this age are not yet having sexual intercourse or engaging in other sex acts, the development of their sexual self is certainly on its course. By the age of 13, 55 percent of kids are masturbating regularly, a number that increases to 80 percent by the age of 15. Masturbation is the most common sexual expression in early adolescence in both boys and girls. Masturbation allows early adolescents to explore their changing bodies and the accompanying sensations as they become reproductively capable and sexually aware. Discuss masturbation in view of your family values to help your child take responsibility for his or her choices. (Please see the discussion of masturbation in Chapter 8.)

In early adolescence most girls' bodies begin to mature: menstruation begins, armpit and pubic hair grows, the uterus grows bigger, and body shape becomes curvier. Boys also experience changes, though often a bit later than girls. Their voice cracks and deepens, their penis and testicles start to grow larger, muscles develop, and facial hair, armpit hair, and pubic hair begin to grow.

Middle Adolescence (Ages 15–17)

Middle adolescence marks a transitional time when kids move from daydreaming about sex to actually beginning (or wanting!) to experiment. Though most high school students do not engage in sexual intercourse, this is the age at which many will begin doing "everything but." Traditionally, middle-adolescent girls have been thought to be more mature and thus more interested in loving relationships than boys, who have been characterized as only interested in physical relationships. However, research is beginning to reveal that this is a highly emotional time for all adolescents—both boys and girls are struggling with their needs to love and be loved and with how to express these needs in healthy ways.[4]

Variations in sexual behavior occur across socioeconomic, racial, and religious lines. In general, fewer and fewer girls and boys feel tied to their virginity because of a value system. Nevertheless, sexual intercourse is not as common among middle adolescents as might be assumed. In fact, today's adolescents in general engage in intercourse somewhat less frequently than earlier generations.[5] This is not to say that sexual behavior has declined overall; kids are just finding other ways to explore their sexuality—shown by the fact that oral sex is on the rise. Figure 4.1 provides the results of a 2002 study on the prevalence of various forms of sexual behavior among teens, ages 15 to 19.

	Female			Male		
	Hispanic	White	Black	Hispanic	White	Black
Any opposite-sex sexual contact	58.7%	63.7%	67.5%	66.5%	62.8%	74.7%
Vaginal intercourse	48.8%	51.7%	62.3%	56.6%	44.6%	66.0%
Oral sex (gave)	33.7%	51.4%	25.0%	36.5%	44.5%	20.2%
Oral sex (received)	41.1%	53.1%	52.4%	48.1%	53.5%	57.4%
Anal sex	9.5%	11.7%	10.3%	16.1%	10.1%	11.2%
Same-sex sexual experience	5.5%	12.7%	9.9%	7.0%	3.5%	5.2%
No sexual contact with another person	40.2%	35.3%	30.3%	32.2%	36.7%	24.1%

Figure 4.1 Sexual Behavior in American Teens, Ages 15 to 19 (2002)

Source: William D. Mosher, Anjani Chandra, and Jo James, "Sexual Behavior and Selected Health Measures: Men and Women 15–44 Years of Age, United States, 2002," *Advance Data from Vital and Health Statistics,* no. 362 (Center for Disease Control: September 15, 2005).

Late Adolescence (Ages 18–21)

In late adolescence, kids are entering young adulthood, a time when they generally determine how sexual behavior fits in with their overall identity. A wide range of philosophies exists among parents, ranging from those who let late adolescents bring sexual partners into the bedroom to those who value sexual abstinence and have a "no sleepover" policy.

Holistic Responses to Sexuality (Ages 12–21)

Physical: Milestones in Development

Normal Sexual Changes as a Result of Puberty

Changes in Girls	Parental Response
Uterus and vagina grow larger; hips widen; breasts grow bigger.	"You're going to start having a lot of changes in your body now—they're good and natural—but you'll start to notice different feelings and even become more conscious of your movements and stride."
Menstruation begins.	*Help her feel normal and know what to expect in advance of physical changes:* "This is going to be a new part of your life—it means you're becoming a woman!—but there are some things you should know about how to prepare for and manage your period."
Changes in Boys	
Penis and testicles get larger and the scrotum darkens in color.	"While these changes are happening, you might find it helpful to check your 'parts' and to understand how this relates to growing into a man."
Voice cracks and deepens.	"I promise I won't laugh—unless you decide to laugh first!"
Erections are frequent.	"It may make you feel awkward when you're in class or public and out of nowhere you get an erection that you wish would 'calm down.' Think of sitting in ice water! If it bothers you, it might help to wear jeans or khakis instead of sweatpants."
Wet dream ejaculations begin as genitals produce semen and sperm.	"Don't worry, this happens to most guys—there are plenty of sheets in the linen closet, and I can show you how to run the washing machine."

Changes in Boys	Parental Response
Hair begins to grow on chest.	*Discuss feelings about hair growth—which can be signs of achievement or points of embarrassment, depending on both personal and social factors. But don't be afraid to have some humor:* "All right! We'll be sure to take pictures and help you count them if you want!"
Changes in Both Girls and Boys	
Body sweats more.	"It might be time for you to start using deodorant more regularly. Do you want to try the kind I use?"
Pimples and oily skin appear.	"There are some products at the store that can help. If you want, we can set up an appointment with the doctor to get some recommendations."
Weight gain or loss occurs.	"You know, sometimes this comes from physical changes and activity levels, and sometimes it's due more to our choices when eating." (See Chapter 6 for information about discussing social expectations and personal attitudes about body self.)
Growth occurs to full height, and strength increases.	"Let's go shopping."
Hair grows around the genitals; body hair grows longer and thicker; hair grows around arms.	*Talk with your kids about the fact that people have different feelings concerning the management of body hair.*
Sexual and romantic feelings are strong and frequent; dreams occur about friends and sex.	"You know, these feelings and dreams are natural, but they can sometimes be confusing or scary. I'm here whenever you want to talk about them."
Nipples may darken in color.	"Don't worry, these color changes are normal."
Body produces sexual hormones.	"Your hormones are important. They affect your physical and emotional changes, including feelings of closeness and love."

FEMALE DEVELOPMENTAL STAGES

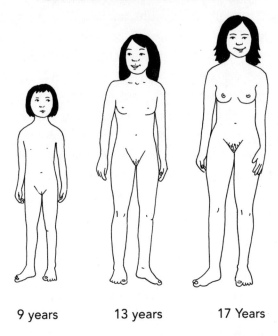

9 years   13 years   17 Years

MALE DEVELOPMENTAL STAGES

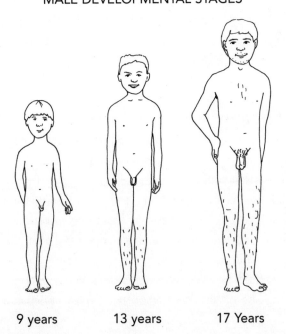

9 years   13 years   17 Years

Emotional: Unexpected Reactions for All Involved

Adolescents are naturally faced with complicated and important feelings, urges, and decisions. Their own personal yearnings for emotional connections can create a wedge in your relationship with them; these feelings can also cause kids to react in ways that surprise both you and them! Discussing and being present with your adolescents is a great gift you can give them as they experience the various desires for sex, intimacy, and love, and as they sort out the connections between these. Emotions and love are not intellectual: they cannot be taught but have to come through experience, and include feelings, needs, and desires that need sorting, guidance, and direction. Your caring presence and empathetic ear can be an invaluable resource for support and understanding as your adolescent goes through these challenging times.

Relational: Making Sexual Choices

Your adolescent will inevitably feel at some point the desire to be sexual with other people. Learning how to love another invites the experience of emotional and sexual intimacy, so beginning in the teen years, he or she will consider options ranging from abstinence to sexual intercourse, including a range of sensual experiences and intimate sexual pleasures in between. Being available to discuss these options and other topics as they come up will communicate your love and understanding—far more than just setting rules—as your child ultimately learns to make his or her own choices. Supporting your adolescent's healthy friendships and providing a loving home make seeking your advice more inviting.

Social: Taking Responsibility

Society will offer your child various options and possibilities for sexual exploration and interaction. If your messages are oblique and vague, and you fail to address the realities that your adolescent confronts, he or she will be left to sort out these crucial matters alone. You need to closely discuss the significance of STIs, sexual abuse, sexual harassment, pornography, prostitution, and sexual responsibility. It is important that you create an open and reality-based exchange about sexuality for your child. Their choice of magazines, books, movies, and social activities should be material for this open conversation. As your child ages and matures, he or she is going to need more independence and less direction from you about values and decision-making. Your dual roles as trusted parent and confidante will hopefully unfold naturally as both you and your adolescent recognize that these roles can exist separately, and that leaving one behind does not mean the other disappears.

Spiritual: Personal Contact

Given the significant challenges of the teenage years, those adolescents who connect to a spiritual core within themselves will find less turbulence and stress and are less likely to make choices they will regret later. Helping your children develop a personal spiritual life empowers them with a "sustaining dependency"—a source of strength, not a weakness—that they will be able to come to trust even more than you or themselves. Through a meaningful spiritual tradition that affirms their chosen path, they will be able to make decisions anchored in solid trust. As love and sex may be confused in adolescent minds, clarifying different forms of love and helping your child understand the responsibilities and benefits of these different forms will be useful. (Chapter 9 discusses sex, intimacy, and love in terms of how we are guided by faith and belief, how we express intimacy in relationships at home, and how our natural sexual expressions reflect our histories and beliefs.)

What can I expect of my adolescent?

Ages 12–14

- Is informed about sexual functions, sexual problems, and the meanings of intimacy and love.
- Develops a healthy acceptance of his or her body.
- Overcomes guilt, shame, and fears associated with sex.

Ages 15–17

- Develops identity to feel comfortable with his or her self—to find consistency between the inner self (feelings and thoughts) and the outer self (actions).
- Recognizes the options of abstinence and celibacy.
- Grows in awareness as a sensual person.
- Distinguishes that sex, intimacy, and love are not the same, and begins to understand when and how to engage each.

Ages 18–21

- Learns how to loosen ties with family and begins to find intimate and loving ties with others.

- Recognizes what sexual pleasure feels like and can express his or her desires through sexual actions.

- Resolves relationship conflicts and addresses concerns about sexuality.

- Feels encouraged in pursuing a satisfying sexual life.

With adolescents, do not:

- Compare your child with others.
- Become either overprotective or too remote.
- Think you have all the answers—consult appropriate sources as needed.
- Violate confidences and privacy unless the adolescent is at risk.

Recommended activities:

- Invite adolescents to discuss how they "put it all together"—how they make sense of sex, intimacy, and love.

- Share pictures, yearbooks, stories, and follies of your own teen years in the interest of communicating how you managed things and what you learned, always keeping in mind the differences between the challenges of growing up then and now. However, don't get carried away reminiscing—get your child's take on how your stories may relate to his or her life.

- Discuss friendships that have continued over time and relationships or intimacies with others: what worked, what didn't, and why.

- Explain how dating doesn't necessarily mean sex—and become a caring advocate as your teen takes on this challenge; discuss dating, its joys and challenges, and always advocate maintaining personal control.

This chapter has given you an overview of tasks and milestones to cover with your kids as they mature sexually, from birth to adulthood. In the next chapter you will find detailed examples of what to say to your child to keep the conversation flowing from both ends. These examples illustrate how to present information in ways that encourage kids to take control of their questions, feelings, and experiences, rather than deny them or disengage. Building on the idea that sexuality is a normal part of being a healthy person, you can assist your children as they grow and keep guilt or denial about sexuality from setting in. As children naturally look to advance beyond their parents' control, you can help them do so in a positive and healthy manner.

FIVE

That's Disgusting, Dad!

The time to stop talking is when the other person nods his head affirmatively but says nothing.

—HENRY S. HASKINS

Talking about sex for the first time with your child is bound to make you anxious. However, if we let anxiety get the better of us, our talk is likely to be clumsy and unsuccessful. Our kids are uncomfortable enough with the idea of this conversation, so they certainly won't be the ones to keep it flowing.

Any one who teaches middle school boys' health classes will tell you what I mean. In the typical "health" class on puberty, half the boys are quiet and serious and the other half can't stop giggling and cracking jokes. But no wonder kids are confused! Usually they get in trouble for saying words like *penis* and *sex*—and now a teacher is saying the words and encouraging them to talk about these topics. The poor teacher at best is able to convey a little information. The larger impact is generally made by the wisecrackers who boast that they have the largest penis in the class or loudly ask if it's possible to drown in a nocturnal emission.

As a parent, however, you are going for something different than the one-time awkward talk about sex. You have the honor and challenge of shaping an ongoing exchange with your child about sex. In this context, your children may bring you their questions and anxieties that come up in everyday life. During middle school, you'll want to ask what's going on in their health class, so that you can help deal with any questions they felt uncomfortable asking about in school. Regardless of what's being taught at school, it's helpful to review details so that you know what points have stuck and what's still not so clear. There may be a lag between sex ed and what's going on with your own child, so tune into your child and tailor your comments accordingly.

"Isn't puberty class hysterical?"

As I previously mentioned, kids' bodies usually start changing and developing mature sexual features before early adolescence. Most kids are aware of the changes and may raise some tough questions for you to answer, such as: "Why's this happening?" "Am I normal?" "How does this change things?" And others may be afraid to say anything to their parents at all. While kids probably already know that these changes affect their ability to create babies, they may also know that the changes have a lot to do with the power to create sexual pleasure.

Given the inherently strange mixture of playfulness and anxiety in sex-ed class, your child should find your relaxed conversation particularly welcome. Having a more focused, open, and comfortable talk about having babies is an excellent way to deepen your communication.

A child's home should feel like the best and safest place to learn about sexual matters. Giving children privacy, within a safe, personal setting, is an important prerequisite. These private talks should be just the two of you.

When we talk to our children about sex, it helps if we keep the language and tone consistent with our everyday relationship so that our kids feel comfortable. Don't expect the conversation to go exactly as you had planned. Be prepared for the inevitable digressions and questions (that's one of the advantages of having more conversations to look forward to). Often, not all of your kids' information will be accurate—on some points they will be well-informed, but don't assume they have correctly connected the dots between the bits of information they've collected from here and there. They're often on target in some areas and totally off base in others.

The following conversations are generally more comfortable for a child when conducted with the same-sex parent. With care and preparation, however, opposite-sex parents can also have these conversations successfully with their kids. Alternatively, single parents may wish to find trustworthy same-sex adults to have these conversations with their children.

Getting Down to Details . . . with a 10-Year-Old Boy

Here's an example of how a conversation might go with a young boy about the male anatomy. This is the approach I used with my own son a few years ago. Of course, you will adjust this to fit your own personal style and relationship with your child, but this may give you some ideas of how to start. I began by bringing in an illustrated textbook. (Visuals make things clearer, more concrete, and therefore less mysterious, and they also give you something to lean on in case you're feeling a bit unsure of the anatomical details.) There were a lot of details to cover, so I spread the conversation out over several talks so my son could better absorb the information. Our conversation went something like this:

I know that you have some ideas about how babies are made—we talked about this before, and you also learned some things from your friends and your health class at school. But it's important to understand how your body works so that you will feel comfortable and confident with it as you get older. So let's begin by talking about how a boy is different from a girl—how does that sound to you?

Of course, my son's response wasn't at all consistent with the script that I had going in my mind. He exclaimed, "That's disgusting!"

Ah, children.

This response was totally age-appropriate, but it's important that you don't simply take it at face value—it doesn't necessarily mean that he wasn't ready to hear this information. It was really just a typical defensive reaction from a young boy to a subject that stirs anxiety. I could tell from his body language— he was wide-eyed and looking attentively at the book I was holding—that he was curious.

But sometimes words do mean that you shouldn't proceed. A child's body language can also communicate a genuine "No, please stop." I can recall the time my dad and uncle decided to fill me in on the facts of life. I was sitting, rather bored, in the living room, thumbing through a magazine during a family visit. Winking at each other—we were the only three in the room— they zeroed in on the subject.

"So Stan, when you were around 12, did you start noticing girls?"

I was totally uncomfortable as sex had always been a suppressed, secretive topic in our home. Their casual approach felt completely out of step. I was 13, and until then I had hardly ever talked about anything very personal with my dad. Most of what I knew I had just stumbled across on my own. Suddenly, I felt like a hostage between these two old codgers bombarding me with the facts of life. I buried my head in a magazine, pretending not to hear their very indirect chat about how kids need to know "their job" in "making babies." Their attempt to communicate now strikes me as funny. Be assured, however, that you can see the signs that indicate when your child is listening—check out eyes, face, words, and body language to tell if you're getting through.

After my son had declared, "That's disgusting!" I decided to forge ahead, based on his body language. Our conversation continued as follows.

The Penis

I've heard you and your friends call the penis at least a hundred different names, but regardless of what you call it, you should know that it's technically just called the penis. But more important than the names you give it is your understanding of what it is and how it works because it's a very important part of your body. A man is usually very concerned about his penis because it's the body part that most distinctly says that he's a man and also because if it gets hurt, it really hurts! Now, you know that your penis is soft and smooth on the outside, but what do you think it's like on the inside?

Remember that this is a conversation, not a lecture, and the back and forth—asking questions and listening—makes all the difference in the world.

Inside, there's a spongy tissue that fills with blood and becomes hard at certain times. When the penis hardens, that's called an erection. You may have noticed this happening to yours, maybe even without your doing anything to make it happen. It even happens to guys sometimes during their sleep! Of course, the most common reason this happens is that the guy becomes turned on—aroused, or excited—sexually. We'll talk more a bit later about why it's really useful for the penis to become hard like this when a guy gets sexually aroused.

Although your son probably already knows that sex happens for many reasons—for pleasure and for creation of new life—it may feel appropriate to save the discussion of sex as purely for physical pleasure until a few years later—when you will follow up on these initial talks.

On the inside, the penis has three layers: two make up the shaft while the third holds the urethra—the tube that carries urine (your pee), semen, and sperm. All of this stuff comes out of the penis at different times. So that urine does not come out of your penis when you ejaculate (which means to release sperm), a special muscle shuts off the bladder. That's kind of a relief, isn't it, because otherwise we'd have a mess! Do you know what the difference is between semen and sperm?

Semen is a filmy, white fluid that contains sperm—reproductive cells that can fertilize a woman's egg. When a baby is made, half of the genes come from the mother, and the other half come from the father—and the dad's half is in the sperm. In a minute or two, we'll talk about how semen gets a chance to get in there and fertilize a woman's egg.

Now the very top or "head" of the penis—called the glans—*is very sensitive. When we're born it is covered by* foreskin, *which may be removed in a procedure called* circumcision. *And circumcised and uncircumcised penises look different.*

At this point I opened the book to pictures of a circumcised and an uncircumcised penis, and I asked my son if he had noticed differences between the penises of other boys when changing in the locker room during gym at school. This would be a good time to mention whether your son's penis is circumcised or uncircumcised and to discuss why parents make these choices, specifically the reasons behind your decision.

The Testicles and the Scrotum

Now, the testicles—*I know you know about these—are often called* nuts *or* balls. *These produce the sperm. The* scrotum *is the bag or sack that hangs under the penis and contains the testicles. The surface of the scrotum is almost always rough and wrinkly. I know that you learned in school that the scrotum hangs outside the body so that the sperm in the testicles don't get too hot and die. In fact, the scrotum also tightens and pulls closer to the body when it gets too cold out: we can't be roasting or freezing the sperm if they're going to live! In general, the scrotum is one to five degrees cooler than the rest of the body. If the temperature in the scrotum is raised above ninety-eight degrees, you can become temporarily sterile, which means that, right then, the sperm are not able to fertilize a woman's egg to make a baby. But don't worry, you make millions of new sperm every day!*

You've probably already heard about testosterone—*the male hormone made in the testicles. Testosterone is a chemical that your body makes, which creates lots of changes in you. The effects of higher levels of testosterone in your body have already begun to kick in for you, and you'll really start to notice them when you enter your teens. In part, it's testosterone that's putting the hair under your arms. More than any other chemical, this hormone makes you develop manly features: a deeper voice* (you can both speculate about what he'll sound like in a few years, possibly adding some welcome humor to the situation), *hair on your chest, face, legs, arms, and around your penis.*

The Prostate

So while the testicles make the sperm, there's another part of your body that makes semen, which carries the sperm: it's called the prostate. *The prostate is a little gland that's just for making that milky white fluid called* semen. *When a man releases semen and sperm, it is called* ejaculation. *When this happens, a man shoots out about 500 million sperm! There's no way we can imagine that number of sperm, but they will nevertheless come out of you.*

The changes we've been talking about really step up during puberty—usually at ages 11 to 12 although boys often move into puberty more slowly than girls. When puberty begins, you are actually physically able to get a girl pregnant! This may be hard to believe because when kids start going through these changes, they're still kids themselves and too young to take care of a baby. So although this topic may seem disgusting to you, it's important to understand because it involves a new kind of responsibility. All right, now that we've covered the basics about how your body functions, let's take a minute to talk about how all this stuff works in practice.

Intercourse

I know you've heard about intercourse already. You and your friends probably call it sex *or* doing it. *Or do you call it something else? Intercourse refers specifically to an act that a man and a woman do together sexually. There are other kinds of sex too, but intercourse is the kind that can lead to a baby, so let's look at that right now.*

This kind of intercourse is also called vaginal intercourse *because it involves a man putting his erect penis into a woman's vagina. Do you remember discussing a few minutes ago how the penis works? I mentioned that the penis's ability to erect when a man is sexually excited is a very useful thing. Upon erection, the penis can fit into a woman's vagina—an opening in her body near to where the penis is located on a man's body. It's important that the penis can fit into the vagina because babies are made when male sperm and a female egg get together, and this all happens inside the woman's body. In order to get the sperm to the egg, the man has to do what we discussed before, which is ejaculate, inside the woman, and then the sperm can swim around and go find the egg. When the sperm and egg meet up, the egg gets fertilized, and this is what grows into a baby.*

Does this make sense to you? Sometimes it's a little hard to understand, but you don't have to worry about getting it all right now. We'll talk about it again, and you know that you can always ask me about anything that's confusing.

If you haven't already spoken with your son about values and how they guide sexual activity, this would be a good opportunity to "sow the seeds," so to speak, about topics like abstinence and safe sex. While your son at age 9 or 10 will probably find the explicit references to sex a little too much to handle without intensely reacting—whether by squirming around or verbally protesting—letting him know that such issues are fair game for your talks is valuable. Mentioning the subject now may break the ice for future discussions.

Question Time

When I had this talk with my son, he took me up on my invitation to ask questions and raised a few good ones.

"What makes the semen come out?" he asked.

I explained how the excitement builds up in your body during sex from rubbing against (and into) your partner. I explained how the excitement hits its highest level when you have what's called an *orgasm* and you ejaculate. He also asked if orgasm was painful or if it felt like urine coming out, and I responded that it felt really good. This, of course, led to a future conversation.

Another question that came to his mind involved what happens to all the other sperm when they go into the woman's vagina. I explained to him that they either spill out or get washed out with the fluid (called *seminal fluid*).

As you can see, it's important that you convey accurate information, but it's just as valuable to use these talks as an opportunity to enhance the quality of your relationship with your children—and to encourage their questions and promote their understanding. These conversations feel natural when you've already built a foundation of trust and openness with your child. By contrast, the well-intentioned yet awkward conversation between my father, my uncle, and me was not based on a foundation of openness, particularly on the topic of sexuality.

Conversations like this should occur in similar detail regarding the anatomy of both sexes. While it is helpful to use an anatomy book for structure, being sensitive to what your child already knows, or thinks that he or she knows, is crucial.

Though I chose to have a conversation with my son, there are several different ways to review this information. If you're not sure about sustaining a conversation at length or if your kid is shy about these things, you can watch a video and discuss it together. Or, as previously suggested, you could try taking shorter parts of the script above and have shorter talks that begin to build a foundation for an open relationship between you and your child in the future.

Getting Down to Details . . . with a 9-Year-Old Girl

Similar conversations with girls usually take place around the age of 9. But because the age of onset of menstruation is growing increasingly younger, some girls may need to hear it sooner—even as early as age 7 or 8—so that you are sure it comes before their first period. Depending on your daughter's personality, she may communicate with you about changes in her body, such as noticing her breasts beginning to develop. However, because she may be too shy to bring this up, you need to be observant of your daughter's bodily growth. If you notice that she seems to be physically maturing earlier than you expected, don't be alarmed—but you may want to ask your pediatrician's advice on whether it's time to begin a conversation about periods and puberty. If the pediatrician indicates that now would be an appropriate time, based on the pace of your daughter's physical changes, find a good time to have a talk with her.

Here's a sample of what a conversation with a 9-year-old girl might look like. As with the boy, the conversation can be divided up into several talks according to your daughter's responsiveness and attention span. A book with anatomical drawings will be a useful reference in this conversation, especially when it comes time to explain the mechanics of menstruation. Don't be discouraged if she is reluctant to have this conversation. However, it would make good sense to discuss her apprehension rather than barreling ahead. The talk might begin like this:

Honey, I know that you've probably noticed lately that girls your age are start-ing to have some changes happening in their bodies. A lot of your friends have got-ten a lot taller this year—you've grown a lot too!—and you've noticed that your breasts are beginning to develop a little bit. You've probably learned in health class at school about the changes that happen to boys and girls as they become teenagers and then adults, but I thought maybe we could talk about these changes in case there are other things you want to know. How does that sound to you?

Menstruation

One of the things that will happen is that you'll get your period. You might start soon, or you might not get it for a few years—it varies a lot in different girls. I got my period when I was 13, but one of my best friends got hers when she was 11, and another one when she was 16! But even if you don't get it for a while, you'll want to learn about it because, chances are, your friends are going to start talking about it a lot, and I want you to know what's going on so you don't get confused.

Do you know what a period is? The scientific name for it is menstruation, *and basically, it is when blood is shed from inside your body—from your uterus, where babies grow—and comes out through your vagina. It usually lasts about a week, sometimes a little less or a little more. It's called a* period *because it happens on a cycle—periodically, just like you call your regular classes at school* periods. *Most girls and women get their period once a month, but that can also vary a bit depending on the person.*

At this point, your daughter might express some fear or squeamishness at the thought of blood—reassure her that it's not as bad as she may think.

One thing that's good to know about your period is that the blood coming out doesn't hurt—it doesn't feel like you've been scratched or cut or anything like that. Sometimes you get cramps in your belly or your back that can be uncomfortable or even painful, but, if that happens, we have medicine and heating pads that can help.

The most important thing you'll have to learn is how to keep yourself and your clothes clean during your period. It's not fun to get stains on your pants! Women usually use special pads, tampons, or both to control their bleeding during their periods. (It's a good idea to have one of each of these handy and to show your daughter how they work.) A pad sticks to your underwear and catches the blood as it comes out of your body, and a tampon goes inside your body and catches the blood before it comes out. When the time comes, I can help you learn how to use both of them, and you can decide which one is more comfortable or easier for you to use. Sometimes you might accidentally get some blood on your underwear or your pants, pajamas, or sheets—and that's okay. Just let me know, and I'll help you wash it out or show you how.

All of this probably seems a little strange to you—it's strange to think that our bodies would bleed when we didn't even hurt ourselves. But the reason it happens is actually really neat; it's linked to a whole process that's going on inside our bodies that we can't see or really even feel. (At this point, it's helpful to have an anatomy book that illustrates the female reproductive and sexual organs.)

The process starts in our ovaries, which are two little organs inside of us that do two things. The ovaries produce hormones called estrogen *and* progesterone, which are special female hormones that help some other organs to do their jobs. The other thing that ovaries do is hold lots and lots of tiny little eggs. About once a month, one of your ovaries—they usually take turns—will release an egg. This is called ovulation. The egg travels through tubes called the fallopian tubes, which bring the egg from the ovary to the uterus. Even though the fallopian tube is pretty small, the egg's trip through it can last hours or even a couple of days. The egg then sits in your uterus for about a week. For adults, this is the time when babies can be made—a man's sperm can fertilize the egg while it's in the uterus, and then if the fertilized egg attaches itself to the inside of the uterus, a woman becomes pregnant. But while the egg is making the trip from the ovary, through the fallopian tube, and into the uterus, the uterus is making things ready in case a baby is going to grow there. The sides of the uterus begin to get thicker and soft as a lining made of blood and other cells builds up—this way, if the egg gets fertilized and attaches to the wall and a baby starts to develop, the inside of the uterus is nice and comfy and padded so that the baby is protected. But usually the egg doesn't get fertilized, so then the uterus needs to get rid of the lining it just built up—and that's where your period comes in. Your period is just your uterus shedding this protective lining. The lining travels out of the uterus and into your vagina, which is the part right inside of the opening, by going through a little passageway called the cervix.

The cervix can get bigger when a baby is in the uterus and is ready to come out. But when you're just having your period, it stays pretty small. The blood then comes out of your vagina. It's usually pretty slow at first, so when it first happens, you'll see just a little bit of red or brown in your underwear. Just tell me when this happens, and you can put a pad in to catch the blood. You might feel excited or scared or happy or sad or maybe all of these things when you get your period for the first time. But all these feelings are totally normal.

The whole process of how the ovaries and the uterus work together is pretty interesting and complex, and what it means when your period starts is that your body is able to have babies. That might sound pretty weird to you since you're still a kid and certainly aren't ready to have a baby! It's funny that our bodies get ready for having babies before we're really ready. That's a lot of responsibility for kids who aren't ready for babies but whose bodies are. Before we start discussing the other changes that your body will go through, let's take a minute to talk about what actually happens to make a baby.

Intercourse

Your discussion about intercourse to explain how babies come into being may occur in a separate conversation or as part of a discussion about the changes your daughter's body may soon be going through. Here's how the conversation might go:

Because we've been looking at how girls' bodies become ready to make babies when they go through puberty, it's important for you to know exactly what women and men do to have babies.

Babies can be made by something called intercourse. *You've heard of this before, but probably under the name of sex, or doing it, or something like that. The term intercourse is used to talk about what women and men do together sexually. There are also other kinds of sex, but intercourse is the kind of sex that can lead to a baby, so we're going to focus on this one right now. This kind of intercourse is also called vaginal intercourse because it involves a man putting his erect penis into a woman's vagina. A man's penis becomes firm because lots of blood flows to it when he is sexually excited, and this helps the penis to fit into the vagina. It's important that the vagina allows the penis in because babies are made when the male sperm from the penis meets a female egg— and this happens all inside a woman's body! So in order to get the sperm to the egg, the man has to do something called* ejaculation, *where he releases some fluid called* semen *into the vagina, and then the sperm swims around and finds the egg. Once the sperm and egg meet up, the egg is fertilized and can grow into a baby.*

I hope this all makes sense to you. Please ask questions if you're confused though. I know it's pretty complicated, but don't worry about getting it all right now. We'll talk about it again, and you know that you can always ask me about anything that doesn't make sense to you.

You may have already given your daughter a pretty clear view of your values regarding sexual activity by this point in her life, but if you haven't, this might be a good opportunity to introduce a talk about abstinence or safe sex— pointing out that no method of birth control works all the time. You can remind your daughter that sex isn't something she'll really start thinking about for a while—at age 9 or 10 most kids still think the idea's pretty gross!

A Woman's Genitals

There are a lot of details to discuss here, so remember to adjust the depth and length of your conversation according to your audience. Some kids are more cautious or less interested in the details, but others are incredibly eager, and this may be one of the most engaging exchanges you've ever had with your daughter.

Let's go back for a second to talk a bit more about the changes that are happening to your body now. All of the changes that we've talked about so far are changes that happen on the inside of your body, so they may be a little harder to understand since you can't actually see them happening. But you already know that there are parts of your body on the outside that are related to the parts on the inside—such as the outside part of what you call your vagina or privates—or like you called it when you were little, your pee-pee. Did you know that there are names for the different areas on this part of your body?

Again, use an anatomy book or other illustration to show your daughter what each area is.

The part of your genitals that's outside your body is called the vulva. *The outer part of the vulva that sort of covers everything else is called the* labia majora *and they're also sometimes called* lips. *You've already noticed that a little bit of hair has started growing on this part and above it, and in the next few years, even more hair will grow there, which is a normal sign that your body is maturing.*

Inside the labia majora are smaller lips that surround the opening to your vagina—these are called the labia minora. Majora *means* big *and* minora *means* small—*like major and minor. That's a useful way to remember which is which. Labia can be bigger or smaller—they vary a lot in different girls and women. The color of the skin here also varies a lot—in some women, it's the same color as the rest of their skin, but in others, it's more pink or brown.*

The opening to your vagina is toward the bottom of the labia minora. At the top of the labia is a little spot that looks almost like a button, which is called the clitoris. *The clitoris is covered by a little flap of skin called the* clitoral hood. *The clitoris has lots and lots of nerves packed into it, which is why it feels good when you touch it. And in between the clitoris and the vaginal opening is the* urethral opening—*which* is where urine comes out. Your urine and the blood during your period come out of two different places.

Just inside the vaginal opening is a thin piece of skin called a hymen. The hymen doesn't usually stay there forever—sometimes it stretches out, and sometimes it breaks. It can break the first time a woman has sex, but it can also break or stretch out when girls are younger if they're really active—during horseback riding or gymnastics or dance and sometimes even from using a tampon for the first time. It sounds a little scary, and it might hurt when it happens, but it only happens once.

Urine and blood from your period are two things that come out of your body, but there are other liquids that you might notice coming out as well. Your vagina has a natural way of cleaning itself, so sometimes you might notice some white or gray discharge in your underwear. It may feel a little weird, but it's normal. Also, there are little glands in the vulva near the bottom of the labia minora that produce a bit of liquid when you get excited sexually; that liquid's meant to provide lubrication during sex, but it can also happen when you're just thinking about sex or even out of the blue. The important thing to know is that it's nothing to worry about.

Breasts

All of the changes of getting your period are part of the larger change that your body goes through called puberty—do you remember learning that word in school? We've already talked about one of the other changes that happen to your body during puberty, which is that your breasts begin to grow. Just like different women's vulvas look different, everybody's breasts look different too—they come in all different shapes and sizes. It can be frustrating if your friends' breasts are growing faster than yours because you may want to have them, too, but trust me, they'll grow! Most women like to wear a bra to help give them support, so when the time comes we can make a special shopping trip to the mall to get you a bra.

Other Body Changes

Other changes happen to your body during puberty as well. You'll grow hair in your armpits and on your legs, which many women choose to shave off. You can too—just let me know, and I can buy you a razor and show you how to use it. You'll also keep growing taller, and the shape of your body might change, and you'll start to look more like a grown-up.

I know that a lot of these changes might sound a little scary, but don't worry—they won't happen all at once! They usually take place over a few years, so it gives you time to get used to them and the new feelings you'll have too. And you know that if you feel scared or uncomfortable or have any questions about all these changes, you can always come to me for help—that's what moms are for!

Not all conversations can be well planned. Sometimes topics and issues will take you by surprise. Sometimes your child will bring something up that you haven't prepared for—some conversations will just barrel through the door. As children mature both physically and emotionally, other challenging themes will emerge that involve your child's body, emotions, and desires—we will address some of these topics, such as crushes, body image, harassment, and bullying in Chapter 6.

SIX

Growing Pains

One of the obvious facts about grown-ups to a child is
that they have forgotten what it's like to be a child.

—RANDALL JARRELL

It was one of those moments that parents dread—Ariana, our 6-year-old, lin-
gered at the dinner table longer than the rest of us that night. She joined us in
the adjoining living room about ten minutes after everyone had left the table,
saying she'd eaten everything on her plate. Later, however, I looked into the din-
ing room and noticed something sticking out from under Ariana's seat cushion—
a piece of bread.

"Ariana, what's that?" I asked, pointing at her chair.

She bowed her head, looking ashamed, and walked out of the room.

I sat there for a moment feeling puzzled; this was very strange behavior for
the youngest of our three children. Ariana had always had a healthy appetite,
and had never been shy about telling us if she didn't like a meal or if she felt
sick. She had always thrived on the challenge of keeping up with her older
brother and sister, three and four years her senior. She was proving to be an
excellent student and had carved out competitive gymnastics as *her* sport at
the age of 4, distinguishing herself from her big sister, who had been involved
in figure skating since the same age. Ariana's natural ability had led her to join
an elite club of child gymnasts, and just that week she had taken second place
in her first show.

Later that evening, I went up to her bedroom and asked why she had put her food under her cushion instead of eating it. She stood there, unwilling to look up from the floor, and mumbled, "I don't know."

"Did someone hurt you? Did something happen at school?" I asked.

"Not at school . . ." she answered.

So, something *did* happen, I thought.

"At the gymnastics meet?"

"Yes." And then the floodgates opened and she told me: "After the awards I went to the dressing room with my trophy, and an older girl came up to me and pointed to her tummy. She told me that I'll never be able to win first place unless my ribs show through my skin. She said, 'Sucks to be you!' really loudly and walked off."

Immediately I swooped her up and hugged and kissed her.

"Why didn't you tell me about this before?" I asked. "You don't need to starve yourself to be a winner. And besides, you're already first place to me. I love you, sweetheart!"

I talked with Ariana about what had happened. I wanted to make sure that she realized the danger of not eating enough food and that she understood that she was perfect the way she was. It was an unnerving experience because right under my nose, my littlest angel had already been pressured into potentially self-destructive behavior. This older girl had elbowed her way into Ariana's consciousness and defined a normalcy that wasn't normal at all. In this case, a competitor was influencing Ariana to conform physically. But it also reminded me that, sooner or later, there would possibly be pressures from her peers to conform sexually.

It also reminded me—this time on a very personal level—of the cruelty that our children face from other children day in and day out. I was further reminded of peer pressure's power to destroy all of the esteem-building that parents do with their children. Our efforts as parents to build confidence through establishing our child's sense of adequacy and self-respect can be so easily undone by the ridicule of others.

So what can we, as parents, do to strengthen our children's relationship with their bodies in order to help them manage social pressure? Try to put yourself in your children's shoes to help understand some of what they're up against. In doing so, maybe we can understand how to help them take control of their bodies and their budding sexuality in the challenging world in which we all live.

Peer Groups and Peer Pressure

As soon as we begin developing friendships, we start to view our peers as a source of information as well as for approval. In early childhood, our peer group includes a broad group of people from school or activities while in adolescence friends are usually more self-selected, including people with similar interests to our own. Our peers contribute to our sense of belonging and our feelings of self worth. They also expand our sense of freedom while influencing and reinforcing our views of what constitutes acceptable behavior.

At the same time, peer groups create strong expectations for appearance and behavior that can taint the positive rewards associated with peer interaction. Individuals often find themselves conforming to the group's norms, behaviors, attitudes, speech patterns, and dress code to earn acceptance and approval. If you conform, you're considered "cool." If you don't, you are often ridiculed and expelled from the group. Sometimes peer pressure is exerted through what Freud called "group mind," the mentality of a group of people that takes on a life of its own. While the desire to conform to the demands of peers is known for its role in influencing adolescent rebellion, social pressure affects children much earlier than adolescence. As children begin to demonstrate and establish identity separate from family, the influence of their peers becomes stronger even at young ages.

The Cost of Cool

The following reflection was shared by a respondent to my Survey on Sex Education:

My 11-year-old daughter came home from school all excited because she was now old enough to attend the Friday Night Live Middle School Dance. I was glad that she felt confident enough to join socially with seventh and eighth graders, and I volunteered to be a chaperone to support this new venture.

While most of her friends say that I'm "as cool as moms get," I wasn't quite ready for what unfolded: the blaring music is taken for granted, but the lyrics of the songs and the attire (or lack thereof) of the kids parading to the beat of the drums threw me for a loop! Girls spinning off the floor, shaking their bottoms, thrusting their chests in and out . . . oblivious to the song lyrics they uttered, as if in a trance: "Oh, I'm so stimulated. Feel so X-rated . . ."

As I tried to pick up my jaw and turn to someone to suggest that something was very wrong with this scene, a nearby group of parents applauded and whistled. One mother yelled out, "You're so cool!" to a young girl who had barely entered puberty yet was passionately shaking her body.

I froze. This was a school-sponsored dance with parents, administrators, and teachers all nodding approvingly at this hypersexual display of their kids. We've learned this kind of behavior at college night club scenes, but here I was in a middle school and I felt like I was participating in delivering my precious child to the slaughter.

A study in the April 2006 *Journal of Pediatrics* received national attention, documenting the influence of sexually suggestive music on early teenage sexuality. The study concluded that listening to popular music—particularly lyrics with sexual content—contributes to earlier intercourse.

As a parent, it's important to be aware of what your kids are listening to, what they're watching on TV, and what exactly goes on at those middle school dances they're so eager to attend. Like this concerned mother, don't be afraid to go against the crowd and stick up for what you believe in, and, more importantly, make sure that your child feels the same confidence to stand up for his or her beliefs.

Parents and the Family: Getting Comfortable with Your "Body Self"

From infancy, children are influenced by their family's values; their early sense of self is basically developed through their interaction with their family. Ideally, children experience love, understanding, acceptance, intimacy, and companionship in their family, which helps them to develop a positive sense of their body. Your children's "body self" is their comfort and confidence in their own skin. It's not a matter of having the perfect physique or an ideal face. This confidence comes from taking responsibility for and ownership of themselves and who they are: assessing their strengths and weaknesses, assets and deficits. Thus, they grow up engaging all the spheres of sexuality that we have considered.

Children look to their parents for cues on how they should act and who they should be, so it's not surprising when 2-year-old Lilly makes her way into her mommy's vanity, streaks lipstick over her mouth and blush on her cheeks, and covers herself with every powder and perfume that she can get her hands on. Nor is it shocking when 3-year-old Stevie climbs into his daddy's suit and falls down trying to wear daddy's shoes, uttering, "I want to be just like you, Dad!" Even sad versions of this scenario are familiar as in Harry Chapin's classic song "Cat's in the Cradle," whose lyrics speak of a son who wants to grow up to be just like his dad, despite the fact that his father can never find time for him. In the song, the father finds that what goes around comes around when his son, now himself an adult, cannot find time for his father. The bottom line is that your child "takes in" your actions. How you act today will have a huge impact on who your child becomes as an adult.

"I want to be just like you when I grow up."

A confident stance, conscious of the example you are setting, is the best approach to guiding your children toward a healthy adulthood. For example, if parents don't value appropriate dress, tidiness, and cleanliness, how do you expect their 9-year-old might look? Or if fashion is a vital value for parents, how do you imagine their child will want to dress? Because our physical appearance is often the first signal others pick up from us, we need to help our kids learn how to properly convey whatever message they choose. This pattern for crafting behavior and attitude affects everything from sports to religion and everything in between. If parents are exercise and fitness buffs, won't their 5-year-old be more confident in approaching sports? Parents who are attentive to nutrition and health will likely have children comfortable with making healthy food choices. When religious values and attendance figure prominently in parents' values, their kids will take this part of life more seriously.

So how do your children feel about themselves? How do their behavior patterns reflect what they have learned at home? How do these patterns make you feel as a parent?

Attraction: How Important Is Looking Good?

If you're like many people, you may believe, "It's what's on the inside that counts." Yet research shows that physical attractiveness is a major determinant of interpersonal and sexual attraction. This physical attractiveness, however, is a combination of the looks we are born with *and* the confidence and self-esteem that come from how we feel about ourselves. A person with high self-esteem makes friends easily, is in control of his or her behavior, and feels more joy in life. You can help your children feel in control of their whole person. They can feel proud regardless of how they look, rather than feeling trapped by their bodies.

To support your child's confidence, attuning to your child's positive body image is a major part of the process. Many parents do this by supporting their children's extracurricular activities; participating in the things your children enjoy and do well boosts their confidence and competence and helps them create a positive sense of their bodies.

As we move into a discussion of attraction, it's helpful to use Exercise 6.1 to determine how your children feel about their appearance. It is designed for children 8 to 12 years old, but you can adapt the questions for discussions with younger children.

Exercise 6.1: Am I *Really* Attractive?

Complete the following questionnaire.

1. What people tell me about how I look:

    Name _____ What that person says_____
    _____

    Name _____ What that person says_____
    _____

    Name _____ What that person says_____
    _____

2. What things do I like about my body? _____
    _____

3. What do I not like very much about my body? _____
    _____

4. People sometimes say I resemble (give name of person you look like)
    _____

5. I think I look _____

6. Attractive for me means _____

7. Questions I have about specific body parts:
    Body part _____ Question _____
    _____

    Body part _____ Question _____
    _____

    Body part _____ Question _____
    _____

    Body part _____ Question _____
    _____

For questions 8–15, use the numerical scale below to rate yourself in the category indicated. Add any comments.

```
|___|___|___|___|___|___|___|___|___|
 1   2   3   4   5   6   7   8   9   10
Terrible/Poor           Average        Perfect/Great
```

Lifestyle

8. Manners (How do I feel I behave socially? / How good is my etiquette?) ____ Comments _____

9. Nutrition (How well do I take care of my body through eating?) ____ Comments _____

10. Athleticism / Physical fitness (How well do I take care of my body through exercise?) ____ Comments _____

Self-esteem

11. Popularity (How well do people like me at school and other activities?) ____ Comments _____

12. Friendships (How well do my friends like me?) ____ Comments _____
_____

13. Attractiveness (How good do I "think I look" as compared to others?) ____ Comments _____

14. Relationship with peers (How well do I get along with the people around me?) ____ Comments _____

Images of Attractiveness and Me

15. Comparison with media images (When I see others my age on TV and in the movies, how do I compare?) ____ Comments _____
_____

16. What do I admire about others my age? _____

_____

17. What makes attractiveness in someone "authentic"? _____

_____

18. What makes attractiveness in someone "inauthentic"?_____

_____

19. In what ways am I similar to my parents? _____

_____

20. In what ways am I different? _____

_____

21. What parts about me would I like to improve? _____

_____

22. What's my plan for improving these things? _____

_____

This exercise can be used as a conversation starter. Your child's feelings about his or her body and attractiveness are something you should know about and feel comfortable talking to him or her about.

Now, go back and answer these questions for yourself about your child. Comparing your answers to your child's may give you some interesting insight as to how you can support your child's self-esteem and body image better.

Addressing Your Kids' Concerns

Sometimes talking to our kids about their appearance can be difficult. We may be uncomfortable talking openly about our children's self-doubt. So instead of communicating openly, we gravitate toward indirect methods of dealing with appearance issues. Kids can be wary of meddling parents—especially when it comes to something they're insecure about—therefore, as loving parents we sometimes go out of our way to avoid pushing their buttons. It gets more complicated when kids model themselves after strange or eccentric characters or align with certain social groups, rather than seek their truly individual sense of identity. Parents may be in denial of what's actually occurring, and this makes it harder for us to help our kids in their struggles. Some of this complexity can be seen in the story about one of my patients, whom I'll call Barry.

Barry: A Public Secret

As a freshman in college, Barry came to me to discuss a problem that had bothered him since early childhood. His most painful experiences had come during gym class. Though he was a big guy and a naturally gifted athlete and coaches often encouraged him to join their teams, he always declined. His reluctance was something his parents could never understand.

Barry had a secret. Since birth, one side of his chest had been enlarged due to an excessive amount of fatty tissue. The condition, called pseudogynecomastia, is not a health hazard, so both his doctor and his parents played down the situation, saying the protrusion was inconsequential. His dad said he'd probably outgrow it, so he shouldn't worry. But Barry did worry—especially after other kids began noticing. Barry told me when he was 7 years old, a kid at the beach he didn't know pointed at him, saying that he had a "boob." Barry told me that for the eleven years since that comment, he had avoided any situation where he might have to take off his shirt around others.

Although Barry had repeatedly told his parents about these concerns, they continued to downplay the situation, thinking it would help him feel more normal. However, they failed to see the seriousness of the situation for him, and he was left feeling completely isolated. Throughout his adolescence, he was essentially handicapped in his physical activities and limited in his social interactions, all because he feared situations where someone else might point out his "boob."

After further investigating the situation together, we found that a relatively minor surgical procedure could be done to remove the fatty tissue. After this procedure, it was evident that so much of Barry's pain could have been avoided had his parents taken his discomfort about his body seriously.

This story raises questions about what to do when a situation cannot be corrected by surgery or when the conversation moves to elective surgery to remove attributes that your child does not like. While I do not *carte blanche* endorse surgery, I believe that surgery to boost vanity is different from surgery that corrects a major detriment to your child's self-esteem. The bottom line is that children should feel comfortable in their bodies, and parents should address concerns that their children have regarding their physical appearance.

Understanding Peer Pressure: Walking in Their Shoes

Body concerns can involve all parts of the body, and around peers kids can be particularly sensitive about their appearances as boys and girls or as young men and young women. Freud said that the penis symbolizes power, and for most boys (and, yes, even for grown men) a bigger penis means more power. However, as most women (and even honest men) will tell you, the idea that "bigger is better" has a lot more to do with a man's need to prove himself in society than with his sexual performance. Nevertheless, there is something about size that gets equated with adequacy: bigger equals "I'm powerful!" (Surely you've noticed how the person driving at the wheel of a Hummer usually is a man.)

Similarly, women often get preoccupied with their breast size although such concerns are often driven more by hopes of getting attention from the opposite sex than by the woman's personal interest. Girls and young women don't just come up with this on their own. Societal pressure fuels this issue, particularly media images that continuously reinforce certain body types as more desirable than others.

Avoiding the "Media Diet"

A strong connection has been found to exist between young adolescent sexual activity and exposure to sexual content in music, movies, and television.

The April 2006 issue of *Pediatrics* reports that white 12- to 14-year-olds who were exposed to more sexually suggestive media (television, Internet, magazines, and especially music) were more than two times more likely to have intercourse than 14- to 16-year-olds who were exposed to less sexually suggestive material.

While the sexual activity of African-American teens appears to be more influenced by their parents' expectations and their friends' sexual behaviors than media cues, the study confirmed that for all kids, one of the strongest protective factors against earlier sexual behavior was clear parental communication about sex.

Researchers point out that parents rarely talk with their children about sex in a timely and comprehensive way, and schools are increasingly limited in what they present to students. Meanwhile, the media frequently and compellingly portrays sex as fun and risk-free. In 2002 more than 83 percent of the twenty television shows that adolescents frequently watched included sexual content, but only one in eight of these shows included a depiction of sexual risks and consequences.

The strongest antidote to this potentially destructive impact of the media diet of sex education is for parents to bolster their communications and offer their kids understanding and guidance about sex.

So if you're planning to address your son's concern over his penis size simply by telling him that he shouldn't worry about it, first consider the following story to see how even socially prescribed symbols have a very personal effect on your child's confidence.

Tim: Having It All

Tim was a handsome college soccer jock, but he came to see me because he was having doubts about his masculinity: he said he didn't think "he was man enough." I was surprised by his doubts because his physical appearance certainly didn't suggest this kind of insecurity. He had a model physique, was a starter on the varsity team as a freshman, and had been intimately involved with several girls.

He explained that his feeling came from the sense that typical male things hadn't gone right for him. For example, he took it as a personal failure when he wasn't selected to be the captain of his high-school soccer team. He believed the team and the coach must have thought he was too "soft." He hadn't received a sports scholarship to any of the major Division I schools, and although he was a member of the varsity soccer team as a freshman, he viewed his "rejection" from other schools as a prediction of future professional failure—not just in sports but in business, his chosen field.

Though Tim had had many examples of success in his life, he dismissed them all for various reasons. He had held a managerial position in one of his father's stores, but he saw this accomplishment only as a confirmation that he would never achieve anything on his own.

I worked with Tim for more than ten years, witnessing many achievements—his college and graduate degrees, marriage, and the fathering of three children—yet his lack of confidence continued to resurface.

Throughout his therapy, Tim would frequently revisit the put-downs that he faced in elementary school when the bully in his hometown regularly taunted him, calling him a "weakling" and a "sissy." I came to realize that the bully's words continued to have a hold on him as if the incidents were still occurring in the present day. Tim also complained that having an uncircumcised penis made him feel like an outcast, as it had been the object of his teammates' jokes throughout his high-school sports career. They also made fun of the size of his penis, leaving him worried that his penis was too small.

A young man who has a small penis yet high self-esteem may compensate by making himself into a great lover. But despite Tim's numerous sexual encounters, he continued to feel inadequate regarding this particular part of his body.

The leading source of Tim's persistent insecurity, I came to realize, was that he had never received approval for all his accomplishments from his dad. This emotional wound had been sniffed out by his peers, who—as peers often unfortunately do—exploited his weakness, deepening his wound. Through years of therapy, it became apparent that the noninvolvement of his father in his life had left him particularly vulnerable and sensitive to the ridicule of other males. This lack of adult male approval, combined with his small, uncircumcised penis, convinced him that he was deformed both inside and outside, leaving him defenseless against the badgering of others.

As his therapist, I might have just emphasized that penis size is not so important and that an uncircumcised penis is physiologically a source of enhanced sexual pleasure. But such reassurances would not have tuned into his deeper feelings. In therapy, Tim grew through expressing and understanding his feelings of inadequacy and developing confidence through constructive actions such as catching himself when he dismissed a positive experience with negative thinking, identifying the source of his negative feelings, and permitting himself to celebrate the genuinely positive experiences and pleasant events that came his way through family, friends, and work.

The challenge in helping kids who struggle with feelings of inadequacy or deformity similar to Tim's is to hear and understand what their perceived deformity means to them.

As parents, it's hard for us to hear that our children have negative and painful self-images or feelings about themselves. Sometimes, however, just letting a child express his or her feelings openly in your presence is what the child needs in order to heal. They don't always want to be consoled; they just want to share their pain. Acting as if pain can be magically removed or pretending that peer pressure is easy to ignore can lead kids to suppress their feelings, making them feel even more alone and leaving them even more vulnerable to peer attacks.

We cannot listen enough! The problems or concerns we have with our bodies are felt on many levels. They should not be denied or avoided. Though we want to emphasize to our children that self-worth is more than how they look, we have to take seriously that their feelings about their bodies connect to their self-esteem and begin our work from there.

Don't forget the impact that your support and approval (as well as your criticism!) have on your child. Be keenly aware of what you say to your child regarding his or her body. To help you with this, here are a few pointers about what you should and shouldn't do to help your child embrace his or her body.

How Can Parents Help Build a Healthy Body Image?

There are a number of things you can do to help your kids develop a healthy body image.

Avoid comments on size or weight. This includes comments about your child and other people—especially jokes. If the subject comes up, do not talk about the weight but about the impact that comments like that have on a person. The point is not to make rules about what's okay or not okay to say but to help your child understand the effect our words have on others. Don't just tell them not to make fun of someone's size; explain that comments like that have such a huge impact on the self-esteem of others. Likely, your child will be able to relate to feeling hurt by another's words. Parents, schools, religious groups, and pop culture need to confirm the reality that people come in all shapes, sizes, and colors—and that this is okay: tuning into situations like this is an opportunity to send a positive message that improves kids' understanding and acceptance of diversity—and themselves—overall.

Help your child understand attraction. This includes what specifically he or she is attracted to, and the presence of attraction in all aspects of life: physical, emotional, relational, social, and spiritual. By helping your child identify what elements of something give him or her pleasure, you support your child's enjoyment from the inside, instead of emphasizing looking outside for happiness. Whether it's humor, music, sports, or another person they are enjoying, you can help your kids name out loud what specifically is so pleasing to them.

Shop with your children. Help them develop confidence in taking responsibility for their physical appearance through clothing selection. Explain to them the impact of first impressions and discuss what impression they want to make. When children want to select clothes that are not flattering to their bodies or shapes or are inappropriately revealing, try to tactfully steer them in another direction. If this guiding nudge doesn't come from you, your children may become the objects of pointing fingers at school because of their poor choices.

Help with expectations. Guide your children about what to realistically expect from their sense of attractiveness, in all five spheres of life. Help them understand what attractiveness—in themselves or in others—can help them bring into their lives, and teach them what can't really be known from first impressions. Help them understand that while attractiveness on one level can be very compelling, satisfaction usually feels best when we find it on many levels at once—including physical, emotional, social, and so on.

Pay attention to doubts and insecurities. Children will often leave small clues about their feelings, to see if you'll ask further. Don't minimize their concerns; take them seriously, provide reassurance, and try to place their concerns in perspective.

Nurture healthy relationships and activities. Support your children in friendships and well-rounded activities—physical, social, religious, and academic—that strengthen their sense of attractiveness in a healthy, positive way.

Talk with your children. Discuss the images of attractiveness that they see in their world—from the schoolyard to the big screen. Don't criticize or judge what they are saying—just talk with them so that you both can understand each other's point of view.

And, last but certainly not least, love your child—happy or sad, up or down, big or small.

All Types and Sizes

As we saw in the story of Barry, being present with your children means more than just encouraging them to accept how they are. If there are things about your kids that they want to change that are reasonable to change, help them to do it. When your teenage daughter wants boobs like the groupies following the guys in HBO's *Entourage*, don't immediately dismiss her concerns as trivial; there's a difference between self-consciousness and vanity. The reason behind such a request may be very sensitive and personal. Instead of responding with your first impulse, talk with your daughter about why this matters to her. Maybe there are less dramatic interventions such as finding clothing that flatters her.

Help your kids set up goals and keep track of their progress. If it's about getting into shape, work with them to make a plan for daily exercise and eating nutritiously. Help them to join activities that support their program. Keep in mind that there are bound to be things that they wish they could change but won't be able to. Help your children to realistically assess their attractiveness, and help them realize and value the spheres in which they may be exceedingly attractive—even if it's not the one they are focusing on.

Though a cliché, it's true: nobody's perfect. Even the most idealized celebrities have things they want to change but can't. If your kid has a celebrity up on too high a pedestal, point out that beyond the media fame other problems may lurk—such as drugs, alcohol, and relationship difficulties. Kids must learn to accept imperfections, "extreme makeovers" notwithstanding. Support your children so that they feel positive about themselves, so they take responsibility for and ownership of their bodies, their style, and the people they are choosing to become.

As kids get older, they often come to feel typecast into a certain look, group, or stereotype. At this stage, help them to realize they are the only ones who can decide who or what they want to be. Sometimes kids gravitate to particular groups for social support or self-identification, but often stereotypes keep people from seeing the whole person underneath.

It's true that our dress and style say something about us. They send signals about where we aspire to fit in society (or not), what kinds of people we feel most comfortable associating with, and many other things. While the exterior can send strong signals to others about who we are, the only way we really know each other is through discovering things on the inside, after we scrape beneath that surface a little. Remind your kids that as they get older, their inner sense of self will grow and develop, often through relationships with others. If they feel insecure now, help them understand that it means the inner part of themselves is developing, and that it's a normal and healthy part of growing up.

Attraction: A Two-Way Street

When attraction is kindled between two people, it's a combination of what you find appealing and what others find appealing about you. Because it's such a personal matter—and based not just on your kids but also those around them—attraction is a subject that requires us to listen to and understand our kids. Attractions convey a great deal about our desires, needs, and personality, and children may interpret our criticisms of what they find attractive as criticism of themselves.

I made this very mistake one Halloween when my 10-year-old son raced into a costume store, selecting a monster mask that exuded a blood-like substance when he squeezed a rubber ball inside the costume. I began to say "No way!"—then I saw his face drop.

Immediately, I cut myself off and regrouped—this was not my costume but his. Maybe I didn't like it, but he clearly did, which was okay with me. I kept quiet from then on. He bought the mask, and we ended up with a very frightening, very happy 10-year-old "Screamer" on our trick-or-treat team.

"Sure, that's a great costume!"

Letting our kids embrace what genuinely attracts them shows that we respect them and their decisions. This does not mean that "anything goes;" it simply means that when we start to say no, we should first stop and think about our reaction. Have we tried to understand our kid's needs or only our own? Are our judgments inhibiting them from experiencing their childhood fully—are we wanting them to act as if they are 50 when they're only 10? What are the real costs of supporting or prohibiting the choices they want to make?

Our success in managing these kinds of situations—deciding when to pull out the parental trump card instead of letting their wishes be met—will contribute to the mutual respect you develop with your child. As you consider the topic of attraction, you'll realize that their choices are not just driven by personal decisions, but are also related to social and gender-based norms. By understanding their attraction through the small choices our children make today and as they grow up, we lay a foundation for their ability to consider concerns such as sexual attraction tomorrow.

To help you calibrate your scales, Table 6.1 shows the "norms" of physical attraction for men and women, measured by a few different studies. The results of those studies describe what men and women found erotic in other men and women.

Table 6.1 Physical Attraction

WHAT MEN FOUND EROTIC IN MEN		WHAT WOMEN FOUND EROTIC IN MEN	
Chest	42%	Buttocks	39%
Buttocks	37%	Slimness	15%
Athletic build	22%	Flat stomach	13%
Hair	21%	Eyes	11%
Face	13%	Long legs	6%
Tall stature	13%	Hair	5%
Large penis	12%	Tallness	5%
Youthfulness	9%	Neck	3%
More body hair	8%	Large penis	2%
Less body hair	7%	Neck and shoulders	1%
Eyes	7%		
Large scrotum	7%		

WHAT MEN FOUND EROTIC IN WOMEN		WHAT WOMEN FOUND EROTIC IN WOMEN	
Buttocks	25%	Face, hair, eyes	42%
Face	20%	Breasts	29%
Breasts	17%	Height	23%
Overall body	15%	Femininity	13%
General looks	7%	Musculature	9%
Hair	5%	Masculinity	6%
Eyes	3%	Age	5%
Legs	3%	Body hair	3%
Thighs	3%	Buttocks	3%
Hips	1%	Hips	3%
Waist	1%		

Source: Mary Ann Watson, Suki Montgomery, and Michael Myers, *Your Sexuality Workbook* (Dubuque, Iowa: Kendall/Hunt Pub. Co., 1996), 79.

Now have your child complete Exercise 6.2 to help identify what he or she finds attractive. You may also want to answer the questions yourself to clarify your own experiences of attraction.

Exercise 6.2: What Attracts You?

Complete the following questionnaire.

List three physical qualities that you're attracted to.

1. _____
2. _____
3. _____

Identify three physical qualities that you think others admire in you.

1. _____
2. _____
3. _____

Which three emotional qualities do you admire (for example, kindness, sensitivity, humor)?

1. _____
2. _____
3. _____

Which three emotional qualities do you think others admire in you?

1. _____
2. _____
3. _____

What spiritual qualities do you find attractive in others (for example, reverence, care, piety, love)?

1. _____
2. _____
3. _____

What spiritual qualities do you believe others find attractive in you?

1. _____

2. _____

3. _____

Aggression, Bullying, and Victimization

Our children are born into a world of mixed messages about peace and aggression. These messages are particularly difficult to figure out because of the complicated and often dark history of our country. U.S. history highlights the values that guided the actions of early American settlers who created our great nation, yet often ignores the brute force that was used against Native Americans and black slaves.

Because each of us has the potential for both aggression and gentleness, we must be sure that our children do not get conflicting messages from our behavior or the behavior of those around us. Think about fans at football stadiums and baseball playoffs reacting in mob pandemonium to a win or loss at a pennant game. Or think about a coach of 10-year-old players telling the team to "kill" or "smash" the opponents—or calling his own team "girly-boys" if they don't win the game. Parents who exhibit anger and violence at their kids' sporting events send the message that the kids have to get ahead at all costs.

As a clinician, I estimate that more than half the tissue boxes in my office are used to capture the tears of patients reliving the shame and harassment from their childhoods, recalling agonizing ordeals experienced as victims of parents and peer bullies. This victimization exerts great pressure on a child's sense of body, self, adequacy, and sexuality.

Social Victimization: What Parents Can Do

Bullying happens when intentional aggression from a peer (or group of peers) is exerted from a position of power toward a weaker person. The aggressor's goal is to damage the status and social relationships of another. The victim is often hurt or ashamed and is often targeted in a pattern of aggressive acts.

How large a problem is peer-pressure bullying? In a *kindergarten* sample, 23 percent of children reported moderate-to-high levels of peer victimization. In another sample 10 to 20 percent of 8- to 12-year-olds were identified as "extreme" victims.[1] And 75 percent of school-aged children report being bullied or hurt during the school year.[2]

For the victimized students, the consequences of this violence are devastating: not only do victims report high stress, loneliness, rejection, and the desire to avoid school, but they also experience elevated anxiety, depression, and low self-esteem. The impact often lingers after the bullying ends, sometimes resulting in adjustment and relational difficulties, adult depression, and anxiety.

Sexuality is about positive connecting. With no healthy and supportive relationships to lean on, those with the least self-esteem are the most prone to tolerating abuse. Boys tend to use physical harassment, whereas girls choose verbal methods. But in both cases, harassment includes name-calling, threatening, and bullying.

Although peers witness more than 80 percent of peer victimization, most do not do anything to help the victim.[3] While children often find it difficult to intervene when witnessing bullying, parents must get involved. Silence or tolerance to bullying means empowering the bully. The worst thing for a parent to do is to blame the victim, saying, "What were you doing to create this situation?" or to tell him or her to ignore it. To be sure that bullies change their behavior, parents must speak out. If you feel uncomfortable about confronting a bully or his parents, speak with someone in authority, such as a school official or even a police officer, to address how to best manage the situation.

Children who learn to identify aggression and bullying will be more likely to be able to identify similarly inappropriate behavior when it occurs in the context of sexuality. By becoming aware and skilled enough to manage the inappropriate use of power in social contexts, your child will be better prepared to respond if similar dynamics arise in their personal relationships.

Crushes and Your Child

You're sitting in your favorite chair, reading the newspaper, not a care in the world, when all of a sudden the living room door flies open. It's your 13-year-old daughter. A stream of tears pours down her cheeks as she cries out, "How could I have been so stupid as to think that he could ever be my boyfriend?!"

Right away you know exactly who she's talking about—she's been thinking and dreaming for months about Gary, who recently moved into town. But what can you say? What could *anyone* say to relieve the sense of betrayal you can see her feeling—not because of a relationship gone awry but because a fantasy didn't pan out. Ready or not, your daughter is the victim of her first heart-breaking crush.

You simply hug her and listen because that is what she needs. Once—though it probably seems like centuries ago—you, too, felt the pain of learning that someone you were completely head-over-heels for did not feel the same way. Over the next few minutes, your embrace can provide a bandage to her emotional wound as she begins to talk. As she recounts her "stupidity" over the last few months, it becomes clear that Gary's role in her life was more like snippets from a movie than reality.

Every time she ran into Gary in the hallway at school or saw him in class, she would feel energized and elated. She'd be looking in one direction, talking with friends, but then Gary would pass behind her, and automatically she would lose her train of thought. Whenever he was around, she would fixate on his every turn and gesture. As she speaks, you realize how serious her crush was when she describes his favorite colors, his favorite kind of clothes, how he likes to comb his hair, and how his dimples change when he smiles.

Finally she tells you what burst her bubble: Gary's girlfriend from his home-town, whom your daughter never knew existed, just enrolled at the high school. Not only did Gary greet her excitedly, but he "swirled her around in the hall and then actually came up and introduced me to her as a *friend* who could show her around."

"I felt like my heart was gonna stop!" she exclaims, assuring you that this is no exaggeration. "So I stood there, nodding my head up and down and smiling this totally fake smile. But really I just wanted to disappear."

As she raises her head and looks into your eyes, red but no longer full of tears, you realize that she's finally feeling less overwhelmed and now needs your counsel.

"How could I have been so stupid?" she asks.

Because each person manages disappointments differently, the comfort that you provide your daughter or son will be based on your own past experiences and your unique relationship with your child. This is critical to guiding your response appropriately. At such moments, take these questions as "announced needs"; you need to hear and respond caringly. Your response—

when done well—will instill in your child the confidence that you can help and understand important relational challenges.

So, let's now consider some specific questions and corresponding information that are important to share with your child as he or she matures both physically and emotionally. Let's stick with the subject of crushes, which seems to affect kids' bodies, emotions, feelings, and desires—and can be quite overwhelming.

Are Crushes Common?

Yes. Very. In fact, most people have crushes—both boys and girls. In fact, although popular impressions suggest that teenage boys are more interested in "friends with benefits," recent studies reveal this to be a fallacy. Yes, boys are reluctant to show their emotions—and when they do, they tend not to do it well—but boys may actually be the greatest romantics. While it may not be any consolation that everyone experiences this pain at one point or another, at least this information will give your child confidence. It helps to know that everyone goes through it and survives.

The extent to which we invest and experience joy in a relationship with another person, regardless of whether the relationship is one-sided, will determine the natural counterpart of emotions and sorrow at its loss.

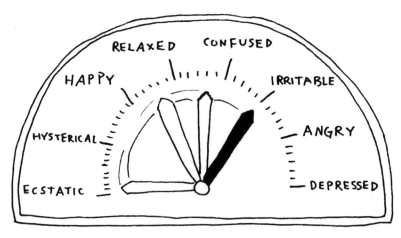

Mood Meter for Adolescents

What Are the Feelings of a Crush?

Crushes are characterized by intense feelings that create all kinds of internal and external reactions when "that certain person" is nearby. When that person isn't around, your child may be unable to stop thinking about the object of the crush; your child may go out of the way to cross paths with that special person and get nervous or even ultra-confident around him or her.

"Will My Pain Ever Go Away?"

As the objects of crushes vary, so too does their length. Perhaps the silver lining to crushes is that though they may last a while, you often get over them before too long. In the story of the daughter who is "crushed," she has been interested in Gary for a while, but not a terribly long time. Occasionally, anxiety from a loss or perceived loss can become overwhelming and may require professional assistance.

Should Crushes Be Taken Seriously?

Sometimes crushes go on for a long time and may include people who are very distant and out of relational range, such as a professional athlete or a television anchorperson. Because crushes usually involve investing emotions in someone without being grounded in reality—or an actual relationship with another person—they are sometimes called infatuations, meaning a relationship "in fantasy." This does not, however, mean that they shouldn't be taken seriously.

Crushes are a means of introducing your child to the feelings—like attraction—that are part of every healthy relationship. Crushes also sometimes lead to a real relationship. All of these factors make it necessary to be kind and supportive about your child's crushes. What's needed is constructive listening, support, and guidance.

How Can Peer Ridicule Be Managed?

It's one thing to have a crush on someone, share it with a friend, and deal with that friend's response; it's quite another when you have an interest in someone—or don't even have such interest—and other kids start giving you a rough time. These days, painful gossip and rumor can spread especially quickly via the Internet. Because all kids start experiencing new feelings about relationships around the same time, they often feel unsure, anxious, embarrassed, and even guilty. Some of their insensitive reactions result from their own vulnerability and uncertainty. Yet these jokes, which can even be driven by jealousy or fear, may be insulting or painful. In fact, your child may have delivered such cutting or unkind remarks. Talk with your kids about how they respond to cutting remarks from others and how they manage harassment by peers as well as how they respond when others are being bullied in their presence. Try modeling suggested responses through a little role-playing—switch the characters around so your child tries out different roles.

What If Someone Has an Unreciprocated Crush on Your Child?

If someone has a crush on your child and your child is not especially interested, your child may not know what to do. It's helpful for your child to develop empathy early. Guide your child to place himself or herself in the shoes of the other person, and then describe what a sensitive, constructive response would be. Learning how to be respectful and sensitive to another's feelings is a valuable lesson by which to live. This lesson of empathy is yet another way that crushes are excellent learning experiences. While your children shouldn't encourage the feelings of another if they are not interested in developing a relationship, responding politely and being a good friend is a way to potentially smooth things out. It may be helpful for kids to discuss their feelings about the relationship with the person who has a crush on them. However, when someone has strong feelings, logic is not always the best solution. Sometimes the best approach is for your kids to just keep their distance to give the person with a crush a chance to cool off.

What about Same-Sex Crushes?

It's quite common for kids to find themselves having a crush on a person of the same sex. Especially common is a child being enamored of someone older, perhaps a teacher or coach.

Because these emotional feelings are intense and hard to sort out, same-sex attractions and crushes may lead them to wonder if they are bisexual or even gay—terms that tend to carry a derogatory meaning at school. The fact is that attractions toward the same sex in adolescence are rather common among both boys and girls. As kids are trying to sort out their identity, they find themselves attracted to those whom they admire.

The important message about crushes is that they are intense emotional feelings driven by the physical, psychological, and social changes of growing up. They require direction and guidance—steps for moving from feelings and desires within one's own self to maintaining relationships with another.

In this chapter, we've considered several concerns our children encounter as they grow up—and have looked at particular social situations that affect how the "facts of life" are driven home. Yes, *home!* We must now take a more careful look at homes today. It's not easy to generalize in the modern world about the home and the family that serve as the conduits for talking about sex. In Chapter 7 we'll take a closer look at families and their variations, and discuss how they can all support "the conversation" with sensitivity.

SEVEN

Ask Your Mother, Ask Your Father

Call it clan, call it a network, call it a tribe, call it a family.
Whatever you call it, whoever you are, you need one.

—JANE HOWARD

We hear a lot of trite and contradictory wisdom about the family in modern society. While William James Durant calls it "the nucleus of civilization," Shere Hite says it's "outdated and not worth saving." Still others opt for George Burns's take: "Happiness is having a large, loving, caring, close-knit family in another city."

While the modern family continues to diversify into ever more unique forms, the status of family in our modern culture remains strong. This is why many people worry that "nontraditional" living arrangements may be harmful to kids' development. Popular literature and the media tend to blame parents for the high rate of teenage sexuality, pregnancy, delinquency, and alcohol and drug use, while single parents or families with both parents working outside the home are often accused of not instilling "proper" values in their children because balancing jobs leaves little time to provide guidance. However, while poor parenting is no doubt connected to a variety of social problems, traditional homes don't necessarily contain competent parents. In any case, research shows that to blame social problems entirely on family structures is unwarranted.[1]

Before turning to the special challenges that arise for parents in various types of family structures, it is important to first review the responsibilities of all families regardless of the specific family arrangement.

The Purpose of Family

In family life, be completely present.
—TAO TE CHING

Commitment is at the heart of effective parenting. Parents need to nurture and provide the love, care, and attention that promote a child's development. Our relationship with our kids must not be theoretical or superficial but grounded in concrete expressions of love and respect for how each child develops uniquely as his or her true self.[2] Specifically, children need to have certain qualities encouraged, ones that will no doubt also contribute to their healthy sexuality. I defined these qualities in my previous book, *True Coming of Age:*

- *Spontaneity:* being able to access their emotions
- *Reasoning:* developing sound judgment
- *Creativity:* awakening of their talents
- *Free will:* choosing openly and without hindrance
- *Spirituality:* responding and communicating with the spirit of God
- *Discernment:* distinguishing right from wrong
- *Love:* engaging in meaningful connections with self, others, and God

When families empower children to develop these qualities, children receive tools for life. However, encouraging these qualities in our kids' development is more than just talk; we must remember to also provide positive models that show how sex, intimacy, and love work together. In one recent poll, over half of the young people surveyed said there were times when they wished they could talk with their parents about sexuality, but they feared that they would not be understood or that their parents were too busy.[3]

The *Tao Te Ching* had it right: presence *is* the key to family, but mere presence isn't everything—we also need to communicate. Listen carefully. Ask questions. Talk *with* your child.

Family Values

When it comes to the specifics of teaching children about sexuality, parents are often vague: "I want them to develop a healthy sexual life when it's appropriate." Parents are often clearer about what they *don't* want to occur, such as, "I don't want my kids to be hurt sexually," or "I don't want them to get pregnant outside of marriage."

Our personal anxieties concerning sexuality often guide how we discuss specific issues in our child's development. But to guide our children to a truly healthy view of their sexuality—one that does not merely reproduce the fears we acquired from our parents or our life experiences—it is important to bring a positive view of sex to the table as well. Often, we can find a more balanced, positive perspective by turning to our larger religious and spiritual values.

Some universal values may include the following goals:

Family Credo on Sexuality

- We speak openly, confidentially, and respectfully with our kids about any sexual matter.

- We promote a healthy acceptance of our and our children's bodies and recognize what is sexually pleasing.

- We embrace sexuality and understand how to avoid guilt, shame, or fear about sex, aiming to bring our actions in line with good judgment.

- We take charge of our decisions and actions so that we express sex, love, and intimacy in appropriate ways.

- We encourage our kids to resolve conflicts and concerns about sexuality.

- We help our kids take charge of developing a satisfying sexual life that grows and evolves over time.

- We promote the belief that our kid's identities are growing or are in the process of growing and are reflected in their sexuality.

- We desire to help our kids integrate their feelings of sex, intimacy, and love as they develop their identities and take responsibility for themselves.

Do these values sound right to you? How would you modify them? What might you add?

The idea of celebrating sexuality with your kids may sound uncomfortable, but your ability to instill an open, positive, and honest approach toward sex is vital. Furthermore, talking about sex does not need to distract your child from your morals and values. Rather, it gives you the opportunity to help shape your child's moral understanding of sexuality; *not* talking about it leaves them open to the influence of other, more questionable sources of information. You as a parent have a responsibility to create a comfortable and values-rich way to talk about sexuality with your child.

When kids do not feel connected to home, family, and school, they are more likely to engage in risky sexual behaviors. A study reported in the *Journal of the American Medical Association* showed that when parents engaged in positive communication to help their children make sexual decisions, kids were more likely to delay sexual intercourse.[4] Young people who reported a lack of parental warmth, love, or caring were more likely to report sexually risky behaviors, in addition to several other emotional and physical dangers. Numerous studies have confirmed that effective parent-child communication about sexuality promoted healthy behaviors. Again, it's vital to remember that it's never too late to begin communicating positive values. The parent-child relationship lasts a lifetime; while earlier is better, honesty can never come too late.

Studies show that when parents make consistent efforts to know about their kids' whereabouts, those children reported fewer sexual partners, fewer coital acts, and more use of condoms and other forms of contraception.

Shifting Values

During the past several decades, substantial value shifts have occurred in the American home. Parents in the 1950s and '60s stressed the importance of obedience, while parents in the 1970s and '80s emphasized greater personal autonomy and responsibility. Although adolescents had little regard for their parents' opinions during the mid-'60s to mid-'70s (which corresponded with an increase in the value of their friends' opinions), studies showed that teens began placing more value on parents' opinions in the '80s; today, this trend has only continued to grow. Parents, however, often perceive that they have less influence on their teens than teens actually report. Though parents *feel* that kids are more autonomous than they themselves felt thirty to forty years ago, kids actually care *more* about their parents' opinions now than they did in the past.

For many people, sex seems split off from intimacy and love because of the way sexuality is portrayed in the contemporary media and in the home. Many children in the United States will experience the divorce of their parents, and some will never know one of their parents. Some kids spend their entire childhood in a one-parent family and never observe a connection of sex with intimacy and love between parents. However, many kids from intact two-parent homes still don't witness a positive connection of parental intimacy and love.

It is vitally important for parents to promote positive views of intimate relationships by figuring out ways to bridge the gap between sex and love. This should be done regardless of the parents' own experience with romantic relationships. If parents suspect that their own example is not the one they want their child to follow, the vital connection between sex and love can be shown by pointing to other relationship role models, such as grandparents, aunts and uncles, godparents, and close family friends.

Women's and Men's Roles in Sex Education

Let's now review some traditional roles and expectations in the parental unit— roles that for alternative families may be filled by grandparents, aunts, uncles, guardians, and same-sex partners.

Sex education in the home is often perceived as the responsibility of the woman. This assumption is clearly problematic as many studies confirm that while fathers may be less involved in sex education, they are no less important than mothers in this critical aspect of child development. For more than fifty years, fathers have taken active roles in the delivery room, sharing the responsibility and joy of birth. Fathers should share as well in all of the responsibilities of sex education, with both its challenges and rewards. Just as mothers do, fathers offer a significant and unique voice for helping children understand sexuality, and they can and should take a full partnership in sex education, whether or not the parents are together as their children grow.

In a two-parent, heterosexual family, talking with your kids about sex should be undertaken equally by mom *and* dad, and you may determine that one spouse is more adequately prepared than another to talk on particular themes. Similarly, in a situation of divorce, parents should communicate to make sure they are on the same page in terms of sex education and discuss openly what they each are teaching the kids—especially to ensure that a topic isn't overlooked because either parent assumes the other is taking care of it. In situations where one parent is absent altogether, or in same-sex parenting situations, parents can think about asking another important adult in their life to help with certain tasks with their kids—for example, a single mother might ask her son's grandfather, uncle, older male cousin, or close male family friend to be involved in some discussions that may seem best addressed by a man. A two-dad family might ask their daughter's aunt, godmother, or a close female family friend to talk about menstruation and other topics with their daughter. Of course, the parent or parents should still be the primary communicators with their children, but reinforcements can always be brought in for specific topics that seem best addressed by a same-sex adult.

Today, most kids learn at school about the developmental changes that they will encounter. However, even with classroom education as a foundation, discussions about puberty between single dads and their daughters may feel a bit awkward. Women's bodies often remain a mystery, even to the most sensitive or experienced of men. For a single dad, or any father, broaching the topic of puberty with his daughter may create uncertainty, confusion, or embarrassment for both of them. This awkwardness for dads may also be related to the social "tradition" that women take care of sex ed—though it's often just as difficult for single moms to broach sexual topics with their sons.

Certain basic discussions—like the anatomy talks presented in Chapter 5—may be covered by a male parent, depending on your ease and your daughter's comfort with the various topics of change, sex development, menstruation, and intercourse. Nevertheless, it might be useful to enlist a female relative or another woman to assist and support you in reviewing particular details that may feel intrusive for you to pursue. In any event, whether you and your family have access to female adult counsel, you should explain your availability and openness more generally to assure your daughter that you can and will personally, or with the help of another, arm her with the information and support she needs and desires.

Beyond specific and sensitive biological details, surely there will also be social issues that you should be prepared to help her manage and understand, from questions about her body to dating, sexual feelings, values, and acts.

Often, we frame our conversations about sex with our kids as a situation in which we're providing information and they're learning. However, one of the most important collaborative realities for families to appreciate is that sexual development affects the whole family. The natural affection that you encouraged in the young toddler you played with will be growing into flirtatiousness, while you, too, also experience changes just by witnessing and guiding your daughter's growth and maturity.

One final comment: sometimes fathers express concern as they recognize that their daughter is getting older. They often feel "different"—their daughter's sexuality starts to not feel "safe," "comfortable," or "right" because it stirs sexual feelings within them. This feeling is not unusual and should not overwhelm fathers. Because of these kinds of feelings, fathers sometimes back away from their daughters, almost as if protecting themselves and their daughters from their feelings and the taboo suggested by them.

If such feelings arise, they do need to be managed. However, your daughter could interpret your self-distancing as a consequence of her development at a time when she needs your support the most. If necessary, discuss this situation with your spouse, a respected friend, or a trusted counselor, and get back in there in your role as dad.

Cultural Sex Rules

When sexuality mixes with culture, we find entirely new sets of signals about how, when, where, why, and with whom to be sexual. Just as we've seen how an individual is unique on physical, emotional, relational, and spiritual levels, the social aspect of sexuality also includes cultural influences and provides scripts for us to use. Each culture provides encoded ways of thinking about and talking about sexuality, which kids absorb as they develop, just as they pick up signals from their families.

In American cultural groups—including but not limited to African-Americans, Asian-Americans, Hispanic-Americans, and Arab-Americans—cultural ways of thinking about sexuality are shaped also by the intersection between the norms of the dominant culture (usually white American) and the expectations of the nondominant cultural group. The result in many communities can be sex rules that are complex and contradictory, as the messages and values of the dominant and nondominant cultures clash with one another.

Our "Big Fat" Cultural Identity

The blockbuster movie *My Big Fat Greek Wedding* gave most of us plenty to laugh about regarding the clash between cultural traditions and mainstream Americana. The lines in the film would run essentially the same whether the culture in focus was Italian, Chinese, Latino, Indian, or any other.

The film makes the point that straddling the values of different ethnicities in America is tough—and real life, unfortunately, is not always as funny as the movie. When it comes to sexual expectations, you can feel not only the clash between cultures but also the impact of double standards for men and women.

As a Greek-American, I couldn't help but feel "gender guilt" as the main character in this movie, Toula Portokalos, explained that she, like all Greek women, was put on this earth for three purposes: "to marry a Greek man, to have Greek children, and to feed everyone until the day she dies." Greek men, on the other hand, are served and doted upon by the women as well as given more social and sexual freedoms.

Frumpy Toula worked hard, and we cheered her along as she jumped hurdles put in place by Greek cultural traditions that blocked the path to her discovery of her identity and sexuality. Eventually aided by the flexibility of her parents, love fused differences between Toula's family and her non-Greek family while our hearts, in the spirit of the American melting pot, warmed and bubbled.

Ethnicity and values do not have to be sacrificed while negotiating cultural challenges and differences. By offering understanding and counsel, alert parents can show kids that they do not have to sever their cultural roots and make all-or-nothing choices—they can fit in with their peers while maintaining the richness of cultural traditions. The moral of the story: you can decide what you will eat—you can figuratively take in what you want—at the Big Fat Greek Wedding without having to be consumed or subsumed.

Our kids are often guided by the perception that to be cool, they have to do what they think other kids are doing, which may contradict their family's standards as well as their own. Kids want to be "normal"—they don't want to miss out on what their peers are doing even if it's not something with which they are entirely comfortable. So it's not unusual for kids to find themselves in confusing and alienating situations. Without guidance, kids may feel marginalized, misunderstood, or unaccepted by one or another of their social groups.

I recall one girl in my eighth-grade class who was the popular self-appointed sex-education instructor of our peers. She used what I thought was a weird come-on that went something like, "Hey, big boy, why don't you come on over so I can peel you a grape." To this day, I don't really know what she was talking about, but I knew whatever it was, it was sexually loaded. I'm sure the lingo in each generation is partly designed to sound alien to parents. Sometimes it remains alien even to those it was intended for! Parents need to help their kids recognize their culture's particular idioms and jargon, decide their intentions when communicating, and determine whether or not they're actually communicating the message they desire.

Parents can help their kids understand that messages can contain various levels of meaning, including sexual innuendo. Sometimes the cultural messages that kids share with one another will be sexually loaded. And sometimes peer exchanges can have nothing to do with sex but still be very confusing. As in the example above, the eighth-grade girl was probably more interested in asserting herself as an alpha female or popular girl than engaging in sex, but how many different ways was her message received by others? Of course, there's no end to children's use of sexual jargon, but you want to make yourself available to help them decode language and become conscious of what they are communicating.

Children's Developmental Needs

It is helpful to keep in mind the different developmental needs of your kids at each stage, recognizing that each child experiences peer pressure differently. Here are some general guidelines regarding how children understand family structures and what to say to children about the family experience at different ages.

Infants (ages 0–2). The family structure is unchallenged, particularly if love and affection are shown to the child.

Toddlers (ages 2–4). Depending upon several factors—access to others, observations, person-to-person contact, the child's will and the will of others—conflicts may emerge. Keep your messages simple, and be present and supportive to help your child participate with others and engage with others' views.

Preschool (ages 4–6). Group or cultural differences are introduced and start being noticed. This can happen in areas ranging from ethnicity to different religious traditions and holidays. Building on themes of tolerance that are hopefully supported in your child's educational system is important. Nonetheless, confrontations over family should be anticipated, so you should introduce skills to manage distractions and differences.

Primary and middle school (ages 6–12). Full-blown challenges will emerge in this period when peer pressure and the need to relate or compete with others as equals become priorities. Not only will your child feel challenged by others, but self-doubts about being different will emerge.

Regardless of your child's love for you, at this stage the issue can arise of feeling weighed down by the features that come from his or her particular family. Questions such as "Why me?" or "Why did I have to be born into this family?" may be heard. This is natural though you may find it difficult not to take it personally.

You don't want to suppress your child's feelings. But you might feel like your kid has punched you in the gut when you hear statements like "I hate our family!" "Do you have to hold hands in front of people on the street?" or "I wish I could live with my real parents!" or simply "Why can't I just be normal!?" The deeper issues surrounding your child's frustration require attention—not a short, quick answer. Avoidance or belittling when such powerful emotions arise is never a good idea.

Adolescence (ages 13–19). Most of us begin to clarify our own identities during adolescence. While peers and peer pressure remain a constant, the tendency to have one foot at home and one foot out the door is common for most teens. Parental understanding of the need to explore the world makes it easier for kids to feel they're always welcome at home and that they get to decide for themselves—as they ultimately will—that home is much better than "not bad" after all.

While guidelines like this can be useful for all parents, concerns may arise that are specific to certain family structures or to certain cultural backgrounds. Addressing concerns as your child experiences them can aid you in talking successfully with your kids about sex, intimacy, and love. So let's take a look at some of the specific concerns that can come up for different families.

Different Family Structures

In American society, we seem to have idealized or generalized broadly about what many would mistakenly call the "traditional family"—the family with two heterosexual, happily married parents, in which the father works full-time and the mother works part-time or stays home to run the household and raise the children. In reality, only about 30 percent of American families fit this description.[5] Families in America are already diverse and are increasingly becoming even more so. Families can be single-parented or same-sex parented; they can have stay-at-home dads or be led by grandparents; they can include several different households because of divorce and remarriage; they can include siblings, half-siblings, adopted siblings, and step-siblings. Chances are that the majority of parents who read this book won't come from a traditional family. That being said, because this idealized stereotype of the nuclear family still exists in our society, it is important that families of all types address the topic of different family structures throughout the child's developmental process so that children can sort through any feelings of difference that they may experience from their peers.

Two-Parent Families

Studies have shown that the traditional family structure encourages sexual behavior patterns that are different from those created by other family types. For example, girls raised by both parents are less likely to have sex as teenagers or become teen mothers than those who grow up under any other family struc-ture.[6] However, these findings should not necessarily lead to the conclusion that two-parent heterosexual households always raise children "correctly" or that alternative households cannot do so. Much of your child's behavior as an ado-lescent and as an adult depends on the particular relationships and experiences fostered by you, the parent or parents.

Parents exert significant influence. The extent of this influence results from the quality of the relationship that they have established with their kids as well as the strength, influence, and insight of their counsel. While parents can-not determine their impact in a purely objective way, research has confirmed that the quality of the relationship developed by a parent with his or her child offsets the risk of teen pregnancy. Teens themselves say that parents influence their sexual decision-making more than any other source.[7]

In the end, such findings do not show that a "traditional" two-parent, het-erosexual household is the necessary ingredient to raising kids with a healthy and holistic view of sex. Rather, it is the specific commitment and involvement of the parent or parents that matters most.

Adoptive Parenting

The general approach to conversations about sex and sexuality is the same with adopted children as it is with biological children. Nonetheless, it is important for adoptive parents to recognize that topics concerning sex, intimacy, and love may stir up special concerns for adopted kids. Such conversations may arouse curiosity about the child's birth parents, which can create feelings of loss and anxiety. "Can I be normal?" may become a pressing question for adopted kids.

Helping your child to understand the possibility that his or her birth parents may not have been able to take care of *anybody* is important, and attending to the feelings that can arise from such an understanding requires particular patience, care, and attention. Uncertainty often creates negative feelings, and your ability to listen, rather than "reassure too quickly," is critical.

Because of such complexities, avoiding this subject—or avoiding topics of sexuality at all—may be tempting for adoptive parents. However, when you talk about sex, intimacy, and love, it is especially important to attend to, embrace, and be present with your adopted child when such painful and uncomfortable feelings occur—and to do your best to provide honest and loving responses.

Single-Parent Families

In the United States today, about 18 percent of families are single-parented by a mother, and another 5 percent are single-parented by a father.[8] Family life can become incredibly more demanding when one parent shoulders the whole load.

Kids in single-parent families sometimes feel cheated or feel a sense of loss. Because single-parent families result from different circumstances, it is important for single parents to recognize the specific needs of their children. The feelings your kids have will create dynamics that affect the trust you try to build with them. The hostility and anxiety of children during divorce is an entirely different kind of anger than the feelings of grief and resentment a child will feel if a parent dies. In both of these cases, however, feelings of abandonment and loneliness may interfere with a child's ability to trust and invest in deeper relationships.

In the case of divorce, children often feel torn between their allegiances, and many struggle to balance or negotiate a connection with both parents. Parents are often unaware of how much of a strain their marital plight puts on their children.

Teens' volatile and frequently changing moods in families of divorce can set

"Sis, I need your help. Katie just got her first period, and I'm not sure about this female stuff . . ."

parents into a tailspin. It can help to keep in mind that many teens are in the throes of adolescent angst and defy parents even in the most stable homes. When a divorce occurs, such expressions may intensify as symptoms of a child's anxiety and fear of the future. This is why it is important to remember that for children, divorce means the dissolving of one of the most basic foundations in their lives. No matter how our children act out, it will help if we can sympathize with their needs and offer reassurance about love and intimacy. It's true that without direct experience of intimacy and love between their own parents, this discussion may feel theoretical or distant for children of divorced parents. Building blocks for intimacy and love, however, are created through our own relationship with our children and through talking about appropriate loving and intimate experiences in relationships that we have with others or in relationships that exist around us.

To appreciate the subtle impact that a single parent can have, take a look at how the feelings of one mother affected her son, a patient of mine.

Lou: Never Quite Good Enough

Lou, a handsome young man in his early twenties, came to therapy because of erectile dysfunction. A competitive kickboxer, Lou had created a macho public persona that many women found attractive. However, he had deep feelings of inadequacy that caused him to overcompensate in school and work. Lou was a classic perfectionist, never letting up on himself. He knew that Viagra wouldn't help him with his erectile issues because he knew the source of his dysfunction was not physical but emotional.

Lou's mother had become pregnant with him after being raped. In his home, sexuality was viewed as a harmful act, and men were identified as hurtful and aggressive perpetrators. In his mind, understandably, sex was something that men needed and to which women, at best, reluctantly agreed. Lou's feelings about sex and sexuality conflicted and tormented him. It was this inner conflict about sex that rendered him impotent. Although he had never acknowledged how his home life affected him, Lou had grown up with very negative feelings about his own sexuality. He firmly believed sex was an act of violence and destruction. He saw all male bodies (including his own) as "monstrous," "disgusting," and "unattractive." He didn't even think it was possible for a woman to experience anything sexually pleasing with a man.

Lou's treatment required overcoming his negative views of himself and his sexuality, his negative body image, and his doubts about intimacy. By working to understand those feelings, Lou came to see the negative assumptions he had internalized from stories he had heard of his mother's rape. Whether his mother knew it or not, she had impaired his sexual development both through the story she told about his conception and through her residual distress with and contempt for men. Counseling helped Lou open himself up to appreciate and develop the joys of an intimate relationship.

Situations like these are indeed sad and complicated. We can hardly blame Lou's mother for his problems, as she herself must have been doing her best to heal from a devastating trauma while raising an unexpected child alone. However, we can see from this story how easily pain is passed on. Parental attitudes have a huge impact on children, whether positive or negative, conscious or unconscious. No matter what our backgrounds, we have the power as parents to help our kids gain a positive understanding of sex. Through doing our own work and passing on the self-love and perspective we find, we as parents can help our children avoid many unforeseen and destructive consequences that may loom down the road.

We can also see from this story that a parent's general attitude toward the other sex plays a big role in the formation of a child's identity and confidence. Lou's mother's contempt for men created within her son a feeling of self-contempt because of all that he had heard about his gender.

Because divorce evokes powerful emotions in parents, they forget the impact of describing *all* men or *all* women as *sick, evil, disgusting,* or some other negative term. They often rationalize that kids can distinguish between their anger and their actual beliefs, but this expectation is irresponsible. While they may claim to exempt their own child from the rest of the gender under attack, even a child can see the problems with such logic. Reassurances such as "Of course, this doesn't apply to you—you're wonderful!" can't be expected to be taken seriously after a daughter hears her father proclaim, "All women are $!#&%!" or a son witnesses his mother announce, "All men are &*%#$!" Your children will remember your anger and your judgments about the opposite sex, especially because those come across so much more powerfully and sincerely than what you might say to make them feel better.

At times when you honestly feel that your emotions are getting the better of you, find someone in your extended family who is of the child's same gender who would be willing to help develop the trusting relationship that is necessary to communicate with your child about sex. A godparent, grandparent, aunt or uncle, or close friend might be a good choice.

Gay and Lesbian Parents

Today an estimated 1 to 6 million children in the United States are raised by same-sex parents.[9] Like all families, gay and lesbian families come about in many different ways—some of them adopt children, some have children from previous relationships or marriages, some conceive children on their own using in vitro fertilization or a sperm donor, and some raise the child with the biological father or mother, often a friend or relative, as part of the child's life.

Children with same-sex parents usually confront discussions of homosexuality much earlier than their peers in heterosexual homes, so those parents must be open and available to provide answers. While children should not be prematurely flooded with information about sexuality, parents should feel comfortable providing adequate information when questions are raised or discussions opened.

There is a lot of controversy right now in the United States concerning same-sex parenting. However, despite cultural stigmas surrounding same-sex parenting, most studies show no developmental differences between children raised by heterosexual and homosexual parents.[10] Good parenting is influenced most significantly by a parent's ability to create a loving and nurturing home, rather than by a parent's sexual orientation. Yet while children of gay parents grow up just as happy, healthy, and well-adjusted as kids with heterosexual parents, it is still important to recognize that kids with gay parents may encounter particular challenges.

If the child's birth parents are divorced, it is important to keep in mind the advice given to all divorced couples: that the parents should continue to communicate with each other regarding their children's sex education and overall well-being.

If your children have been raised in a same-sex home since birth, talking with them about all different types of families will answer questions they will want to ask from the time they are toddlers, and prepare them for questions that will be raised by others.

For parents, it is important to discuss your thoughts and apprehensions, even rehearse your comments. Listen to your children carefully to confirm your mutual understandings, and get your partner's thoughts about effectively communicating.

It also makes good sense to prepare your kids that schoolmates may be confused or critical about the fact that they don't have a traditional "mom and dad." Helping your kids anticipate and manage the criticisms of others is part of the parent's role. When kids with same-sex parents are teased or feel different from others because they don't have both a mom and a dad, you will need to pay attention to their feelings and help them learn to respond to their critical peers.

I suggest role-playing situations with your kids to help boost their confidence. You can play the role of your child in order to model responses as well as the role of the other kid to learn with your child how he or she will feel and respond, giving your child an opportunity to improve the responses.

These are the kinds of questions the children may encounter:

"Are you weird? How can you have two moms and no dad?"

"Why doesn't your mom ever come to pick you up?" (for a kid with
two dads)

"I don't want to play at your house because your family is strange."

Whenever you're in a minority, you have the double burden of advocating
for your child and educating others in addition to all the "normal parenting"
responsibilities. The tasks are large, and if it's not in your temperament to
address or even confront situations that seem insensitive or unfamiliar, your
child may face the consequences of others' ignorance.

Families are critical in sex education. Their efforts to build meaningful
connections with kids set the stage for understanding the relationship between
sex, intimacy, and love. Modern times have reconstructed the family unit, but
regardless of the family's formation, its role is essential in building a healthy
and grounded experience for children's sexual development. Having explored
the role of the family, let's press on to address some specific issues in your child's
sexuality—the so-called *nitty-gritty*.

Part III

Sex Out of the Closet

EIGHT

Getting Down to the Nitty-Gritty

Sex lies at the root of life, and we can never learn to
reverence life until we know how to understand sex.

—HAVELOCK ELLIS

Parents often struggle over how to deal with sex and values with their teenagers
and often end up falling into one of two extremes—permissiveness or restrictiveness. Remember the parents from Chapter 2? John and Mary were at the permissive extreme, automatically putting their daughter on the Pill when she was
16, while Paula and Martin fell at the other extreme, cutting sexual contact or
exposure from their daughter's life altogether. Both sets of parents, however,
avoided direct and open talk about sex with their daughters.

It's always hard for parents to talk about sex with their kids, and it certainly
doesn't get any easier with "taboo" topics such as masturbation, same-sex attraction, and sexual abuse and incest. It can even feel complicated to talk about
seemingly tame issues such as abstinence or sexuality and the Internet. Even
though masturbation is a normal part of growing up, social norms and cultural
or religious values can make it feel weird to bring up.

So while crossing into this awkward territory may be difficult, it really is
important to get clear about our views on sexual issues. Communication is
key in guiding children to take an informed position on sexual issues rather
than being drawn in or persuaded by others. As a parent, your role can be to

give your children the tools and empowerment to consider these issues from all angles, and help them to know what position their parents have come up with through a similar process. Instead of just telling your child that such things are *good* or *bad*—giving *yes* or *no* answers—ask and discuss with them how each topic affects them personally. While doing this, keep in mind the five components of sexuality that we have considered—physical, emotional, relational, social, and spiritual. Help them anticipate and navigate conflicting attitudes about sexuality, and encourage them to continue to pursue personal answers to questions about sexuality.

Of course, you as the parent may not feel 100 percent sure about your position on these topics either—especially if, as is the case for many in our generation, your own parents did not speak with you openly about sexuality. In this chapter we'll explore some of the more complex, difficult-to-discuss topics that affect sexual health. By creating a space in which these topics are discussed openly, you will enable your children to feel comfortable and confident with these subjects. You will help them establish the foundation for their opinions within the safe, value-rich environment of your home, possibly obviating the need for them to look outside or experiment just to discover where they stand. The information in this chapter will help you explore challenging topics with your children so that you will be better prepared to understand their concerns and offer your own advice.

Masturbation

Masturbation involves stimulating one's own sexual organs for pleasure, often to the point of orgasm. While many parents associate masturbation with puberty or adolescence, as we've mentioned, children discover the pleasure of fondling their genitals long before this time, and self-pleasure can continue into adulthood as well. If you watch infants, you'll observe that they discover self-pleasure when they are four to six months old, and usually continue the practice in some form throughout their life.

Nevertheless, masturbation is not openly accepted or understood. Some religions hold strong positions against masturbation. You may even have heard the scare tactics of claims that masturbation has negative physical consequences. Even in the information age, myths survive out there about masturbation—

from getting warts to having three-headed kids. I have been asked by college students if masturbation can cause blindness. And while, of course, none of these are true, guilt often surrounds the act of masturbating because people have internalized the notion that it is intrinsically bad or harmful, or, at least, undeservedly self-indulgent.

Because of the misconceptions that surround masturbation, self-pleasure deserves our careful consideration. Despite the reigning stigmas, just about everyone masturbates at some point in his or her life—by the age of 15 about 80 percent of people have done it.[1] It's important for parents to be aware of these facts as well as to encourage their children to ask questions about masturbation and be ready to provide thoughtful responses. Don't, for example, emulate the parents who, in a story I heard a few years back, told their son that he should never masturbate. When he asked why not, they said, "Well, if you do, you know you'll go blind." After pausing for a moment, to their surprise, their son responded, "Well, can't I just do it until I need glasses?"

The motivation for masturbation, as with most sexual behaviors, can be strong, and the motivations vary. Is it driven by loneliness? Sexual obsessions? Or simple sexual arousal? Other factors can also come into play. By talking directly with your kids, you can consider and address the drives that may affect them personally as well as give perspective from within your religious or spiritual tradition (such as whether it is acceptable to find enjoyment in sexuality for pleasure). We also need to be realistic and acknowledge that most kids masturbate regardless of what religious authorities say. Thus, rather than suppressing or denying the existence of their sexual desire or making them feel guilty, it is healthier to acknowledge their sexual feelings and understand masturbation and other expressions of sexuality. Through our conversations we inspire positive attitudes in our kids toward their sexual nature and, ultimately, toward themselves.

Because some people distinguish touching the genitals from masturbation that leads to orgasm, there remains some controversy among specialists on faith and sexuality about whether childhood pleasuring is, in fact, masturbation. While it is true that a young child may not have a *sexual* understanding of the act, and that self-stimulation obviously advances with time—eventually culminating in orgasm—in my view, childhood pleasuring is on the same continuum as masturbation: I support the idea that self-stimulation is a normal, healthy part of human sexuality that may serve some basic purposes of sex, as discussed in Chapter 1.

So masturbation (or self-stimulation) begins early in a child's life. This means it's usually the first big sexual challenge parents confront with their kids. Here's what makes it difficult: if from the time our kids are very young, we consistently send them the message that pleasure is not an appropriate goal in sex—or if we teach our kids that sexual behavior should only emerge after marriage—then masturbation raises some very genuine dilemmas. Like most sexual issues, masturbation does not warrant being presented as an all-or-nothing proposition. To help you sort out the issues at stake in shaping views and discussions on masturbation, let's consider the facts in light of the areas of sexuality used in this book.

Physical

Masturbation usually begins through unintentionally stimulating the genitals and realizing that it brings pleasure. It's from this innocent place that kids usually begin to self-stimulate before puberty's onset. While you can discourage masturbation for religious reasons if those are your family's values, masturbation is a topic that can be addressed as an outgrowth of behaviors observed in your child or when discussing sex developmentally.

In general, masturbation causes no negative physical consequences. It can be a great guide to developing awareness about what one finds sexually pleasurable. Further, it can provide a safe release from stress and sexual tension. Masturbation provides a way—without the threat of STIs and the need for birth control—for kids and adolescents to become familiar with their growing bodies, fostering a sense of ownership of one's sexual self.

Meanwhile, there can be damaging psychological or physical consequences to forbidding masturbation altogether. Commonly, the anxiety that children develop from the message that masturbation is bad or wrong can foster more compulsive sexual behaviors throughout life. At the more dramatic extreme, I worked with a 19-year-old boy following a near fatal illness, who shared with me that when he was around 8, his parents told him he should never touch himself "there." While they meant he shouldn't masturbate, he took it literally to mean he should not touch that part of his body. Burdened by guilt, he very privately masturbated and never dreamed of broaching the topic at home.

Unfortunately, he'd also been hesitant to tell his parents that one of his testicles had swollen to the size of an orange—he believed his masturbation might have created the problem, and he didn't want his parents to find out he'd been doing it. After the pain became too much and he finally disclosed the problem, he was diagnosed with testicular cancer. Luckily, he was able to get successful treatment in time. The story poignantly emphasizes how unclear communication and parental anxieties can be not only counterproductive, but sometimes quite destructive.

Our kids need to learn how to take charge of their bodies. From a young age, they must know that understanding their bodies—from showing us their lumps, bruises, pimples, and pains to any discomfort with their sexual organs or personal issues—is important and that they need to make us listen.

Helping Kids Sort Things Out

The ability to distinguish between private thoughts and actions, sexual secrets, appropriate boundaries, and inappropriate acts develops over time. It's especially difficult when sexual images and information bombard our kids left and right. If we are to strengthen their confidence and minimize confusion and unnecessary guilt, it is imperative that we as parents provide information to help children sort things out. For example, even if you don't have a problem with the idea that your child may masturbate, you may want to inform him or her that some people masturbate and others don't—or that some masturbate at one period of their lives and not in others. You should also explain that although masturbation is a private way of experiencing sexuality, privacy doesn't mean that it has to be a secret or that it's wrong; rather, privacy is merely respecting one's own boundaries and those of others.

Emotional/Social

Some people reason that masturbation is a staple of adolescent sexuality because it can be done alone and is free, always available, and quick and easy to learn. Another camp argues that masturbation interferes with human social nature and development—and possibly even undermines the drive to find a mate. Certainly, if someone does it frequently every day, masturbation is an obsessive-compulsive behavior and can well be an isolating activity. But when understood as a part of one's developing sexual self, masturbation can also enhance the sexual confidence that enables one to relate to others.

Some people also see masturbation as part of a less mature, underdeveloped sexuality. David was an 18-year-old who consulted me about premature ejaculation. I mentioned a treatment that required masturbation exercises to correct the sexual difficulty. Surprised by the suggestion, he blurted out, "Masturbate? I would never masturbate! I haven't masturbated since I was 13." It turns out David had been taught that "little boys masturbate; men don't." The cultural rules he had been taught clashed with my treatment advice, leaving him uncomfortable with the plan. It's important to recognize and respect how others' values guide different sexual practices—and to feel comfortable and confident enough to establish your own.

Relational

How can you relate to another person sexually if you haven't realized and experienced what sexuality means to you? Because masturbation provides valuable information about how we achieve sexual pleasure, it helps foster communication between partners, who are both then better equipped to talk about their sexual needs and desires.

Spiritual

Some religious traditions teach that sex should be confined to marriage—done for the sole purpose of procreation. It follows that these religions also often view masturbation negatively, condemning it as a sin. The argument emphasizes that sexuality is the ultimate bond between two people and that masturbation is therefore wrong because it leads to self-absorption and the exclusion of others, including God. Other religious viewpoints, meanwhile, support sexuality and masturbation as a means to thrive as human beings and connect with ourselves, each other, and God because all aspects of the self—including our sexuality and spirituality—must be able to coexist in harmony. You need to decide whether or how your religious beliefs will guide your feelings and behaviors about this issue—but it's important to address them openly with your kids.

One young candidate studying for the priesthood confided in me: "You know, if I didn't feel the desire to masturbate, I would really be holy, probably even a saint." Because of his take on the conflict between religion and sexuality, this young man had dissociated from his sexual feelings rather than trying to understand them.

Ironically, by actively fighting his sexual desires, he became *spiritually* self-absorbed. In our therapy sessions, we uncovered a set of deeper issues that his sexual urges had symbolized—but which he had blocked by simply denying those urges. I believe that attuning to our sexuality leads to a genuine and deeper understanding of our reality—physically, emotionally, and spiritually. Often, the picture of ourselves that our sexuality can open us to stretches beyond the impression of who even *we* think we are.

Am I Gay?

Sometimes we think that our choices about sexuality are purely rational and moral. But in making choices about sexuality, there's a lot more involved and at stake than just what you think and want. Let's examine the forces that can come into play by looking at this dialogue between Jake and his father.

(A father finds his 14-year-old son sobbing in his bedroom.)

DAD: What's the matter?

JAKE: Dad, I think something's wrong with me. Guys keep saying I'm gay, and they call me a faggot! I don't think I am. Do you think I am?

DAD: It sounds more like a put-down. Do you think they call you names more than other guys?

JAKE: No, not really. But it still bothers me. I don't think I'm gay, but I guess I hadn't really thought about it that much. Why would they call me that?

DAD: It doesn't seem like something to use as an insult—but sometimes people can be insensitive. Anyway, you should know there's nothing wrong with you. It's normal at your age, very normal, to question your feelings and wonder about your sexuality. Your body and your brain are just changing so much, and that's part of becoming a man. These changes cause a lot of hormones to race through your body, and it can make you feel confused and unsure of your feelings. That's normal. I went through it. Every guy goes through it. And sometimes this questioning inside makes guys so nervous and uncomfortable, they take it out on others, throwing around words such as *gay* like it's an insult. This kind of teasing happens a lot, but it's never okay. Figuring out who you're attracted to is just part of everybody's growing up. It's something you might spend a lot of time thinking about because it's not as obvious to some people as it is to others. It's especially hard because the culture we live in often assumes everyone is or should be straight—meaning heterosexual. Who knows—it may take a few years before you've got yourself figured out. But just remember that no matter what, whether you're straight or gay, your mom and I will love you and support you.

Now, there's nothing easy about a conversation like this for either the father or the son. But it is a crucially important conversation because, more than anything, Jake simply needs to know that, even though it's not right, kids often use sexual orientation as an insult. Comments such as "that's so gay" resound in schoolyards everywhere. Our culture still tolerates and even encourages the view that straight is normal, gay is abnormal. It is important for parents to counteract these harmful ways of thinking and assure kids that any uncertainties within themselves about their sexual orientation are completely normal and okay.

Sexual orientation is a loaded subject—especially with the modern debate over gay marriage and ordination of gay clergy. It's understandable if you feel nervous about broaching the topic. The important thing to remember is that you can't just assume that your child is straight. This assumption could create a wedge that undermines the development of a genuine relationship. That wedge, if created, can take decades to heal; often individuals undergo a long and torturous process of self-acceptance completely without parental support—simply because they assume their parents will not accept them.

And yet many parents who had staunch views against homosexuality have learned, after a child "comes out," that the power of love for a child wins out and will melt strictly held views. With love for your child in mind, you can ask yourself: Would I rather go through that process after decades of emotional separation from my child or do the work now of opening my heart and mind for the sake of enjoying the reward of a continuously open and supportive relationship?

The Heterosexuality-Homosexuality Continuum

Society tends to polarize sexual attraction as if only two distinct orientations exist—homosexual or heterosexual. This dichotomized treatment of such a complex subject is not only unrealistic but also harmful to people as they try to understand their sexual attractions. Designations such as straight, gay, lesbian, or bisexual may serve a purpose for identifying the sexual orientations of particular persons, but they are unhelpful when used to marginalize and stereotype people, judge them, or assign qualities to them. The assumption lives on, mostly unchallenged, that we can determine a psychological profile of a person based on who they are sexually attracted to.

In fact, sexual orientation and attraction appear to exist along a continuum, a theory confirmed by several studies that show a bell curve of sexual orientation with fewer people fitting exclusively heterosexual or homosexual definitions though most define themselves as heterosexual. It is noteworthy that in recent years a growing number of people with bisexual orientations have been acknowledged to exist in all sexual, racial, socioeconomic, religious, and vocational groups.

Same-Sex Attraction

Estimates of the prevalence of strong same-sex attraction hover in the range of 3 to 8 percent of the population.[2] Thus, relatively few parents will have the experience of a child coming out as gay, lesbian, or bisexual. Nevertheless, it is important for parents to keep in mind that children may be experiencing feelings of attraction for members of the same sex—which, as mentioned earlier, can also be manifestations of admiration for someone the child wants to emulate or sees as a hero. The less open we are to listening to the range of feelings our child may be having, the more likely a child with these feelings is to conclude there is something wrong with him or her. Rejecting a child who understands that he or she is homosexual will not change sexual orientation. Indeed, while there remains disagreement over the causes of same-sex attraction, attempts to convert or alter the sexual orientation of homosexuals have largely fallen flat.

I believe that the causes or sources of sexual attraction are too complex for scientific explanations from one field alone—whether genetics, developmental psychology, or psychoanalysis—to satisfy. Because "heterosexual" and "homosexual" are not necessarily distinct categories, there exist in each group people who have had same-sex and opposite-sex experiences. The complex overlapping of experiences and identity point to multiple potential origins of sexual orientation: physical, emotional, and social—and possibly also relational and spiritual.

Some people who experience periods of same-sex attraction ultimately identify as heterosexual. Also, some people who have had heterosexual relationships and experiences ultimately identify as gay or lesbian. People also often experiment sexually during their high school and young adult years as a means of coming to understand their own orientation. Thus, homosexual experiences don't necessarily hold the final word regarding a person's sexual orientation. However, keep in mind that while experimentation is normal and not necessarily a clear predictor of long-term sexual orientation, same-sex behavior may be a true expression of your child's sexual orientation. In fact, as the average age of "coming out" as gay or lesbian is getting younger and younger, you should not be surprised if your child seems confident about their orientation (straight *or* gay!) at a young age.[3] Again, the most important thing is to offer unconditional love and support and to be available to talk with your child about any concerns he or she brings up along the way.

Issues of Sexual Orientation

Though teens are often very accepting of their own sexual orientation, incidents of bullying based on kids' actual or perceived sexual orientation (as in the case of Jake) are still very high and have resulted in increased absenteeism from classes, higher suicide rates, and reports by teens of feeling unsafe in school.[4] Bullying and peer pressure are, unfortunately, an ever-present part of a child's growth in sexual awareness, and sometimes kids are pressured to have sex with a member of the opposite sex to prove that they are not gay. It is always important to stress to children that they can and should make their own decisions about sex—that sexual experiences will always be better and more meaningful when they aren't in response to pressure from someone else.

Archbishop Desmond Tutu: Sexual Differences and Equality

Archbishop Desmond Tutu, a leader in the struggle against South African apartheid and a winner of the Nobel Peace Prize, spoke with me in an interview and explained how he understands sexual orientation and God's take on the matter.

One of the wonderful [directives] we have comes from the words of our Lord before the Crucifixion: "I will be lifted up . . . I will draw all . . ." That "all" is absolutely inclusive—inclusive of us in our racial differences, our gender differences, our status differences, and our differences in sexuality. Sexuality is, in fact, a gift that comes to us from God. I've frequently said that it is very odd if sexuality is a matter of choice, very odd for anyone to want to choose a style of life that attracts so much hatred and that exposes them even to the possibility of death.

We have inflicted on gay and lesbian couples the pain of having to live a lie or face brutal rejection if they [decide] to reveal their true self. But oppression cuts both ways. Behind our "safe barriers" of self-righteousness, we deprive ourselves of the rich gifts that lesbian and gay people have to contribute to the whole body of Christ. . . . Each one of us is of infinite worth. We are all children of God with different gifts, different makeups. We belong in God's family.

The archbishop believes that rather than being judgmental, we should embrace others who may be different from us in a spirit of understanding, acceptance, and openness. This is truly a valuable lesson to pass on to our kids.

Even if your child has assured you that he or she is straight, it's important to discuss sexual orientation and to offer assurance that being gay is nothing to be feared and that name-calling, teasing, and bullying based on sexual orientation are *never* okay. Though your own child may not be gay, chances are high that someone he or she knows at school is, so it's important to educate all kids about sexual orientation so that they are familiar with the reality. This information sharing helps make things easier for *all* kids.

Sexual Abstinence

Both girls and boys will feel and encounter social pressures to have sex. Both will also have the sometimes uncomfortable experience that members of the opposite sex are "sizing them up." To reduce this group pressure, they may often decide to have sex. However, many people choose sexual abstinence because it reinforces the fact that we *do* have choices regarding our sexual behavior. Sexual abstinence is the choice to not give in to those pressures and instead to take control of one's sexuality. By discussing the available alternatives to giving in to sexual pressure, you can help your teen tell the difference between their own needs, wants, and curiosities, and the pressures of others.

Abstinence: A Time for "Do's"

"It's okay not to have sex," a man advises his younger friend. "You, uh . . . what are you, 25?"

"I'm 40," is the reply.

"Holy $*@#, man. You got to get on that."

Sound familiar? If you haven't already recognized it, this snippet of dialogue is from the popular film *The 40-Year-Old Virgin*. In the film, Andy Stitzer is a bumbling, painfully nerdy, action-figure-collecting electronics store employee who is also, at age 40, a virgin. What's so funny about that, you ask? Ask and the likely response is, "Come on. This is the twenty-first century. No one stays a virgin until they're 40, right?"

Is that right? Though mainstream culture might try to depict abstinence as antiquated or even absurd, in addition to religious advocates, some media figures have publicized their vows to abstain from sex. Whether for a period of self-reflection or until they say, "I do," these celebrities have shown abstinence has a lot going for it—regardless of what pop culture might say. Basketball player A. C. Green, for example, held out until he was married at the age of 38, and Rivers Cuomo, lead singer of the band Weezer, vowed to remain celibate for two years.

What's the motivation here? For most, abstinence represents a time of self-reflection—a period to get to know yourself and your needs so that sexual intimacy later on is more rewarding. Pop culture likes to paint abstinence as utterly obsolete, monastic, or, as we saw in the case of *The 40-Year-Old Virgin*, the terrain of oddballs and social disasters. But if your child has chosen abstinence, or if abstinence is a value you promote, try to encourage abstinence not simply as a list of "don'ts," but as a positive and dynamic time for "do's"—*do* spend time getting to know yourself, *do* get to know what you might want in a partner, *do* nurture your physical and spiritual health in ways other than sexual. If viewed as an opportunity for growth and not as a prohibition, abstinence can be a time of significant self-discovery.

With the spread of AIDS and increased awareness of STIs and teen pregnancy, sexual abstinence has become an increasingly popular option for teens. Only about half of teenagers become sexually active by the time they are 17—a percentage that is significantly lower than what is commonly assumed.[5] Though abstinence is still largely thought of as an option called for by religious institutions, it has gained a wider following. Some teens today choose abstinence to assert that they are mature and responsible enough to decide for themselves when to have sex, rather than letting pop culture dictate the decision.

In either case, abstinence needs to be clearly defined because it means different things to different people. Some people think of abstinence as staying away from *any* sexual activity, including "making out," petting, oral sex, anal sex, and even kissing. For others, abstinence simply means not going all the way—but allowing "everything but." This second form of abstinence is sometimes chosen as a means of avoiding pregnancy and STIs or for preserving virginity (an equally loaded term).

Because of the wide range of definitions of this word, it's important to discuss with your kids what abstinence means to them. Though I have outlined a few definitions at the extremes, many variations fall somewhere in between. You'll want to ask your teens about their personal boundaries and how they came to those decisions. Ask them what sexual acts are acceptable or unacceptable for them at this point in their lives and why. Such clarification is necessary and helpful because if you make incorrect assumptions, you may neglect to talk to your teen about certain topics, such as the STI risks associated with oral and anal sex.

Relationships via the Internet

While some people still date in the old-fashioned, face-to-face way, meeting and getting to know each other over the Internet is growing quickly. The advantages of Internet dating include efficiency, the ability to reach out from the comfort of home, the ability to test compatibility before investing time and money in personal meetings, and a sense of safety before the pressure of appearing before another. However, our children are the most Internet-savvy generation yet, and their pervasive presence on personal web portals such as MySpace, IM services, and chat rooms has rightfully drawn the concern of parents interested in guarding the safety and privacy of their children.

So what's our parental strategy when online dialogues transition into the possibility of personal meetings for our kids? How do we protect them from sexual predators or others seeking to exploit our children's youth and innocence? How do we guide our children to choose boundaries that reflect their level of readiness when the Internet opens possibilities of accelerated sexual exposure and encounters? What follows are some suggestions for dealing with Internet communications and dating.

First of all, remind your child that real facts are hard to obtain over the Internet. Just because a person's online profile says that they are 16 doesn't mean they really are, and pictures they post could easily not be of them. We're inundated daily with news stories about shady characters who seek to manipulate children over the Internet. Use these events as real-life instructional material—a more effective vehicle for getting through to your kids than your three-point sermon.

Ask your child to be open and honest with you about Internet communication. It's not unusual or unreasonable for parents of kids under 18 to monitor all their online activity—including knowing what their profiles say on Web sites like MySpace and who they talk to on these sites. It's best to be direct about your policy on Internet privileges. Be sensitive to the fact that kids may want to keep their contacts secret because it's unpleasant to discuss relationships that they're trying to figure out. But if your teen really avoids sharing any information with you, chances are there's something going on you need to know about. Find ways to talk to your teen about what their Internet contacts mean to them, and spend time on Web sites like MySpace to get a feel for the particular appeals and challenges they may present to your child.

Even if your kids have moved off to college or away from home, and you and your child agree that arranging a personal meeting with an online friend is okay, set ground rules focused around safety: meetings should be during the day, in a public place that's familiar to your child, and with a group of friends rather than one-on-one. Arrange a time for a "check-in" call or text message to ensure things are going as planned.

For all dating, Internet-based or otherwise, it's a good idea to rehearse your teen's sexual plan. While going with the flow sounds easy, moving into uncharted waters with an unknown partner can run into unexpected problems. Practicing with your child, reminding him or her to take a few minutes before an action to think about how they will feel the next day—given its potential implications—is a rehearsal well worth its time.

Go over with them ahead of time questions about the possibility of sexual pressures: Is kissing okay? French-kissing? Intercourse? Other sexual practices? Of course, this will be an awkward conversation, but the risks are real on several fronts, so it is a conversation you shouldn't avoid.

If you sense they are planning to have sex, it's reasonable to suggest that they think about the consequences before it happens rather than panicking afterwards. Can this activity lead to an STI? If so, what does it take to have sex safely?

Remind your child that first dates are not about deciding on an idealized perfect match. Really, it's just a chance to check things out. A self-respecting approach suggests trusting the person a little the first time, and if the person responds caringly and appropriately, trusting a little more the next time. By moving at the natural pace that feels right at all levels—not just physical, but also emotional, relational, social, and spiritual—a lot of angst, pain, and loss can be avoided if the date turns out to be disrespectful, manipulative, or inappropriate along the way.

Providing strength and a healthy sense of control will enhance your child's confidence on that first date so that he or she feels empowered to choose to get closer or to move away, based on a responsible assessment of the situation. We'll come back to the topic of dating in Chapter 9.

Sexual Abuse

While for most of us the thought of sexual violation by a family member is hard to imagine, it happens all too frequently, and the impact on a child lasts a lifetime. Sexual abuse, incest, and sexual deviation are among the most difficult topics for parents to address with their children—and yet they are frighteningly too common. It's critical that we discuss these matters openly, for the safety and long-term welfare of all children. The last thing you want to do is make your children feel ashamed or afraid to talk about abuse. Consider the experience of a young woman whom I saw in psychotherapy.

Megan: It's Worse Than You Think

Megan had reached her early 30s without experiencing a loving relationship. Every partnership in her life had turned out abusive in one way or another. During one of our sessions, she described her childhood and, based on the things she said in the conversation, I decided to ask if she had ever been subjected to sexual abuse as a child.

She looked a bit taken aback by my question, and it was clear I had touched a sore spot. She began crying and said, "When I was a teenager, my uncle would force me to have sex with him, and my father did the same thing to my sister."

I gave her a few moments to regain her composure while I took in what she had just revealed. I asked what she thought about the abuse. Her answer was chilling, but, sadly, not unusual: "I always wondered why my father picked my sister and not me."

Though sexually assaulted by her uncle, the biggest issue to Megan was not that she had been violated by a family member, but that she had been rejected by her father, who chose her sister over her. Though we can consider the behavior deplorable, for Megan the worse insult was that her father had not "chosen" her.

Megan's judgment was distorted. Her perspective on the desire of her father, at the supreme cost of the dignity of her body and person, reflects the deep neediness of a child and the emotional price paid when a child is the subject of incest. And it does indeed occur far more often than we would like to admit—in fact, one in three girls and one in six boys are sexually violated before the age of 18. Statistics show that 25 percent of incest perpetrators are uncles and 15 percent fathers, but there are no clear predictors of which types of families will experience incest.[6] Incest and sexual abuse may occur in the most unlikely of situations, and by the most unexpected persons. Another of my patients shared this experience with me.

Marilyn: Struggling beneath a Facade

Marilyn was an attractive student in her early 20s who came to see me because she was experiencing restlessness, insomnia, and muscle tension she attributed to her career path and relationships.

Very adept and able to reflect articulately on her experiences, she quickly undertook relaxation and assertiveness training and readily reviewed her early development to gain insight into her relationships. The daughter of a renowned physician, she said that she appreciated having been able to enjoy life to its fullest and felt good about her parents and her eleven brothers and sisters. She effortlessly explored and shared all the major areas of her life, details of her personality and experiences with her family members.

Though citing stress as her primary reason for seeking therapy, Marilyn always seemed to possess a pleasant, warm, and affectionate manner. As the months of therapy ensued and she solved problem after problem for herself, I began to wonder: Why, if she seemed stress-free, did she want to stay in treatment after a year and a half? What had we missed?

Marilyn had already volunteered information about her sexuality; she had described a healthy sexual relationship with her fiancé. It felt like she continued to want to talk about various topics, but the conversation always seemed somewhat friendly and topical rather than problem-focused. I finally shared these impressions and asked if she felt we should continue to meet. Was there something that she hadn't been able to discuss but should?

For months she had dodged such questions, saying that she found our time together useful and supportive. This afternoon, however, in a quiet voice and a subdued manner, she finally said there was something else.

Between the ages of 11 and 14, her older brother had forced her to perform sexual acts. Though initially her recollection was vague, her eyes welled up as she disclosed the surfacing details. Beneath the buoyant and delightful veneer was a depressed and guilt-ridden woman, deeply in pain. She felt that only after building a trusting and open therapeutic relationship with me, was she finally ready to share this most deeply held secret.

No longer feeling the need to circle the issue or hold back memories, torrents of emotions broke forth. I learned of the intimidation, humiliation, and sexual abuse she had suffered. We finally located the hidden, central source of Marilyn's various psychological struggles.

Only in looking back did it become clear to me that Marilyn had, consciously or not, talked with me for almost two years to establish the safety needed to confront her vulnerability. Our therapeutic rapport provided her the safety she needed to reveal what had knotted up her life below the surface. She had known from the beginning what "the issue" was. But she first wanted to be sure she could talk to me.

I will not go into detail here about how Marilyn's brother, fiancé, and family members participated in her treatment and therapy over several years, resulting in a positive reconciliation and healing for her. Instead, I want to return to the importance of being open with our kids about such issues so that they can avoid the horrible experience of repression and guilt that Marilyn went through.

Feeling safe to speak out in general is essential for a victim to feel safe discussing sexual violation—particularly if the perpetrator is someone we are expected to trust, such as a member of the family, teacher, or member of the clergy. Typically, perpetrators of sexual crimes will be very careful about covering their tracks through intimidation and threats to the security of the victim. They stalk—not unlike predators in the wild—choosing as prey the most vulnerable and unsuspecting.

Who's Guarding the Children?

Picture a blonde 23-year-old woman, a graduate of the University of South Florida with part-time professional singing and modeling experience. Sure, she might sound like the ideal Saturday night date, someone any guy would want to show off to his buddies or take home to mom. What you wouldn't expect is that this is the profile of a convicted sex offender. In 2005, Debra LaFave, a reading teacher in Temple Terrace, Florida, was charged with several counts of having sex with a 14-year-old student. That same year, Beth Geisel, an English teacher in an all-boys high school in upstate New York, pleaded guilty to third-degree rape of a 16-year old and admitted to having sex with two 17-year olds. And eight years before that, Mary Kay Letourneau, a sixth-grade teacher in the state of Washington, pleaded guilty to two counts of second-degree statutory rape. What do all these women have in common? All attractive young women, they're the last people you'd expect to have a criminal record—much less people you'd label with the term *pedophile*.

There's something about watching a beautiful young woman being led out of court in handcuffs that rubs us the wrong way. We like to believe that all little girls are angels—but we can't ignore the opposite end of the spectrum: the pervasive fantasy of the *hot* librarian or the scantily clad nurse reflects a cultural attitude that an element of danger, even illicitness, in "good girls" is, well . . . sexy. This gender double standard was expressed by former Secretary of Labor Robert Reich, who said of Letourneau, "Where were teachers like she when I went to school?" And, even more shockingly, the judge in the LaFave case said, "Don't you wish you were in her class?" Contrast this with the wrath incurred by male pedophiles, who regularly receive threats of castration or partial lobotomies. The gender double standard is stark—men are potentially dangerous predators, and women are potentially their victims—and so pervasive it is nearly invisible.

It's crucial that as parents, we recognize our own preconceptions about whom we are willing to trust with our children. We might *want* to view our day care providers or ballet instructors or softball coaches as saintly, salt-of-the earth folk, but we cannot be blinded by our own prejudices. This is not to generate frenzied paranoia but to encourage parents to remain alert and continually aware of our assumptions. When it comes to the safety of our children, we can afford no double standard.

Addressing incest and sexual abuse with your own children is not easy, particularly if you feel you might be planting unnecessary fears concerning the behavior of relatives, family members, and acquaintances. I suggest using the opportunity of the unfortunately all-too-common related news stories to raise the topic. Let your kids know that these things do occur, and that you are available to discuss any situation they encounter that they feel uncomfortable with. As we've mentioned repeatedly, keeping the lines of communication open is not just a matter of advertising their freedom to "talk to you about anything." Rather, show them your openness through noticeable efforts to discuss personal matters and be helpful with their feelings and concerns. They need to know that you believe them and care enough to consider what they might be going through. This shows them not just that you care, but that you know *how* to care. When facing so powerful a violation as incest or sexual abuse—either personally or in response to the news—you may feel beside yourself with rage and despair. But it's vital to remember that your child needs to know that *their* feelings are your preeminent concern.

Explaining the Risks of Sexual Assault to Your Kids

In the United States, someone is sexually assaulted every two and a half minutes. There are approximately two hundred thousand sexual assaults each year. Close to half of all sexual assault victims are under the age of 18. The Department of Justice estimates that even more assaults occur than are officially reported.

These are very scary statistics. Sexual assault happens, and happens often. And it happens often to children.

Do these statistics mean that your child will be sexually assaulted? While we all hope and pray that it does not, the risk exists, and we can take action. Parents need to educate their children about what is appropriate sexual behavior between themselves and others and begin discussing such issues at a very young age—in small ways, concerning touch and boundaries—in their earliest conversations with toddlers. When children are young, it's vital to talk with them about their control over their body, the differences between appropriate and inappropriate touching, and how to ask an adult they trust for help when they're unsure if they have been touched inappropriately.

Parents can also explain to their preteen daughters the unwanted and potentially dangerous attention that wearing certain types of revealing clothing can bring. It's important to explain to your children the risks of being alone with others, regardless of their age and position (for example, teachers, coaches, clergy, family, and friends). We must also discuss scenarios for handling situations that make them feel uncomfortable or threatened. Similarly, it is critical to talk to your children about appropriate sexual behavior and the very real legal implications of their actions, as they may be quite unaware of what is proper behavior.

More than anything else, though, it's important to love your children, support their developing self-awareness of their body, and encourage them to love, respect, and protect their own body. This *will* help to prevent your child from being a statistic.

We also need to keep in mind that abuse can be very subtle—sometimes hidden beneath seemingly innocent acts of taunting, kidding, or even having fun. The process we spoke about in the beginning of this book—helping your children understand and own their physical bodies, set boundaries, and recognize when lines have been crossed and how to respond—is especially essential when we consider its importance in helping our kids say no to situations of abuse.

Abuse can take on subtle forms yet create significant damage. Though we've already considered the impact of bullying and harassment, sometimes it occurs right in front of us in family settings, and we feel immobilized.

Greg: And No One Intervened

Greg was a junior in college who came to see me because he felt "insecure with girls." As we talked about his past, one incident caught my attention. When he was 8 years old, Greg's large extended family would get together each weekend during the summer for family picnics. One time, his aunt offered to teach all the kids how to play volleyball. Greg wasn't interested as he wanted to fish in the stream for crayfish instead.

About an hour later, Greg heard his aunt yelling his name. She found and cornered him, yelling, "At picnics everyone is supposed to be together." She then pushed him to the ground and pulled down his pants and underpants. He recalled that this happened with most of the adults within viewing distance and his cousins even closer. Some stood in shock while others laughed at him.

Greg called this the most embarrassing moment in his life. Though his mother confronted her sister later about what she had done to Greg, he felt alone and disgraced. The young man cried in front of me: "I couldn't believe that no one came to help me."

Greg was sexually violated in the presence of his entire family. While it's hard to conclude whether there's a connection between this incident and his insecurity with girls, there's no question that the profound pain inflicted on him left him still wounded many years later.

Greg's aunt should have been stopped immediately and held accountable for her actions. But Greg could not recall a single one of the more than twenty adults who were present coming to his aid. The story exemplifies, in a particularly striking and painful way, how easy it is for adults to overlook and thereby tolerate occasions of abuse that may have devastating effects on our children. Both morally and sometimes legally, inaction in the face of abuse makes us party to that abuse. When we have not carefully considered issues of boundaries and what constitutes right and wrong behavior, we can fail to act in situations when our children most need us.

The Many Roads to Sexual Knowledge

You may have been exposed to many sexual situations in your life. Many of them were probably incredibly private, and perhaps a few crossed into the category of secretive or questionable experiences. Can you recall sexual situations that you prefer not to remember or that you wish had never occurred? Imagine your child confronting similar situations.

In sixth grade, I recall my buddy Duke telling me he had already had a girl-friend. "And," he asked, "do you know what a girlfriend can do for you?" Duke was a year older than me and already had peach fuzz around his upper lip. While previously he could be counted on to show up for a game of softball, he had lost touch with our group of friends when he started seeing this girl. He would tell us they were "not really dating"—yet he told stories about how the girl let him "do things" he said wouldn't make me proud of him. Duke treated me as a walking conscience because, although he made a point of sharing the fact that he was regularly having intercourse, he at the same time felt guilt about entering these explorations. The "secret" Duke carried was that he was growing up—and sexually engaging in a way he wasn't proud of. Your kids will hear about such exploits from others and may even them-selves act out in ways that they're not proud of. If you make clear to them that sex isn't a "public secret," they will be more likely to ask for your help as they work to make sense of growing up. Talking about daily events or even reflect-ing on the range of material aired on television can be ways of letting your kids know that you want to hear what's going on in their lives and that you're available to help them understand it.

The same year that Duke shared his tales with me, two tough and popular kids, Tony and Erik, developed their own sexual secret. In shop class, when the instructor left us alone with our woodworking projects, they would pressure Brian—one of our more docile and compliant classmates—into giving them oral sex. I told them to knock it off, but they ignored me, leaving me feeling quite helpless. I asked Brian why he went along with this without getting help, but his response was passive—either his will was defeated or he didn't know what to do. Meanwhile, Tony and Erik bragged about how they wouldn't date or have sex with another classmate of ours named Denise, but they would "let her" give them blow jobs as they knew she would do pretty much anything for their atten-tion. As I look back, I don't know why my classmates and I felt like we couldn't take some kind of action—maybe we feared being victimized ourselves, or maybe we were just unsure that it was any of our business. These stories serve as reminders that when we, as parents, have an open relationship with our kids, they will feel more comfortable telling us about disturbing situations that they experience. We will thus be in a better position to strengthen their confidence as their sexuality develops by helping them distinguish appropriate and inappro-priate behaviors and understand their role in the face of abuse.

As reflected in these memories from my childhood, sexuality and aggression often come together, especially for adolescents. We all have sexual and aggressive impulses and must learn how to manage them. This means not taking advantage of others through greater strength or sexual maturity, but tuning in and responding to the feelings, impulses, and behaviors of others. It also means letting our kids know who they can turn to, in addition to you, for support and guidance. In social settings where confusing, new, and disturbing things occur, such as drinking, bullying, or sexual improprieties, kids are often caught off guard with no clue where to turn or what to do. We have to use the many opportunities we have—whether watching the news, reading the paper, or catching a film—to underscore the resources and strategies for proper, constructive, responsible action.

Classic Issues and Questions

Phew—that's some of the toughest stuff for most of us parents. Issues such as masturbation, abstinence, homosexuality, sexual abuse, and incest are very delicate and, therefore, tend to be the most challenging for parents to discuss with their children. With that hurdle cleared, we can move on to some of the issues and questions that parents have about their kids that qualify as classics, due to relatively consistent interest in these topics across time and place. Below are several of these classic questions to which I've responded. I invite each of you to weigh in, based on your own values and beliefs. Note that although some of these questions refer specifically to a boy or girl, most answers are equally relevant to both sexes.

Toddlers, Preschoolers, and Kindergartners (Ages 2–5)

Q: *We have two kids: our girl is 3 and our boy just turned 5. Since they were very young they've bathed together, and we haven't made much of an issue about their being naked together. My sister visited us recently and was quite upset that we were so casual about their nakedness. Are we making an error in judgment?*

A: Usually toddlers are not very distracted by nakedness and don't perceive seeing their toddler brother or sister—or even a naked adult for that matter—as provocative. However, at around 3 years of age, kids do begin seeking privacy. So in my view, while shared bathing can provide an early opportunity to discuss the differences between boys and girls, around three years of age is an appropriate time to introduce discussions about privacy and boundaries— demonstrate the boundaries for both kids by having them bathe or shower separately. I'd also check with the older child and see for yourself if he has thoughts about privacy. Your 5-year-old may welcome boundaries consistent with what he is learning at school and that support his own need for privacy. Everyone in the home may benefit from establishing house rules about privacy, such as knocking when doors are closed, not walking around naked, and other such guidelines.

If it were my son, I'd open the transition so that he could sometimes shower with me, and maybe the mother could shower with the daughter. This will offer stimulus for new conversations about sexuality and differences while also supporting gender distinctions and identities.

Q: *I've heard that it's inappropriate for parents to walk around the home either nude or in undergarments. Does this behavior cause problems or stimulate the kids too much?*

A: The effects on a child of exposure to nudity often depend on where he or she is developmentally. In other words, a 2-month-old baby boy isn't going to have any feelings about being in bed with his naked mother, whereas a 5-year-old very likely might.

I think that parental nudity requires thoughtful judgment. Overstimulating a child sexually can shut down a child's natural curiosity. At the other extreme, severe modesty can create undue sexual apprehension and anxiety.

I would ask the question, "What's the intention of this nudity?" Is nudity consistent in the child's society? What happens when friends come over? What double standards might the child perceive if the parents put clothes on only when friends come around? How well are we empowering our child's sense of taking control regarding sexual boundaries and privacy in a manner that is comfortable and socially appropriate?

When children start vocalizing questions and becoming self-conscious, which is usually around 2 or 3 years old, discretion should begin to guide matters of privacy. Children should be respected, supported, and encouraged to develop integrity as they grow into confident individuals.

Primary School Kids (Ages 6–8)

Q: *I recall reading that elementary school was not a time when kids develop that much sexually, that they really get going later in middle school. So I'm worried that if I bring up any sexual matters at this point, I'll risk overstimulating my child. Are there any big concerns that I should be addressing at this stage in their development?*

A: You probably did read somewhere that kids aren't developing much sexually during their elementary school years. This theory, which is often called *latency*, suggests that children in elementary school are in a kind of sexual development holding pattern, and that their sexual growth recommences around the time they enter middle school. While there is some truth to the theory of latency, it's certainly not 100 percent accurate.

Up to around age 5, kids are developing incredibly rapidly, from tiny babies to small people who can walk, talk, laugh, cry, articulate their emotions, have likes and dislikes, and so much more. During this time, they also learn the basic facts of life, including that people have different kinds of bodies and that body parts have different functions. Yet their bodies don't usually begin to show any secondary sexual characteristics until closer to when they become teenagers. So does this mean that they are not developing sexually *at all* between ages 6 and 10, and that it's not necessary to talk about sexuality during these years? Not at all. These may be years when your kids wonder more specifically how babies are made. They may be exposed to some more involved sexual material from movies, books, or friends. These years are an excellent time to build strong, open, loving, and gentle relationships with your children. Your children are not yet entering puberty, but there is still a lot of sexual material for them to sort out, and there are still many important conversations to have during these childhood years.

Q: *My second-grade daughter came home and told me she has a boyfriend. What does this mean at this age?*

A: Kids are amazing at picking up adult terminology; they use words that seem light years beyond their maturity levels. Yet these words can make sense when understood in the context of their current growth and development. It's extremely unlikely that your daughter has romantic feelings for her 7-year-old boyfriend in the way that teens and adults think about dating. Kissing tag, played with friends, is probably the extent of their romantic activity, if any. What your daughter probably means by *boyfriend* is that she likes a particular boy for some reason or reasons—maybe because he's very sweet or great at doing flips—and they play games together during recess, share snacks at lunch, and enjoy each other's company, giving each other a sort of special status. Your daughter is, in essence, learning about friendship: she's practicing intimacy with a person of the opposite sex. To her, *boyfriend* means *special* friend or someone she's excited about and really likes. In some ways, it's sad that we don't all choose our partners using such earnest and innocent criteria.

However, it's important to make sure your daughter is doing things that make her feel safe, happy, and healthy. Ask her about what *she* thinks having a boyfriend entails, what they do together, and why the friendship is important to her. Be happy that she has a friend she enjoys, but make sure she's making choices that she feels comfortable with. It's unlikely that she would be doing otherwise, but by acknowledging her happiness and making sure she knows that you're there to talk about it, you'll be in a good place to find out if there's any trouble in 7-year-old paradise.

Preadolescent Boys (Ages 9-11)

Q: *My 11-year-old son has been asking why men have their penises circumcised. How might I go about answering his question in an age-appropriate way?*

A: It's perfectly natural for your son to be curious about circumcision at this age, whether he is circumcised or not. At this point in his development, he may be exposed to other male genitalia in the locker room or in other situations, and he will probably notice that all penises don't look alike. The best answer to this question about circumcision will incorporate information about biology, your values, and positive acknowledgement of the many varieties of human bodies and choices. You might answer as follows:

To get your penis circumcised means that a doctor, or, in some traditions, a person performing a religious ceremony, cuts off the foreskin, the area that covers the tip of the penis. You can tell pretty easily if a boy or man's penis is circumcised because if it is "cut" there is a ridge close to the tip. People used to circumcise baby boys for health reasons or because of religious customs. It's not necessary to do this and doesn't make a huge difference for the function of a penis—either for urinating or in sex—if it's circumcised.

If, as an expectant parent, you're trying to decide whether you want to circumcise your son, it's a good idea for you and your partner to consult with a pediatrician, your spiritual adviser, and anyone else whose opinion you value and trust.

Q: *On several occasions, when my son's close soccer buddy visits, I've overheard him share graphic dirty jokes. Should I let my son be friends with this boy?*

A: One of the toughest parts of being a parent is learning to acknowledge and accept the amount of influence that your child's friends may have over him. It can be very scary for us parents to discover how easily our children can be influenced by children who have not been raised with the same values we have worked so hard to instill. Peers can and do powerfully influence a child's development. But does this mean that your child's friends all need to be screened by you to ensure they promote positive values?

Of course not. The important thing when it comes to peer influence is that your son or daughter always remembers the option of coming to you whenever hurt, confused, curious, or excited feelings come up about something a friend did or said.

True, some kids really can be negative influences, and you'll want to speak with your child and share what you feel is a threat to his or her happiness. In some cases, you may be able to speak with the friend's parents, but this can be difficult if you don't know them personally or if they become sensitive to what they perceive as criticism.

If you feel your child's safety is threatened, don't hesitate to remove him from the situation. But in general, what's most important is that your child knows that you are open to discussing anything and that his feelings about his friends' behaviors are of great importance to you.

Preadolescent Girls (Ages 9–11)

Q: *My daughter has been complaining of aches and pains. I remember my mother telling me that these feelings were "growing pains," but is that true? Does puberty— or these body changes—hurt?*

A: As puberty begins, all kinds of things can happen. Sometimes breasts can be sensitive—especially when they're first developing. For this reason, as well as for general comfort and appearance, many girls choose to wear bras.

The other normal change that sometimes produces physical and emotional discomfort is menstruation. It's important to see how your daughter feels with the cycles because sometimes it's possible to get medication. But puberty should not be painful in a big way, and if your daughter feels pain, talk about it with her and help her find a solution, possibly by means of a medical consultation. Make sure to figure out with your daughter whether she wants to see her regular pediatrician or whether she's ready to go and talk to a gynecologist. Check in with your daughter about whether she's comfortable seeing a male physician or whether she'd prefer to talk to a woman. While these may seem like small details, it's very important to ensure that your daughter is as comfortable as possible when discussing such sensitive issues. (Similarly, if your son has been seeing a woman pediatrician, at around age 10 ask if he'd prefer to have a male doctor.)

Adolescent Boys (Ages 12–18)

Q: *My son's voice is in the process of changing, and I want to help him understand that what he's going through is a healthy part of growing up so that he isn't constantly embarrassed or caught off guard. How should I approach this discussion? Would it be insensitive to inject humor into the situation?*

A: It may be really tempting to laugh when you hear the crack of a boy's adolescent voice, but if your son's not yet ready to find his voice change funny, it's crucial to be sensitive to his feelings when you discuss what's going on with him. Watch his reaction to his voice cracking; does he make fun of himself, or does he turn beet red and try to change the subject? Once you've gauged how he feels, you'll have a better idea of how to approach the conversation. But whether you take a lighthearted or serious approach, be as open and clear as possible. Your explanation might go something like this:

When boys get to be a certain age, their larynx—also called a voice box or Adam's apple—grows larger. As the vocal cords get thicker and longer, we hear a deeper voice. As you go through these growth changes, every so often your voice will crack—it suddenly becomes squeaky—not the best situation if you're giving a speech or presentation. But hang in there; it's just part of the change from boy to man.

Q: *I was doing the laundry last week and noticed that my son had piled several sets of sheets in a ball on the floor of his room. When I asked him why he had changed his sheets multiple times, he blushed, mumbled incomprehensibly, and left the room. My guess is that he's having wet dreams, and I want to talk with him about what he's experiencing, but I'm not quite sure how to begin the conversation.*

A: Wet dreams (technically called *noctural emissions*) are normal experiences for boys growing up, but they are certainly sometimes awkward to manage. Neither you nor your son should be embarrassed though. Wet dreams occur for both boys and men. Sometimes boys and men recall ejaculating after having a dream about sex, but other times wet dreams are not connected to a sexual fantasy.

If you and your son have not yet talked about wet dreams, there's clearly no better opportunity. However, you don't want to put him on the defensive by appearing critical of his behavior or calling attention to the soiled sheets he dumped on the floor. You also don't want to bombard him with information he already knows, or you'll just elicit an eye roll or two. Chances are, your son and his buddies have been swapping stories and making hypotheses about this bedtime phenomenon. This may be a subject that is more comfortable for a boy to discuss with his father in greater detail—although his mother, too, should certainly be available to discuss the topic.

It's a good idea for boys and their parents to anticipate the possibility of wet dreams and to plan to manage the situation respectfully and privately. You and your son could brainstorm solutions together. For example, if your son discovers that he had a wet dream, you and he may have agreed on a plan where he can toss the soiled clothing and bed sheets into the wash or hamper and, without discussion, get clean linens and pajamas.

Q: *While cleaning out the family computer, I found out that my 12-year-old son has been viewing pornographic Web sites. Is it normal at his age for boys to be interested in pornography? And what's a helpful, appropriate response?*

A: Pornography is a difficult topic to address at any age, with your kids or with your partner. Usually it's not a single occurrence. An interest in pornography may run the gamut from harmless exploration to problematic sexual compulsivity. Pornography can mean different things and serve different purposes. If you find out that your adolescent son has been viewing nude photos or videos of people having sex, it doesn't mean that he's out having intercourse or that he has unhealthy desires or urges. It can simply mean that he's starting to be interested in exploring or fantasizing about certain expressions of his sexual development.

However, it is also important to note that while an interest in sexuality isn't unhealthy, parents can and should address the topic with their children. Pornography cannot substitute for open discussions about sexual maturation, and you certainly don't want pornography to replace normal relationships. Unfortunately, disturbing and violent material is easily accessible on the Internet, and talking with your young children after they have been exposed to such disturbing pornography will not erase their trauma and distress. That is why safeguards such as instituting parental Internet controls or monitoring your child's computer use make a great deal of sense.

It's a good idea to have a preemptive conversation with your child about pornography: tell him how you feel about pornography; discuss whatever knowledge, feelings, and experience of pornography he has; and let him know that you're always there to talk about these kinds of issues. When it comes to a topic like pornography, it's important that you bring it up first: no matter how open you are or how close you may be to your child, it will be a difficult subject for a child to raise himself, as there are so many taboos surrounding the topic.

Some people believe that pornography is always an inappropriate medium; if that is your view, you need to communicate openly and clearly why you, your faith, or other value system takes the stance that you subscribe to concerning pornography.

Q: *Last week, I overheard my two teenage sons talking in the den. They were boasting about all of the sexual things they do with girls. As their father, I feel unsure about how to appropriately involve myself in their conversation so that I can make sure they're being safe and only doing what they and the girls are comfortable with. How should I approach joining their conversation?*

A: While it's right for you to try to remain involved in their sexual development and exploration, fight the urge to swoop in. The last thing your boys want is for Dad to come dashing in from the kitchen, spatula in hand, butting into what they thought was a private conversation. The same goes for conversations you might overhear between your teen and friends, or from your teen's end of a telephone conversation. It's crucial that siblings bond without their mom or dad constantly looking over their shoulders. Wait for the right time—driving them to the mall, or after the game on TV—and bring up what's on your mind. Be honest about what you've overheard: "I couldn't help but catch some of your conversation the other day, and I want to make sure you boys are being smart about the things you do with girls—and that you treat girls with respect." Make sure they know your values regarding sexual activity. Then wait and see where they'd like to take the conversation.

The challenge with teens, of course, is that usually they don't want to hear any of your advice. Teens often like to think that they've got it all figured out and that parents "just don't understand." If you have waited until now to have "the talk" with them, it shouldn't be surprising that they've been having this talk with each other for quite a while! So instead of delivering a long-winded monologue, simply offer a little wisdom, and see if they want to move forward with the conversation. By sprinkling small seeds with your teens, you open the chance of a larger ongoing conversation, letting them know you want to remain involved but showing that you respect their boundaries as well.

Q: *My son borrowed my car to go on a date, and when I got in the car the next day, I found a condom. I didn't know that he was sexually active. What should I do?*

A: As tempting as it might be, don't jump to conclusions. Just because your son is in possession of a condom does not mean that he is actually using one. For many teenage boys, carrying a condom can be something of a status symbol. Boys may feel pressured to be seen as cool and popular, and having sex—or, at least, the appearance of having sex—may earn him some points among other boys. That said, you may want to reassure your son that there's nothing wrong with abstaining, and he shouldn't feel pressured to do anything he does not feel ready for.

Of course, there is the possibility that your son is sexually active. Approach him gently and not accusingly; otherwise he will shut down and the conversation will be over. Suddenly pouncing on him with, "Are you having *sex?*" will probably only make him defensive. Instead, say something like, "I found a condom in the car, and I think we should talk about it."

Be clear what your values are regarding sex. Do you approve of him having sex at his age? If so, you are likely to be relieved that he is practicing safe sex, and you can use this occasion as an opportunity to show support for that choice and to act as a resource for his questions. However, if you do not condone him having sex at this age, make it clear—with gentleness, but also with resolve. Don't alienate him by saying something like, "Don't ever let me find condoms in my car again," because you'll probably get precisely what you ask for: you'll never *find* condoms—or worse, he will stop using them. Don't give him reason to become more and more secretive at a time he needs you most.

Communicate as clearly and honestly as possible what your values are regarding sex. In addition, sex inevitably carries significant responsibilities and consequences in all the spheres of sexuality we've addressed. Discuss the consequences as you see them, both practical and emotional, that can accompany sex at his age. And most of all, keep the communication going.

Adolescent Girls (Ages 12–18)

Q: *I found out that my daughter was asked about her breasts during a conversation with someone on MySpace.com. What should I do?*

A: During the preteen and teen years, forming social identity is a vitally important step in your child's development. It's no wonder, then, that online social networks such as MySpace and Facebook are especially alluring to teens. While we can't always hover over our children's shoulders when they surf the Web, we want to be sure that they are navigating these tricky waters carefully. Ask your adolescent what she thinks are appropriate or inappropriate ways to describe herself to the online community. Mention that responsible communication includes making conscious decisions about what we intend to communicate as well as considering the impact of the messages we send.

In this situation, make sure to relate these important reminders to the message you'll give about handling the question about her breasts. You have an important opportunity to discuss with your daughter the possible intentions of the questioner as well as the scenarios, fantasies, and dangers that can be stirred by engaging in such personal communication in a public and anonymous network. For example, the personal pictures that we choose to post and the self-descriptions we write form this representation. You will want to talk about "safe" sites that only allow preapproved people to view your personal information and why it is essential that she use only such sites.

Make sure your adolescent knows that any online behavior that confuses or upsets her is not okay, and that if she encounters such behavior, reports can be made to MySpace or the authorities. (You should also know that MySpace carries an option for parents to delete their child's account, and there are many online monitoring programs parents can use, such as Software4parents.com and k9webprotection.com.)

However, what's most important is the conversation with your children, and not just having the authority to delete their accounts. You need to learn about the online community that you are allowing your child to enter. Do the research, talk to them, and stay involved!

Q: *I read a document that my daughter had left open on the computer, a poem she had written about a sexual fantasy she had. The fantasy disturbed me. How should I talk to her about it?*

A: Fantasies are funny things—they're intensely personal, usually purely imaginative, and sometimes very different from what you might expect from a person, even someone you know well. Some people like to imagine waterfalls; others, whips and chains. Fantasies often are entirely unrealistic, and other times they involve real people and situations we have lived through. For the most part, fantasies are fantastical, separate from reality, and not intended to be acted upon. Yet the relationship between one's fantasy and reality is difficult to know as fantasies sometimes are rehearsals for reality and desires that might be followed through on.

Some fantasies can seem disturbing to others. If you find yourself judging another's fantasies, just remember the expression, "to each his own"—it was practically invented for this kind of situation. At the same time, if your child is writing about engaging in a behavior that makes you worry for her health or safety, it's important to talk with her about your very real concerns. Hopefully, you will have already laid the groundwork for having these types of very honest discussions.

Your daughter may feel as if you've violated her privacy by reading her poem—although it's possible she left her poem in view because she wanted you to read it and needs help coping with her fantasies or desires. Make clear you found it by accident and that you think it's great she's expressing herself so articulately. Tell her you want her to know that you are a resource for all kinds of questions and impulses she may have. It may be good to remember some of your more unusual sexual fantasies, to help you approach the subject tenderly and without judgment.

It's vital that your children know that while fantasizing is healthy, different rules apply when making a fantasy into reality. This goes for all fantasies, sexual or otherwise: it's fun to imagine skydiving, but you'd be much more careful standing in the doorway of a real plane. The sexual plane delivers a lot of turbulence in real life that doesn't show up in fantasies of friendly skies. When your children are ready to jump into sexual experiences in real life, make sure that you've gone over the risks and backup plans with them and that they bring a good parachute!

Q: *I found a pregnancy test when I was cleaning my daughter's bathroom. This must mean that she is sexually active and that she may be having unprotected sex. She may even be pregnant! What should I do?*

A: First of all, take a deep breath. This situation is incredibly hard for both parents and children, and it's vital not to start feeling angry, sad, scared, or any number of emotions that may be coming from incorrect assumptions.

Having a pregnancy test does not necessarily equal unsafe sex or pregnancy. Your daughter is most likely sexually active, but she may have bought the test only as a precaution, acknowledging to herself that while she's been safe or lucky so far, accidents can happen. Or, of course, the test could mean that your daughter fears she is pregnant and has purchased the test to find out the truth.

To make this conversation as healthy, safe, productive, and loving as possible, approach your daughter gently. Waving the pregnancy test in her face and demanding to know what's going on will only make her unwilling and unable to confide in you.

Tell her that you accidentally found the test and that you didn't mean to infringe on her privacy, but now that you've found the test, you do want to talk about it. Ask her as kindly as you can why she has the test, and see whether she's willing to talk about it. Make sure that she knows that you'll support and love her, no matter what she tells you. This conversation may be very tough— she might have to tell you some difficult things about her private behavior. But no matter how complicated the content of the conversation, what's important is that the tone is focused on her needs and where *she* is, rather than your own anxieties.

Q: *My 15-year-old daughter wants to date a 21-year-old student from the local college. I can't help but wonder what his intentions are. How can I talk to my daughter about this subject without seeming to prejudge her and the situation?*

A: There's something to the common wisdom that six years is a world of difference between 15 and 21, and barely a blip of time between 25 and 31. Regardless of your daughter's level of maturity, the reality is that her 21-year-old boyfriend is operating in a different realm with a vastly different set of expectations. It's vital to talk with your daughter about the problems that could arise by dating someone at such a different place in life. The disparity between them may not only be sexual (although the differences in sexual experience and expectations may indeed be vast), but will likely also include everything from different educational experience (will she be able to relate to his ideas?) and leisure activities (he can legally consume alcohol and visit bars, while she cannot). You may also want to point out that if a 21-year-old is intimate with a 15-year-old, he is guilty in most states of statutory rape and can be arrested.

It's important to present these potential disparities in a nonjudgmental manner. So ask open-ended questions: What kind of a person is he? What is he studying? How did you meet him? What do you like about him? What are his friends like? By understanding why she is attracted to him, you may be able to better steer her toward finding those same qualities (an appreciation for a particular band, an interest in the theater) in someone else, whose age and expectations (sexual and otherwise) are more likely to be appropriate for your daughter.

However, if she is enamored of this man, we should remember our teenage years enough to recognize that a well-reasoned case is flimsy next to the promise of romance. She may insist that this may be one of those one-in-a-million cases. You may decide it is better to allow her to see this man in your home while you are present—perhaps having him over for dinner with the family—and to stress that as she gets older she will be allowed to go on dates outside the home with him, with appropriate curfews.

Behavior over time is one of the most significant measures of what's real, and if this relationship can endure with the restraints that you establish, in a few years she will be able to assess her experiences and feelings and proceed in developing this relationship.

NINE

What's Love Got to Do with It?

For one human being to love another; that is perhaps the most difficult of all our tasks, the ultimate, the last test and proof, the work for which all other work is preparation.

—RAINER MARIA RILKE

Sexuality is not something that just shows up at puberty. By the time adolescence hits, sexuality emerges as a product of our *total* history. The memories, perspectives, and experiences that make up our personal histories all contribute to what sex becomes for us—including the connection between our deepest motivations, our physical expressions of love, and so much more that is beyond language itself. With that wider understanding of love in mind, it starts to make sense that simple rules of "should" and "should not" about sex neither fully satisfy our emotions nor can be a final standard for evaluating our actions. To help us better grasp the complex, multifaceted nature of sexuality, we need to explore the relationship between sex, intimacy, and love.

Sex, intimacy, and love are three of the most powerful sources of connection we will have with others in our lives. In previous chapters we explored a fuller understanding of sex as it relates to the physical, social, emotional, relational, and spiritual aspects of our lives; it's now time to focus on two overlapping aspects of sex—intimacy and love—that give expression to our true self and connect us to our potential.

Defining Intimacy

Some people use the word *intimacy* to describe the act of sexual intercourse. But intimacy is in fact deeper, more meaningful, and more multidimensional than intercourse. It is a long-lasting emotional bond between people that resonates much further than a short-lived physical act. To be an intimate partner requires profound trust and care for someone else. The trust part is this: you allow another to see who you are, and you know that they value you because of—and sometimes, in spite of—your real self (who you are right now). And the "caring" part is that you, in turn, choose to see and embrace another without imposing your own needs, feelings, and thoughts on them. Intimacy is, in short, *knowing yourself through the eyes of another and allowing them to know themselves through you.* True intimacy is really a mind-blowing mystery: you let go of your own demands, and you find your "true self" by taking on the needs of another.

Our first understanding and experience of intimacy comes from the trusting relationship that is developed with our parents during childhood. Through the affection and attention we receive as children, we learn both about ourselves and about the dynamics of interpersonal relationships. Usually, we are the beneficiaries of our parents' love and learn to love in kind. As affection and trust are internalized, we develop our ability to initiate and maintain enduring, intimate relationships with others. Parents are crucial for setting into motion for their kids a model for what it means for us to be intimate with one another.

Defining Love

The English language uses the word *love* to capture a variety of experiences. By contrast, Greek uses at least four separate words to describe love: *eros, philia, storge,* and *agape. Eros* is sensual, physical, all-encompassing love, including sexual passion; *philia* is love shared through friendship or companionship; *storge* describes commitment, as in parents' enduring care for their child; and *agape* is unconditional, altruistic giving to others. The ambiguous meaning of *love* in the English language can cause us (and those whom we love) confusion or misunderstanding. For example, saying "I love you" to another may indicate passionate physical attraction, friendship, familial commitment, or unconditional care. The term *love* is difficult for us to pinpoint in English, as it can simultaneously be one of those experiences, be all of these forms, or a combination of any number of them.

We generally associate romantic love with some form of sexuality. Some express love without sex, just as others experience sexual relationships without love. Usually, what we call romantic love excites the physical, emotional, and spiritual aspects of our selves; however, love can be all of those things without being romantic. For many, marriage is about finding that special person who engages us fully and in every dimension.

In modern society, love is often thought of in terms of function, utility, and personal gain. However, restricting love to these considerations deprives us of the awe, mystery, and reverence that love can introduce. In the same way, when we experience sexuality that doesn't engage us on these higher levels, we are left with a narrow experience of what it means to love.

Looking for Love in All the Wrong Places

"My body's interested, my heart is pounding . . . but is anybody out there for me?" This is a common sentiment of the students and patients I see. Often, out of fear of loneliness, a need for companionship, or an inability to connect in positive ways, people settle for sexual experiences to find short-term comfort and feel what it's like "to be connected." As Tina Turner described in the song "What's Love Got to Do with It?", people sometimes equate sex with love. This was the case with Dena, a patient of mine.

Dena: "Love Is Sex; Sex Is Love"

Dena came to me because she knew her sexual behavior had gotten out of control. Although some people are naturally more sexual than others, as Dena and I discussed her life and sexual history, her stories revealed a sad truth: it wasn't sexual satisfaction that Dena was constantly seeking, but love.

Since childhood, Dena had lacked love and support from her family. Her father had left when she was a newborn, and her mother's complicated psychiatric problems had rendered her unfit to raise a child. Dena had grown up in a series of foster homes, and as she was moved from family to family, her instability increased because of the sexual abuse she experienced in many of the homes. These early, unwanted exposures to sex had led Dena to believe that her sexuality was the only thing that could earn attention or love for her. As a result, she had been having sexual intercourse as often as two or three times a day since her early teens, often with different men.

Because she had never experienced any sort of relationship built on trust or the kind of unconditional love a parent normally provides, Dena believed the only way to get a person to truly care for her was to have sex with them. This was the only form of "care" that she understood. Based on her deep belief that all men want is sex, she had created a motto for herself: "Love is sex, and sex is love." In the end, she was left feeling just as lonely, wounded, and detached as she had felt during her childhood.

Over time, I helped Dena to better understand what her sexual activity represented and to recognize that there were different kinds of men and different kinds of love. Together, we distinguished between her emotional needs and her sexual desires, so she could move forward in a more healthy way. Once she had learned about the differences and connections between sex and love, and developed a clear understanding of her past, she began to experience love on new levels and in new ways. Dena learned to develop relationships with different men based on their personalities and their shared intimacy, rather than solely on their sexual interaction.

As Dena's story demonstrates, when our sexual experiences lack emotional and spiritual dimensions, the physical dimension can become overpowering and destructive. Physicality alone is changing, limited—ultimately not sustaining—and often comes with its own costs and risks. We can help sexuality be healthier for our children if our discussion of sex with them is all-encompassing, embracing what makes us most complete according to our whole nature—physically, emotionally, relationally, socially, and spiritually. In this chapter, we will explore the interconnection between these spheres so we can guide our children in making both the distinctions and the connections between sex, intimacy, and love.

Kids can confuse sex and love, and find themselves "looking for love in all the wrong places," as the classic tune declares. At the same time, if we are not careful and conscious as parents, kids can also easily conclude that love doesn't exist at all. This was the case with another patient, Mark, whose story exhibits again the potentially damaging effects that occur when parents neglect to instruct their children about the connection between sex and love.

Mark: Dancing Alone

When I first began to see Mark, he said he was "unable to have a relationship." But it wasn't because women weren't attracted to Mark; on the contrary, women flocked to him. Mark was a handsome 23-year-old who worked as a Chippendale's dancer. His problem was that while he acted interested in the women he dated, he actually "felt nothing for them."

Mark's childhood had been lonely and isolated. His mother had died of a heart attack when he was 10, and he said he had never known her because she worked "all the time." He only remembered her wanting to buy him clothes, which to him embodied the emotional emptiness of his upbringing. He had no memories of comfort, and he felt his family had been burdened by a lack of money. He also saw his father as remote. By the time he was in his late teens, with only an inattentive father to support him, Mark had been pretty much on his own.

He had soon discovered that his good looks could produce fast money—and a lot of attention—so he had become a Chippendale's dancer. Money, however, was never enough and did little to fill his void. As he clearly articulated:

I always wanted something that would make me feel good. At first, I thought good clothes were the answer. Then it was a trip watching how people would get excited when I took off those nice clothes. I wanted their excitement—their feeling. Yeah, I would smile, but after the show I was empty. Same with sex. For me sex is a gig; it doesn't do much for me. I get off on what others feel, but I feel nothing.

But Mark was only telling half the story. His efforts to relieve his emptiness were more extreme. Later, I learned that he would regularly seduce women so they would take him home after a Chippendale's show. After sex, when the unsuspecting woman fell asleep, he would steal her credit cards, return to bed, and depart the next morning.

Over the course of therapy, Mark realized that his deception of himself and others was caused by inadequate emotional support in childhood and anger at his mother's death. Many of his behaviors—of which his exhibitionism and robbery were only the most pronounced—were cries from a lonely, bottomless pit within him to "get attention." Mark's sexual self was hollow, since he could never feel the emotion he evoked in others; sexuality was a ritual in which he danced alone, without a partner to reciprocate.

Mark had a narcissistic personality disorder. You may remember the Greek myth of Narcissus, the handsome man who was so enamored of his own reflection in a pond that he never left its side and faded away into nothingness. Narcissists become consumed with their own significance, and when we indulge them, we ourselves can also become absorbed in the reflection of their magnificence. Even though Mark seemed indifferent to his seductions, he continuously roped women in, collecting their affections as one might collect novelty coins. Because he wore an automatic facade of affection that never connected to his true feelings, he was unable to discover, build, or accept his true self until he honestly looked at himself, his feelings, and his behaviors. Mark finally came to realize that he needed to get to the root of his anger before he could develop what was essential: a genuine connection with another person.

Hope ignited for him in therapy. His search for consistent, caring support led him to try learning to trust. Eventually, after tapping into his true self, Mark was able to develop real relationships that gave him real opportunities for growth.

Mark's story underscores the importance of genuinely connecting with our kids. While it is not anyone's fault that Mark's mother died and that his father may have had a hard time as a single dad, we have to ask: what commitments are children learning to foster in their earliest relationships? Parents need to listen to their children's concerns and support their children's growth by giving them sound values that help them see how intimacy and love can look and take shape. So how do we express values in our relationships with our kids? And which values are important?

Values and Loving

Values help us structure our connections with others. They give us purpose, meaning, and guidance as we confront challenges that naturally arise in relating to others and the world. We often speak of values as the goals we strive for and the virtues we maintain. However, it's helpful to talk with your kids about what values are starting to guide their sexual, intimate, and loving behaviors and to understand the sources and reasons behind them. Here's one way you might introduce the importance of values to your young child:

Every time we have to make a decision, we use the values that we have in order to help us make that decision. Values aren't things that you hold, like money or candy. They are inside of you. What do you like best about your best friend? Or about your-self? Or your mom and dad? What things do you like about the person you admire the most? Those are all of the qualities that point to what we value because they come from things that are valuable to us. For example, sharing ice cream shows values of giving or generosity and care, friendship, and love. And all of those are things we find important in life.

Values are fundamental to our true sexual fulfillment. To be fulfilled in our sexuality, our sexual actions need to be grounded in our values. Otherwise, sex will never connect with the big picture and deeper parts of who we are. As we saw in Chapter 6, it's possible to be attracted to someone physically and start fantasizing about intimacy and love that just isn't there—no mat-ter how much we want it to be. The fact is that just sharing sex, an activity that can be quite self-focused (we can masturbate alone, after all), is much easier than sharing true intimacy. Intimacy cannot exist unless partners focus both on themselves and on their partner—exhibiting the values of caring, sharing, loving.

Frequently after getting married, people experience an after-the-honeymoon phase, characterized by distance and lack of attraction. Couples sometimes say they feel less attracted to their spouses in this phase, or that they are somehow emotionally turned off. I think in many cases it's likely this lack of fulfillment results from a relationship that grew primarily from physical attraction or from partners seeing what they wanted to see in each other, rather than really tuning into each other's personalities (their wants, needs, desires, who they actually are) and nourishing a deeper connection of shared values and intimacy. If we want our children to have fulfilling relationships, we need to foster in them an awareness and appreciation of their own values, and teach them to be vigilant in assessing whether their relationships reflect those values. The more in tune they are with the deepest aspects of themselves, the more readily they can recognize partners who can engage them on those levels.

Partners must tune into each other, identify shared values, and build up values that they admire in one another—or else the foundation of their relationship is on shaky ground. While sexual desire may decline over time, intimacy sustains a relationship in the long term as partners support and strengthen each other through shared values. Values are indeed valuable! Your preteen and teen children (or you yourself) can complete Exercise 9.1 to get a reading of the qualities and values that they find attractive in others. This is the kind of check-in that may change over time. This exercise will help your children identify their deepest—and often undiscovered—values so they will know what to look for in their friends and partners.

Exercise 9.1: What Qualities Do You Value in Others?

Think about the qualities listed below and use the following rating scale to rate how much you value them in a person who attracts you.

1	2	3	4	5
Unimportant	Somewhat valued	Desirable	Important	Essential

___ Ambitious

___ Attentive

___ Competent

___ Cheerful

___ Cooperative

___ Courteous

___ Dependable

___ Empathetic

___ Enthusiastic

___ Faithful

___ Generous

___ Helpful

___ Honest

___ Intelligent

___ Just

___ Kind

___ Moral

___ Nurturing

___ Physically attractive

___ Sense of humor

___ Sensitive

___ Sensual

___ Other

_____

After your children complete Exercise 9.1, ask them if they themselves embody the qualities they value or if they seek out someone who complements their strengths. Then ask them: Who do you share these values with? Are they shared with your best friend? With those you love? As parents, you may want to review your values and note the particular activities or experiences that put these values into action in the home. For example, if kindness is a value, are expressions of kindness acknowledged and supported? When someone is unkind, is this constructively addressed and corrected? Are you pleased with what you've identified as your values? Do you think your values lead you to meaningful connections? Do those with whom you enjoy relationships share similar values?

Support Systems

Because your kids really need a warm, loving, parental arm (both literally and metaphorically) over their shoulders when sorting through sexual feelings and making choices about dating and intimacy, it should be your top priority to help them identify their values and the support systems that will reinforce those values. Support systems don't always mean formal groups, but rather people or circles of people whose voices have an impact on your kids. They won't always be made up of the genuine, concerned voices you might hope for; sometimes kids settle for less than caring, constructive support in order to feel recognized or accepted. Negative influences from peers, media, and others can lead your child down destructive paths by communicating negative values, so it's up to you to steer them in the direction of constructive support systems.

Who makes up your child's support system? This group can include friends, coaches, teachers, clergy, family members—and, of course, you. The support system will be made up of people whose messages most significantly influence your child's choices, so you have an important role in helping your child recognize the qualities of a healthy support group. Among other things, healthy support groups build the following qualities in your child:

- *Mutuality:* reciprocal giving and taking
- *Positive esteem:* valuing one's identity
- *Empathy:* caring for others
- *Respect for individuality:* supporting personal qualities
- *Support for growth:* celebrating one another's accomplishments

You can't just select your child's support system. Ultimately, children will listen to those they trust and admire. But you can counsel your child in how to choose the people whom they listen to. If your child can understand—rather than be told—why you affirm or feel uneasy about their friends or their choices, they are more likely to consider your input in rethinking their decisions. Supporting and counseling your child through this process of developing a support system generally comes along with a time commitment—getting to know their friends by having them over and going to games or school events. This is time well spent as it allows you to have a presence in your child's social life and to meet the individuals who figure prominently in it. Speaking of those prominent other individuals in our children's lives, let's move on now to the territory of girlfriends and boyfriends: dating.

Dating: Sorting out Love

Since the beginning of this book, we've considered how complex sex is; in this chapter we cast an even larger net to encompass the many levels and dimensions of love. While much is known about how the plumbing of sex works, the question of how love works has eluded the brightest minds and most searching hearts. So you're not alone in wrestling with this ultimate question but a part of the human race!

Throughout this book, we've observed the vast disconnection between sex and love in our culture. Try this fact on for size: before graduating high school, the majority of American teens have engaged in sexual intercourse. Yet how many American teens truly know what "love" is? Common sense (and experience!) tells us that sex is not the best or only way to figure out love. The best way to figure out how to love is through meaningful, intimate relationships and dating.

Kids and Dating

When it comes to navigating the unpredictable terrain of teenagers and dating, most parents feel just as lost and ill-equipped as their teens. In 2005, *Time* magazine reported a study by the National Center for Health that found that more than half of the adolescents surveyed had engaged in oral sex. About 11 percent of girls ages 15 through 19 had reported having at least one same-sex encounter. And in a 2001 article, *Time* touched on the hidden underside of teen dating—dating abuse and violence.

The reality is enough to throw parents into a state of panic. So how do we, as parents, guide our teens (and ourselves!) through the murky landscape of teen dating? Here's one place to start: show them you love them. A study from Advocates for Youth concluded that adolescents who reported feeling connected to parents and family were more likely than other teens to wait longer to have sex. A study also showed that teens whose parents made consistent efforts to get to know their friends and to keep track of their whereabouts reported fewer sexual partners, fewer coital acts, and more use of contraceptives.

The bottom line: stay involved! This doesn't mean you should morph into Boot Camp Mom or Prison Ward Dad by barking orders as your child leaves the house. Resist the urge to plant that surveillance camera in the family car! But *do* let your teen know that his or her dating life is of genuine concern to you. Make sure you know what your teen's boundaries are—for example, what exactly counts as sex? Voice your values and ask your teen to voice his or hers. Stay vocal. Remember, if your teen trusts and respects the source, they are more likely to heed your wisdom. You may not be able to sit between them at the Cineplex or barricade the doors to the bedrooms when they're at home after school and you're still at work, but you can make sure they've thought about what they're doing while they're there.

There's no question about it, your child's first date is a milestone worthy of excitement and anticipation. But what dating becomes has a lot to do with the kind of significance that we attach to it. Some see dating as a status symbol—access to an elite and sought-after commodity. However, the goal of dating should be to discover what we seek in a relationship—and to refine our understanding of love. In the beginning stages of the dating process, it's quite typical for kids to be unsure about what they expect to happen on a date. So it makes sense that your kids' first date may be centered on an event such as a carnival or concert or on creating a certain atmosphere where they feel in their element. Their goal may be, at this early stage, to simply accomplish this milestone rather than to explore the nuances of an intimate relationship.

So how can parents guide their children through this challenging process? One important way is to listen when your kids tell you about the qualities they like in the person they date—their *values*, so to speak. (Hint: refer to Exercise 9.1.) If you have established yourself as a thoughtful and sympathetic confidante, your opinion will matter to your teens. On the other hand, if you make it clear to your teens that no one is good enough for them, you may not get to hear what they feel and think. Try to suppress your own preferences (who and what you envisioned for that first date) and tune in to the things your son or daughter appreciates about that person and the plans they have made.

When your kids first start to date, it can be a nerve-wracking time for everyone involved. Whether you're the mom or the dad, your support will be very helpful. Make sure to communicate with your teens about details: Is the date starting too early in the evening? Too late? Are the locations and activities to their liking? What time will they be home? These should all be topics for open discussion. You can also provide your kids with some "objective" opinions about their choice of clothing (the red shirt or the blue?) and the activity for this date, and, of course, a few extra hugs before they go.

While you cannot wave a magic wand and turn a frog into a prince, you can convince your child that he or she is "okay" at dating, no matter what. Help them understand that dating is about getting to know other people and letting them get to know you—the *real* you, not the "you" you think they want to see. At the same time, talk to your kids about the ways a date can go seriously wrong, whether through misrepresenting information (for example, lying to create a certain impression) or doing things against their better judgment (for example, breaking the law, drinking, taking drugs, or having sex). While intimacy, particularly in later years, may for some kids include alcohol and sexual activity, the point is that you can be a guiding light to help your child make smart choices.

Try to keep the dating process in perspective in your own mind and as you discuss expectations (and possibly disappointing realities) with your child.

Remember that no one figures out meaningful relationships on a first date! Often what we look back on as superficial qualities or attractions were what led to accepting or initiating the date in the first place. However, as your kids refine their understanding of their needs, they will more solidly establish their expectations and standards, and they will know what they hope to experience in a date and more successfully engage in dates that are satisfying for them.

Dating is a developmental process, where we are supposed to learn whether a relationship is right for us. Though a dating relationship is a statement of commitment, it is not a marriage. When one partner starts to feel "stuck" or no longer genuinely enjoys the other's company, it may be a sign that a dating relationship has run its course. If you have a trusting relationship with your kids, they will feel comfortable sharing their thoughts with you as they take their relationship's pulse and grow in understanding themselves and others. You can help jumpstart conversations by asking how a date went and if they enjoyed themselves.

One option to consider when kids are not quite ready to date—much less, go steady—may be to date in groups. Many kids may still not feel ready to date, even well into their teens. Opportunities such as middle school dances, roller rink nights, and community service provide useful and healthy social interaction and can be a creative transition into dating terrain. Don't push— and whatever you do, don't imitate the patterns of Sylvia, the mom who vicariously lived through her daughter in Chapter 3.

Now that we've discussed ways in which you can help your kids make connections between sex, intimacy, and love as they learn about relationships, let's move on and talk about other important ways to connect sex, intimacy, and love—in the realm of spirituality. This is one area where we may need to delve in deeper than usual, to make the connections between the roots of our values and how they show up in practice.

Spirituality and Sexuality

May the outward and inward person be one.
—SOCRATES' PRAYER

Love is dynamic and embraces many things. In its broader meaning, love involves positive growth and supports healthy relationships with our selves, others, and God. Through love, our thoughts and emotions expand beyond our self and incorporate the ones we have chosen. By learning how to draw on spirituality or God's transformative power, we are often able to experience a greater union than we can create on our own.

I recall a couple whose marriage demonstrated the power of love rooted in a relationship with God. Whenever they argued, they would confess their feelings during a time of prayer they shared each night. By inviting God directly into their lives and the problems they shared together, they were able to reframe the current struggle in light of the broader purpose they had named in their wedding vows, including honoring the values of love and respect. Including God in their marriage in this profoundly personal way helped them break away from potentially frustrating deadlocks and continually enhanced their perspective on the commitment to loving one another. Discuss with your children such means of connecting spiritually with their chosen partner. When we have committed to *living out* our spirituality, we can similarly draw on the same spiritual resources and address our conflicts and confusions. Prayer is a direct source for bringing spiritual values into our life.

Most of the world's major religions elevate love as one of the greatest values to cultivate throughout our lives. By loving and strengthening our connection with God, we are able to love and strengthen our connection with others. We are then able to bring the qualities of truth, justice, kindness, patience, and goodness to our relationships—not just for the sake of our partner, but in order to grow into the human beings we were created to be.

Religions largely build their foundations on principles of love, but at the same time, many religions disconnect this love from any expression of physical sexuality. People sometimes have an all-or-nothing approach to sexuality, linking "good" and "spiritual" with "chaste," and placing sexual pleasure and attraction into the category of sin or evil. Do a mental check: if your kids have been exposed to such mixed or confusing messages, there's a good chance they will feel guilty about any sexual attractions, feelings, or actions.

Your child should be at peace with his or her sexuality in view of his or her faith. Remember, sexuality is a process—we're always growing, in many ways, including spiritually and sexually. If your children have sexual feelings that they haven't been able to reconcile with their beliefs or values, you will want to help them resolve such conflicts by examining whether their sexual expectations of

Is it ever possible to be both "normal" and "good"?

themselves are realistic. For example, if your children desire to become physically or emotionally intimate with someone, you need to help them sort out the value of abstinence for them and how they feel about different levels of sexual engagement. Stress the importance of communicating their needs and values to their partners; their partners will also need to communicate their values about moving to deeper levels of sexual intimacy. Oftentimes, religion will affirm that sex is acceptable in marriage, but it insists upon zero sexual activity beforehand. Taken literally, this creates a dilemma in modern times when people often don't marry until they're in their 30s—significantly past their sexual peak, at least, for most men!

When it comes down to it, some religious ideas may make sex more complicated than it needs to be. The simple joy, forgiveness, and acceptance that religions affirm are often much easier to attain than we realize if we see chastity as a choice rather than something that is imposed on us and if we accept everyone on loving terms. Help your kids start to understand sex within this positive atmosphere, so they recognize the potential meaning of sexual abstinence for spiritual reasons, rather than as something that is imposed for no reason or for the purpose of making sex the carrot on the far end of the marital stick. Bringing your love for your child into discussions about sex and spirituality can go a long way toward supporting the connections they will make between sex, intimacy, and love. We need to be proactive in illuminating the connections between spirituality and sex for our children because our current explanatory systems (those found in pop culture, religion, and so on) are likely to fall short on this task. While religious authorities may preach about love, they are often silent on ways to appreciate our God-given sexual feelings in positive ways.

The best we usually hear from religious figures is that sexuality is appropriate in marriage. But this dodges the truth that sexuality exists for all people before they get married. Consider that children and adults typically participate more in religious life than high school and college-age youth. Could part of the reason be that religions ignore or condemn the raging hormones of adolescence and young adulthood—one of kids' major concerns during this developmental period—and primarily suppress, repress, and restrain instead of constructively guiding sexual development? Religiously raised youth are often left to juggle emotional and spiritual comfort with private sexual experimentation.

Simply pointing toward marriage as the antidote for uncontrollable sexual feelings is potentially damaging. If youth cannot be honest about their naturally fluctuating and evolving sexual feelings, the sexuality they carry into marriage can retain the stain of being bad or sinful. Further, we may want to lead our children to consider many different factors in choosing a healthful and appropriate life partner, besides their first intense sexual attraction. We can do this if we help our kids feel it is okay to accept and understand their sexuality, rather than reject or suppress it.

Whatever position your religious tradition holds on sexuality and marriage, this subject should be approached openly with your kids. If marriage is principally touted as the only safety zone for sex, many marriages will be launched for the wrong reasons. Precisely because many religious communities are silent about sex, it becomes a central part of parental responsibility to provide realistic and appropriate guidance.

How Do I Love Thee?

We know one of the most basic openings for discussing sex with our kids is by explaining its relationship to having babies. But procreation is rarely the main motivation for a couple to have sex. More often, couples enjoy sexual intercourse to share their feelings of love. Couples not only enjoy the pleasurable physical feelings of sex; for many, sex is also a confirmation of their emotional and spiritual connection and oneness.

Love and Marriage, Love and Marriage . . .

". . . go together like a horse and carriage," croons Frank Sinatra in the famous song. Sure, this equation might be taken for granted today, but until the mid-twentieth century, this just wasn't so. Next to decidedly unromantic factors such as politics and economic stability, love was seen as a pretty flimsy reason to get married.

The sixteenth-century French essayist Montaigne wrote that any man in love with his wife must be a bore, since no one else could love him. Around 1700, a Protestant minister in a Virginia colony warned spouses that loving each other too much or using endearing nicknames undermined husbandly authority. And as late as the Victorian era, adultery and friendship kindled a much hotter fire than did the marriage bed, as marital relationships were often passionless.

Though Christianity is essentially a religion about love, love in the traditional Christian sense meant something spiritual, as opposed to the physical expression of love. Only over time was love actually practiced as empathetic, intimate, and reciprocal. Though over 78 percent of the population in America marries, studies show that 50 percent or more marry for reasons other than love: because of loneliness, desire for children, financial security, or simply the status of being married.

Because saying "I do" isn't always the same as saying "I love you," we should take care that different expectations about marriage don't cause undue conflict between spouses. We also need to talk to our kids about what we want from marriage and our reasons for getting married—and discuss with them what *they* want and expect, or don't want and expect, from marriage. Most important, we need to guide them into marrying for the reasons they value most.

Our kids, however, are at an early age exposed to a culture that promotes "getting it on"—so they need someone to help them figure out if this behavior is right for them. This is where *you* come in for one of your most important roles. The decision to be sexually active ultimately lies in their hands; however, you can play the crucial part of equipping them with notions of love and sex that will improve their chances of experiencing sex and love together in fulfilling ways.

Sexual Experiences

We've covered how special and complex sexuality is by drawing attention to personal boundaries, vulnerability, and the dangers of engaging prematurely in sex. While it is unlikely that your kids will speak with you before having sex, being there as they make this decision is very helpful. It makes sense to treat this subject head on, shortly after dating begins.

Just as you'll make time for a discussion before a date, be sure to be available later for a follow-up talk. The goal is to have your teens honestly explore the feelings, experiences, or situations they feel will make them ready for love or maybe intercourse with another person. Before you begin, start thinking of similar feelings you have had and what your experience has taught you about the connection between sex and love. What follows is an excerpt from the kind of conversation that should prompt a proactive, positive exchange of ideas about getting ready for love or sex.

MOM: So you've been seeing John for some time now. What do you enjoy about spending time with John?

TEEN: You know, when we're together, I feel all excited in my chest, and I just want to get closer with him.

MOM: Yes, I remember feeling that way too. It is pretty common to get the butterfly feeling at the beginning of a new relationship, and it can even sometimes be taken for very strong feelings, like love. But sex is most fulfilling when you know someone very well and trust him completely.

Be ready for a range of responses from your teen. And as in this exchange, be sure to let your kids know you see them, care for them, and understand them.

Attraction and Balance

Honestly and compassionately talking with our children about their sexual attraction (feelings, thoughts, desire, actions) sends the message that they are normal and starts them on the road to taking responsibility for their actions. In this way, we bring love and sex together. Attraction comes from a desire for intimacy with another as well as from a sexual feeling that is more visceral. It may well be that the ancient Greek value of balance is an especially useful maxim to guide sexuality. Much that we consider useful about sexuality in our communications with our kids involves balance, as we saw in Chapter 3.

The ancient Greeks perceived that what most disturbed the gods was *excess*, so they emphasized a life that reflected balance: "Nothing in excess" was a rule for life that assured fulfillment. They also crafted stories of extremes that represented ends of the sexual continuum. Dionysus was the god of wine, associated with the unrestrained, often irresponsible, pursuit of pleasure and fun. Apollo, on the other hand, the god of the sun, music, and medicine, held to a rational, stolid vision of the world, distancing himself from the passions. The Greeks used these images of flawed gods to symbolize the problems we invite if we live too much at either end of the spectrum. By maintaining balance, however, attraction and pleasure do not pose problems, but become healthy, appropriate expressions of the fullness of human experience that lead us to higher levels of love. By maintaining sexual balance, we avoid the all-or-nothing extremes of Dionysus and Apollo—and enable ourselves to grow into deeper levels of love.

Talk with your teens about maintaining balance in their relationships and discuss how extreme behavior or restraint ultimately leaves us unsatisfied. (If you think it will engage their interest, you can use the examples of Apollo and Dionysus to help illustrate these points.) Discuss how, on the one hand, indulging every sexual attraction with acts of sex ultimately draws us away from our deeper needs. If your kids seem to be moving in this direction, they need to monitor themselves so they will not be pulled away from genuine connections. But on the other hand, distancing from and denying sexuality in our lives will leave our physical and relational needs unsatisfied. If your kids have this tendency, they may need to lighten up a bit, in the interest of enjoying their relationships more freely and encountering love. Point out to your kids how both of these extremes bring the same experience of loneliness.

Rather than treating all kids the same way and expecting their sexual desires to be managed through some single, ideal design, we must reflect on their natural variations. This doesn't mean giving them carte blanche to act on every impulse. Instead, it means consciously crafting yourself to be a sustained, accepting guide so you can help your kids embrace a positive sense of self-discovery, self-awareness, and self-esteem. If you have more than one child, you will see that they engage relationships differently based on their unique temperament and personality. Whether or not you identify with each of their expectations, they still need your counsel and love. The act of parenting is making contact with them when they need you the most.

Relationships: Sex, Intimacy, and Love

Those of us who have loved one person for a long time don't expect relationships to be easy. Love is the spiritual truth that transforms our human experience into something divine. It has the potential to change negatives to positives and problems to solutions. It transforms darkness to light, anger to joy, and tears to laughter.

So help your children look to their spiritual resource as one true source of love and as a resource for the hard times in relationships. Help them see God as part of their support group, from whom they are able to receive acceptance and experience care, and teach them to share this acceptance and care with others.

Love is a learned response and emotion. By pointing out instances where you see people demonstrating care and love for others, you can help your child adopt patterns of intimacy and sexuality based not on the self-centered vision often promoted in our culture, but on the wider experience of embracing others.

As parents, we shouldn't let pop culture, science, philosophers, or even religion define love for our children. Your children must know your love for them as clearly as they know that they are alive. While love's mystery is too awesome to be confidently defined, your children will discover it through watching and learning from you and from their relationship with you.

There is no greater responsibility of parenting than to love. So let's find the truest form of love, and let this spill over to our love for our children. This is the greatest gift we can give to their ongoing human and sexual development.

Notes

Introduction

1. Dale Kunkel et al., "Sex on TV 4," Kaiser Family Foundation http://www.kff.org/entmedia/7399.cfm. Accessed December 2006.

2. Center for Disease Control and Prevention, "Youth Risk Behavior Surveillance—United States, 2005," *Morbidity & Mortality Weekly Report* 55 (2006): 1–108.

Chapter 1

1. Associated Press, "Special Report: Clinton Accused," Washington Post Company (1998); http://www.washingtonpost.com/wp-srv/politics/special/clinton/stories/whatclintonsaid.htm#Edu. Accessed December 2006.

2. World Health Organization, "Sexual Health—A New Focus For WHO," *Progress in Reproductive Health Research* 67 (2004): 3.

Chapter 4

1. Lynn Barnett, "Keep in Touch: The Importance of Touch in Infant Development," *Infant Observation* 8 (2005): 115–123.

2. Elisabeth Casparian and Eva S. Goldfarb, *Our Whole Lives: Sexuality Education for Grades 4–6*, (Boston: Unitarian Universalist Association, 2002), 23–58; and Makanah E. Morris and Jerry Agate, *Sexuality and Our Faith: Grades 7–9—A Companion to Our Whole Lives* (Boston: Unitarian Universalist Association, 1999), 39–54, 139–166.

3. Tricia K. Neppl, "Social Dominance and Play Patterns among Preschoolers: Gender Comparisons," *Sex Roles* 36 (1997): 381–393.

4. William S. Pollack, *Real Boys' Voices* (New York: Penguin Press, 2000), 149–153.

5. Center for Disease Control and Prevention, "Youth Risk Behavior Surveillance—United States, 2005," *Morbidity & Mortality Weekly Report* 55 (2006): 1–108.

Chapter 6

1. Laura D. Hanish, Becky Kochenderfer-Ladd, Richard A. Fabes, Carol Lynn Martin, and Donna Denning, "Bullying among Young Children: The Influence of Peers and Teachers," *Bullying in*

American Schools: A Social-Ecological Perspective on Prevention and Intervention, edited by Dorothy L. Espelage and Susan M. Swearer (Mahwah, N.J.: Lawrence Erlbaum Associates, 2004): 141–159.

2. John H. Hoover, "Bullying: Perceptions of Adolescent Victims in the Midwestern USA," *School Psychology International* 13 (1992): 5–16.

3. Ibid.

Chapter 7

1. Connelly M. Goodstein, "Teen-age Poll Finds a Turn to the Traditional," *New York Times,* 30 April 1998.

2. Nicholas Lagina, "Parent-Child Communication: Promoting Sexually Healthy Youth," www.advocatesforyouth.org. Accessed December 2006.

3. Michael D. Resnick et al., "Protecting Adolescents from Harm: Findings from the National Longitudinal Study on Adolescent Health," *The Journal of the American Medical Association* 278 (1997): 823–32.

4. Ibid.

5. Rosemary Radford Ruether, *Christianity and the Making of the Modern Family* (Boston: Beacon Press, 2001): 182.

6. Debra Kalmuss, Andrew Davidson, Alwyn Cohall, Danielle Laraque, and Carol Cassell, "Preventing Sexual Risk Behaviors and Pregnancy among Teenagers: Linking Research and Programs," *Perspectives on Sexual and Reproductive Health* 35 (2003).

7. National Campaign to Prevent Teen Pregnancy, "America's Adults and Teens Sound Off about Teen Pregnancy: An Annual National Survey," http://www.teenpregnancy.org/resources/data/pdf/wov2003.pdf. Accessed December 2006.

8. U.S. Census Bureau, "From Birth to Seventeen: The Living Arrangements of Children, 1998," *Population Profile of the United States: 1999* (1999): 23.

9. American Psychological Association, *Lesbian and Gay Parenting: A Resource for Psychologists*, http://www.apa.org/pi/lgbc/publications/lgparenting.pdf. Accessed December 2006.

10. Ibid.

Chapter 8

1. William D. Mosher, Anjani Chandra, and Jo James, "Sexual Behavior and Selected Health Measures: Men and Women 15–44 Years of Age, United States, 2002," *Advance Data from Vital and Health Statistics* 362 (2005).

2. John Cloud, "The Battle Over Gay Teens," *Time Magazine,* 10 October 2005: 42–51.

3. Ibid.

4. Massachusetts State Youth Risk Behavior Survey, 1999, http://www.doe.mass.edu/cnp/hprograms/yrbs/99/letter.html. Accessed December 2006.

5. Center for Disease Control and Prevention, "Youth Risk Behavior Surveillance—United States, 2005," *Morbidity & Mortality Weekly Report* 55 (2006): 1–108.

6. Diana Russell, *The Secret Trauma: Incest in the Lives of Girls and Women* (New York: Basic Books, 1986): 216.

Glossary

Talking about sex is not easy. Words mean different things to different people. This glossary includes technical terms relating to sex as well as slang and colloquial words. Warning! You may find some words vulgar or offensive. Such words are added not to suggest that they become standardized but to equip you as parents to understand terms that are often used in popular culture. In turn, you can help your child understand the meanings of these vulgar or offensive terms as well as important vocabulary terms about sex when the need arises. Read through this glossary to get familiar with the words. In some instances, whole new levels of awareness will occur as you more fully understand the meanings of these terms. I also invite you to stop and think about the words you use to casually talk about sex—what values and assumptions do you convey with your language?

Please note that a separate list follows for Slang Expressions for Sex (see pages 269–270). Also note that the contraceptive technologies listed here, such as Depo Provera and hormonal birth control pills, are not necessarily effective prevention against STIs. Be sure to check whether a given birth control method also serves as protection against STIs.

Explanatory Notes

Colloquial: informal but vulgar.
Slang: informal, may be playful, but also may be vulgar or derogatory.

---

abortion: removal or expulsion of an embryo or fetus, which can occur spontaneously (miscarriage) or be artificially induced through chemical, surgical, or other means.

abstinence: avoidance of sexual behavior. For some this refers exclusively to intercourse; others define it broadly as avoiding all forms of sexual activity.

AC-DC: (*slang, often derogatory*) a person who engages in sexual activities with members of both sexes.

addiction, sexual: uncontrollable sexual compulsivity.

adolescence: the period between childhood and adulthood when the physical changes of puberty initiate a transition in all spheres of development.

adultery: sexual intercourse when at least one partner is married to someone else.

afterbirth: the placenta which is discharged after delivery.

agape: Greek term referring to unconditional love that does not involve sexual relations.

AIDS: acronym for acquired immune deficiency syndrome, a virus spread through the exchange of bodily fluids that destroys the immune system.

amenorrhea: absence of menstruation.

anal intercourse: inserting a man's penis into the anus of his partner. Also any sex act involving the anus.

anal stage: Freud's second stage of psychosexual growth, in which pleasure is derived from holding or releasing bowel movements. Freud believed that this holding style in physical behavior was related to one's emotional management of control.

analingus: oral stimulation of the anus.

androgen: male sex hormone secreted through the testes of men and adrenal glands of both men and women, which enhances masculine characteristics. From the Greek *andros*, meaning "man."

androgyny: having psychological and physical attributes of both men and women.

aphrodisiac: chemicals considered to enhance sexual arousal.

arousal: stimulation toward sexual desire and erotic behavior.

artificial insemination: medical intervention to inject sperm into a woman's uterus, for the purpose of conception.

asceticism: philosophy originating with ancient Greeks, emphasizing that wisdom and virtue can be achieved by avoiding passion.

asexual: experiencing no sexual attraction toward either males or females.

attachment: emotional connection between people, e.g., parent and child, or quality of connection in an intimate relationship. Attachment theory points out that romantic relationships are greatly affected by the connection of a child with his or her parents.

attraction: interest in others based upon particularly desirable characteristics. What is considered desirable will vary from person to person and from historical period to historical period.

autoeroticism: self-stimulation or masturbation.

balling: (*vulgar slang*) having sexual intercourse.

balls: (*slang*) testicles.

BDSM: acronym for bondage, domination, sadism, and masochism.

bestiality: having sex with animals.

birth: beginning of a new life.

bisexuality: sexual attraction toward both men and women.

blow job: (*colloquial*) oral sex; specifically, the oral stimulation of a man's penis.

blue balls: (*slang*) testicular pain created by excitation without ejaculation or the need to ejaculate.

bondage: the practice of tying people up or restraining another person for sexual pleasure.

bottom: (*slang*) submissive partner in a sexual relationship.

brothel: the location where prostitutes provide sexual services. Sometimes called a cathouse.

buggery: (*slang*) anal intercourse.

butch: (*colloquial*) a lesbian who assumes a dominant or masculine gender role or masculine dress or behavior.

call girl: prostitute who arranges sexual contacts by phone. *Call* refers both to a telephone call and to being "on call."

Casanova: a man with bravado about sexual virility who seduces women. Eighteenth century adventurer Giovanni Giacomo Casanova's name has become synonymous with his infamous seductions.

castration: removal of a man's testes; *castration anxiety* in psychoanalysis refers to a man's fear of losing his genitals and erotic interest.

cathouse: see *brothel.*

celibacy: sexual abstinence or a vow not to engage in sex. Sometimes this refers to being unmarried or vowing to remain single.

cervix: the lower, narrow end of the uterus that projects into the vagina.

chancre: a painless sore or ulcer caused by a virus or a bacterium. Also the primary lesion in syphilis.

chastity: a state of virginity, not having had sexual relations; purity of mind and body, often equated with the avoidance of all sexual activity.

chat rooms: live online discussion sites where people communicate by typing messages.

chlamydia: the most prevalent sexually transmitted pathogen, causing infection in the genitourinary tract for both men and women.

circumcision: surgical removal of the foreskin of the penis, performed in certain cultures as a religious practice or health measure.

clap: (*slang*) gonorrhea.

climacteric: menopause for women; a period of reduced sexual activity for men.

climax: orgasm.

clitoris: a woman's sexual organ that focuses sexual sensation, often compared to a man's penis but without direct reproductive function.

closet homosexual: one who does not openly express his or her same-sex orientation.

cock: (*slang*) penis.

coitus: sexual intercourse as a man inserts his penis into a woman's vagina.

coitus interruptus: withdrawal of the penis during intercourse as an attempt to avoid conception. This method of birth control is highly ineffective and does not prevent STIs.

compulsive sexual behavior: uncontrollable sexual behavior and drive that interfere with daily life.

computer porn: pornography acquired through the Internet.

concubine: a second wife, usually of inferior status. From the Latin word *concubina,* meaning "to lie together." In current usage, it refers to a woman who lives with a man and shares a marriage-like relationship, though they are not officially married.

condom: a sheath made from latex or a membrane worn during coitus (or oral sex) over the penis to prevent pregnancy and the transmittal of HIV and other sexually transmitted infections. Note that there are also female condoms.

congenital: acquired by the fetus in the womb and present at birth, e.g., heart defects that a child is born with.

conversion therapy: practice that attempts to change a person's sexual orientation from homosexual to heterosexual. Also known as *reparative therapy,* this therapy is highly controversial with unproved efficacy.

corpora covernosa: spongy tissue in both the clitoris and penis that becomes engorged with blood and stiffens in sexual arousal.

coprophilia: a paraphilia where sexual arousal is attained in connection with feces during the sex act. From the Greek *kopros,* meaning "dung."

copulation: sexual intercourse. From the Latin *copulare,* meaning "to unite" or "connect."

corona: the ridge of the penis, separating the glans from the body. From the Latin *corona,* for "crown."

covert sensitization: behavior modification in which an aversive fantasy is paired with a paraphilic fantasy in an effort to extinguish the paraphilic fantasy.

crabs: (*slang*) pubic lice.

crimes against nature: legal term used in published court cases in the United States since 1814. It refers to intercourse, cunnilingus, fellatio, masturbation, and paraphilias.

cross-dressing: wearing garments of the opposite sex.

cruising: seeking out a sexual partner.

crush: an infatuation; a state in which one fantasizes about romantic involvement with another person.

cum (come): (*slang*) semen.

cunnilingus: oral sex acted upon a female; sexual arousal involving licking and sucking a women's genitalia (vulva).

cut: (*slang*) describes a circumcised penis.

cybersex: engagement in sex through the Internet.

date rape: rape that occurs during a social encounter in which the perpetrator is known to the victim. Legally, the crime is considered to be just as serious as a rape perpetrated by a stranger.

defloration: rupture of the hymen, particularly associated with first intercourse and certain cultural rituals.

dental dam: a small sheet of latex used to prevent the spread of STIs during oral sex.

Depo-Provera: a highly effective injection that blocks ovulation and conception. Sometimes also used to suppress sex drive in men.

deviant: outside the cultural norm. *Note:* For those whose sexual behavior is outside the norm, this word is offensive because their behavior is normal to them. For those who identify with the majority, describing a sexual behavior as "deviant" may lead to judging such sexual behaviors rather than attempting to understand them.

diaphragm: a shallow rubber cup, fitted to the contours of a woman's vagina, that is coated with spermicide and inserted before coitus to prevent conception.

dick: (*slang*) penis.

dildo: a sex toy that can be inserted vaginally or anally. Often, but not necessarily, shaped like a penis.

doggy style: (*slang*) intercourse when one person penetrates another by entering from behind.

Don Juan: refers to a compulsive seducer or philanderer, or to a man with an insatiable sexual appetite or drive. A fictional Spanish noble, seventeenth-century Don Juan seduced women by disguising himself as women's lovers or by promising marriage; he is often portrayed as absurd or villainous.

drag queen: a gay male who dresses as a female, often for theatrical purposes.

dualism: philosophy that separates physical and spiritual dimensions, often characterizing the spiritual as higher and better.

dyke: (*slang, sometimes derogatory*) lesbian. Can be derogatory, but is also used in the gay community as a way of proudly asserting one's identity.

dysmenorrhea: painful cramps experienced during menstruation.

egg: reproductive cell in women.

ejaculation: the expulsion of semen.

Electra complex: a girl's attraction to her father. In psychoanalytic theory, a conflict of the phallic stage of girls, in which they wish to possess their father and perceive their mother as a rival, as portrayed in the ancient Greek drama *Electra*. This conflict is analogous to the boy's Oedipus complex.

embryo: fertilized egg until eight weeks gestation.

erectile disorder: difficulty achieving erection for men that can be related to multiple and various factors.

erection: the aroused state of a penis because of vasocongestion of the tissue and engorgement by blood.

erogenous zone: a part of the body that produces sexual excitement when stimulated.

eros: sexual passion related to physical passion. In Greek mythology, Eros was the god of love, son of Aphrodite.

erotic: associated with sensual or sexual pleasure.

erotica: literature or art with a sexual theme.

estrogen: hormone produced by a woman's ovaries and in small amounts by both men and women in the adrenal glands and by men in the testes.

eunuch: a castrated man. Historically, these men were often castrated to fill specific social roles such as high-register vocal performers, guardians of women, or religious specialists.

exhibitionist: a person who exposes genitalia compulsively or in inappropriate settings to obtain sexual gratification and to shock and startle victims.

exploitation: the act of using another for one's own advantage.

faggot: (*vulgar slang, often derogatory*) male homosexual.

fallopian tubes: the passageway the egg follows to the uterus.

fantasy: mental imaging used to become sexually aroused.

fellatio: oral stimulation of a man's genitals.

female: the sex that bears children and produces ova; a girl or woman; feminine, lady-like, proper.

feminine: having qualities attributed to a woman.

femininity: qualities attributed to women. Cultural stereotyping identifies women as feminine, meaning that they are soft, frilly, irrational, passive, helpless, and needing a man's protection. The feminist movement has raised awareness regarding the limiting impact of the usage of this term.

femme: (*colloquial*) a lesbian who assumes traditional feminine gender roles.

fetishism: condition in which sexual arousal involves inanimate objects or a particular body part.

fetus: term to describe the embryo after the eighth week of pregnancy.

fisting: (*slang*) inserting one or both hands into the vagina or rectum of a sexual partner.

foreplay: stimulating sexual interactions that set the stage for intercourse.

foreskin: loose skin of the penis that folds over the glans; the foreskin may be cut in circumcision.

fornication: sexual intercourse between two people who are not married to one another. This term is often used in religious contexts.

French kiss: kissing in which one partner's tongue touches the other's.

French tickler: a condom-like device with small protrusions that fits over the penis, designed to give a woman additional sexual pleasure during intercourse.

frigid: (*colloquial*) averse to sexual intercourse. The term carries a negative connotation and can be used to describe men or women.

frotteurism: a paraphilia in which sexual arousal occurs by rubbing one's genitals against another unconsenting person in public places.

gang bang: (*slang*) sexual intercourse (usually rape) in which multiple men penetrate one woman.

gay: describes a person whose attractions are to people of the same sex. *Gay* is more often used to describe men, while *lesbian* is often the preferred term for women. Sometimes used pejoratively for effeminate men. Derogatory slang referring to gay men includes *fag, queen, fairy, homo.*

gender: one's cultural, social, and legal status as a man or woman.

gender dysphoria: the feeling that one's gender does not match the sex of one's body. Also referred to as *gender identity disorder.*

gender identity: one's subjective sense of being a man or woman.

genital herpes: painful herpes infections affecting the genital and genitourinary system. See *herpes.*

genitals/genitalia: reproductive organs of men and women; often refers to external sex organs.

gestation: period of time in the development from conception to birth.

gigolo: a male prostitute who caters to women.

glans: the rounded end of the penis or clitoris.

gonads: sex glands. A man's gonads are testes; a woman's gonads are ovaries.

gonorrhea: an STI caused by a bacterium that creates a burning sensation at urination. From the Greek *gonos*, meaning "seed," and *rheo*, meaning "to flow;" the ancient Greeks erroneously interpreted gonorrhea as a loss of seminal fluid. If untreated, gonorrhea can cause pelvic inflammatory disease.

grinding: rubbing against one another; mimicking intercourse for sexual excitement, often while dancing.

G-spot: a sexually sensitive area on the front wall of the vagina named after Ernest Gräfenberg who identified this as an erogenous zone. Some report that this area provides a "deeper orgasm" and female ejaculation, and men have identified a similar area near the prostate gland.

gynecologist: a doctor specializing in the female reproductive system and women's medical health.

hand job: (*slang*) manual sexual stimulation of the genitalia by one's partner; especially refers to the stimulation of the penis.

hedonism: belief system in which pleasure represents life's highest good.

hermaphrodite: person who possesses both ovarian and testicular tissue (named after the Greek gods Hermes and Aphrodite).

herpes: painful viral infection causing blisters, herpes I (oral herpes), and herpes II (genital herpes). From the Greek *herpein,* meaning "to creep."

heterosexism: thinking in exclusively heterosexual terms about sexuality specifically, and human experience generally, thereby neglecting and invalidating the existence of homosexual and bisexual attraction, behavior, and relationships.

heterosexual: having an erotic attraction to, and preference for, romantic and/or sexual relationships with the opposite gender.

hickey: a red mark, usually on the neck, created on the skin from prolonged sucking and biting. Teenagers sometimes flaunt these as status symbols of their romantic involvement.

HIV: acronym for human immunodeficiency virus, the virus that is the precursor for AIDS.

homophobia: fear of homosexuals. From the Greek *homos,* meaning "same," and *phobia,* meaning "fear."

homosexual: having an erotic attraction to, and preference for, romantic and/or sexual relationships with one's own gender. In certain contexts, it is used as a slur. The term is usually used in clinical speech; in more common usage the preferred terms include *gay, lesbian* (as a noun or adjective), or *same-sex* (adjective). From the Greek *homos,* meaning "same," not from the Latin *homos,* which means "man."

hooker: (*slang*) prostitute.

hooking up: (*slang*) usually refers to a casual sexual encounter that can involve varying degrees of activity ranging from kissing to sexual intercourse.

hormone: secretion from a gland that regulates various body functions. From the Greek *hormon,* meaning "to set in motion," "to stimulate," or "to excite."

horny: (*slang*) having sexual tension.

hottie: (*slang*) sexually attractive person.

hussy: (*vulgar slang*) a brazen, lewd, immoral woman.

hustler: man or woman who serves as a prostitute.

hymen: thin membrane partly covering the opening to the vagina. May be broken during sexual intercourse or other physical activity such as sports.

hypoactive sexuality: less than normal drive that contributes to sexual dysfunction.

hysterectomy: surgical removal of the uterus.

id: from Freud, a mental structure driven by primary drives for gratification.

impotence: difficulty achieving and sustaining erections sufficient for intercourse. Because of the pejorative connotation of this term, this word has been replaced in popular and medical discourse by *male erectile disorder* or *erectile dysfunction.*

impregnate: to make pregnant or inseminate; to cause conception.

incest: sexual relationship or marriage involving those in a family (blood) relationship that is prohibited and illegal. From the Latin *in*, meaning "not," and *cestus*, meaning "chaste."

infatuation: a state of unreasoning, intense emotional preoccupation with another, including sexual arousal.

infertility: inability to conceive a child.

inner lips: labia minora; the delicate folds immediately surrounding the vagina.

intercourse: sexual activity between two people, usually involving a penis inserted into a vagina.

Internet sexuality: sexual connection on the Internet where participants view material with sexual content, or connect with others, both with the object of achieving sexual pleasure.

intimacy: feelings of connectedness marked by sharing innermost affections, feelings, and thoughts. This chosen state of openness and vulnerability occurs in secure relationships.

intromission: penile penetration of the vagina. See also *intercourse.*

IUD (intrauterine device): device (loop, coil, or shield) inserted into the uterus to prevent the egg from implanting.

jerk off: (*vulgar slang*) to masturbate (for a male).

john: a man who hires prostitutes for sexual services.

kinky: having unusual sexual practices or desires.

knocked up: (*slang*) pregnant.

labia: folds (labia majora and minora) that run down the mons along the vulva.

lactation: production of milk by mammary glands for the purpose of breastfeeding.

latency: the fourth stage in Freud's model of psychosexual development between the ages of 8 and 12; "the quiet before the storm" preceding puberty.

lesbian: a female who is homosexual; a girl or woman who has significant sexual or romantic attractions toward other women. From the Greek Lesbos, an island in the Aegean Sea where the poet Sappho ran a school for girls for whom she expressed passion.

lesbo: (*vulgar slang*) a derogatory term for a lesbian.

LGBT: acronym for lesbian, gay, bisexual, and transgender.

libido: psychoanalytic term referring to one's sexual drive and desire.

love: a committed, trusting relationship with another. The word takes on many meanings. Sometimes it means sexual intercourse; other times, it means a spiritual connection.

machismo: Spanish term referring to a man's masculinity, bravado, and virility.

madam: woman who manages the business of a brothel, often a former prostitute.

maidenhead: condition of virginity; hymen.

male: the sex that produces sperm that can fertilize female eggs; a man or boy; masculine, manly, or virile.

man: adult male human; sometimes used generically to refer to a person of either sex (as in *mankind*); a person endowed with strength and characteristics attributed to men; (*colloquial*) husband.

masculine: possessing qualities attributed to men.

masculinity: qualities attributed to men. Cultural stereotyping identifies men as strong, aggressive, dominant, silent, and mechanically competent. Furthermore, the stereotype emphasizes that they should not express tenderness, sensitivity, or pain. This narrow prescription for men has changed as a result of the women's movement.

masochist: person who is sexually gratified by experiencing emotional and/or physical pain and humiliation.

masturbation: sexual self-stimulation by touching or rubbing one's own genitals for pleasure.

mate swapping: sex involving couples' exchanging partners; open marriage.

ménage à trois: sex involving three people. From the French *ménage,* meaning "household," and *trois,* meaning "three"— household of three. The "household of three" comes from the fact that a ménage à trois was typically a husband and wife couple with a (live-in) lover.

menarche: the onset of menstruation.

menopause: the end of menstruation.

menstruation: the cyclical bleeding in females that results from shedding the uterine lining (endometrium).

MILF: (*vulgar slang*) acronym for "mom I'd like to fuck;" a sexually attractive older woman; originating from the film *American Pie.*

miscarriage: a spontaneous, natural abortion.

molestation: sexual assault.

mons: a mound of fatty tissue covering the pubic area in women.

morning-after pill: estrogen pill taken after coitus that inhibits pregnancy by preventing a fertilized egg from implanting in the uterus.

natural childbirth: delivery of a child without drugs or anesthesia.

necrophilia: a paraphilia characterized by desire for sexual activity with corpses. From the Greek *nekros,* meaning "dead body."

nocturnal emission: involuntary ejaculation of seminal fluid while asleep. Also referred to as a *wet dream,* it is not necessarily related to the individual dream content.

nuts: (*slang*) testicles.

nympho: (*slang*) pejorative term for a woman who is sexually interested or active.

nymphomaniac: a woman with an excessive, insatiable sexual appetite or drive.

obscene: refers to sexual material judged by society as being potentially offensive, lacking serious value, and appealing to prurient interests.

obstetrician: a physician who specializes in prenatal care and the delivery of babies.

Oedipus complex: a boy's attraction to his mother. In psychoanalytic theory, this is a conflict to be resolved by boys, who wish to possess their mother yet perceive their father as a rival (the analogous conflict for girls is the Electra complex). Derived from the ancient Greek tragedy in which King Oedipus kills his father and marries his mother.

onanism: coitus interruptus. The term is derived from Onan in the Hebrew scriptures, who interrupted intercourse, "spilling his seed." This reference is the basis for those who point to biblical sanctions against masturbation.

openly gay: describes those who do not hide their being lesbian, gay, or bisexual.

oral sex: sexual stimulation involving the genitals of one partner and the mouth of the other.

oral stage: Freud's first stage of psychosexual development, related to trust. Refers to the infant's oral connection with the mother through breastfeeding.

organ: (*slang*) penis.

orgasm: the climax of sexual excitement.

orgy: unbridled sex among many participants.

orifice: refers to any opening in the body, most commonly the mouth, vagina, or anus.

outer lips: labia majora.

outercourse: forms of sexual activity that do not involve the exchange of bodily fluids, such as hugging, masturbation, and rubbing (sometimes known as "dry sex").

outing: (*slang*) revealing another person's sexual orientation without his or her approval. This may be done in an attempt to discriminate against or discredit an individual, or to combat discrimination by forcing closeted gays to acknowledge their sexual orientation.

ovaries: almond-shaped organs that produce egg cells and the hormones estrogen and progesterone.

ovulation: the release of an egg from the ovary.

paraphilia: a diagnostic category referring to atypical patterns of sexual arousal, which do not conform to social norms. These urges are recurrent and central to a paraphiliac's excitement. From the Greek *para*, meaning "to the side of," and *philos*, meaning "love of another."

passion: ardent desire; strong physical attraction, particularly in sexual relations and romance.

pederasty: sexual love of boys. From the Greek *paidie*, meaning "boy."

pedophilia: a paraphilia involving sexual desire for children.

Peggy Lee syndrome: the letdown that some teenage girls feel when their first sexual experience is less exciting than expected. Named for the song made famous by the singer Peggy Lee, "Is That All There Is?"

penetration: entrance of the penis, fingers, or sex toys into any orifice (vagina, anus, mouth).

penis: the male organ for sexual intercourse. From the Latin *penis*, which means "tail."

perineum: the area between the anus and penis or vulva. From the Greek *peri*, meaning "around," and *ineum*, meaning "to empty out."

perversion: psychological abnormality; compulsive sexual behavior outside the identified cultural norm.

pervert: person who departs from socially acceptable standards of sexual conduct.

petting: physical gestures in romantic exchange; often differentiated as "light" or "heavy," terms which distinguish contact above the waist from contact below the waist.

phallic stage: Freud's third stage of psychosexual development involving the genitalia, specifically the penis, related to pleasure and emotional power, aggression, and dominance.

phallus: the penis or something symbolizing the penis.

pheromones: body chemicals that attract sexual partners, particularly profound in nonhuman species.

philanderer: one who carries on a sexual affair without the intent to marry, especially in an adulterous context.

philia: Greek word for love, referring to friendship based on liking and respect rather than sex.

Pill, the: a synthetic hormonal substance that effectively prevents ovulation. This is an effective method for contraception.

pimp: a man who solicits business for a prostitute and lives off those earnings.

plastic: (*colloquial*) condom.

platonic love: nonsexual relationship; often a close relationship that transcends physical desire or interest.

plays: (*colloquial*) overtures intended to bring a relationship into sexual territory.

PMS: acronym for premenstrual syndrome; the physical and emotional changes women experience during the three to fourteen days prior to the start of each menstrual cycle.

polymorphous perversity: from psychoanalytic theory, openness to all forms of sexual stimulation.

pornography: depictions of erotic or lewd material designed to cause sexual arousal. Soft-core pornography features nudity, sexually suggestive behavior, and simulated or veiled sex; hardcore pornography contains visible aroused genitalia and penetration.

positions: sex positions; the placement of bodies during intercourse.

prick: (*vulgar slang*) penis.

primary sexual characteristics: physical characteristics that differentiate men and women, specifically those directly involved in sexual reproduction, such as sex organs.

progesterone: hormonal substance that prepares the uterus for implantation and maintains pregnancy.

promiscuity: casual sexual activity with various partners.

prophylactic: condom; from the Greek *phylacto,* meaning "to prevent;" so called because of its use in preventing pregnancy and the transmission of various STIs.

prostaglandins: hormones that may cause muscle contractions associated with menstrual pain.

prostate gland: chestnut-sized gland in males, connected to the neck of the bladder and vas deferens, that stores and secretes alkaline fluid and enzymes that make up one-third of the seminal fluid.

prostitute: a person who exchanges sexual services for money.

prurient: tending to excite sexually; lewd. From the Latin *prurire,* meaning "to itch."

psychosexual: relating sexual development to psychological factors.

puberty: biological sexual transition from childhood to adulthood. From the Latin, *pubertas,* meaning "ripe old age."

pubic hair: secondary sexual characteristic of hair around genitals developed in puberty.

pubic lice: small parasitic insects that inhabit pubic hair. Also known as *crabs*.

puppy love: (*colloquial*) passing affection felt by a child or teen. The term may be used pejoratively, to dismiss such feelings as inconsequential.

pussy: (*vulgar slang*) vagina. Also a derogatory term for a weak male.

queen: (*slang*) effeminate or flamboyant gay man.

queer: (*slang, sometimes derogatory*) gay. Historically an insult, *queer* has been reclaimed by some in the gay community as a term of pride. In contemporary usage, it is an inclusive, unifying sociopolitical umbrella term for gay, lesbian, bisexual, transgender, and transsexual people as well as for heterosexuals whose sexual preferences and activities are outside the mainstream.

rape: forcible, nonconsensual sexual act.

refractory period: period of time, such as after orgasm, when person is not responsive to sexual stimulation.

rhythm method: ineffective method for contraception where partners attempt to schedule sexual activity around the woman's monthly cycle, avoiding sex at times when the egg is most likely to be fertilized.

rimming: (*slang*) analingus.

RU-486: drug (mifepristone) that induces menstruation by blocking absorption of progesterone, which prevents the uterine lining from supporting the embryo, thereby inducing abortion of the embryo/fetus. Sometimes referred to as the *abortion pill*.

rubber: (*slang*) condom.

S and M: (*slang*) acronym for sadomasochism; sexual acts involving a partner who derives sexual pleasure from experiencing physical and emotional pain, and a partner who derives sexual pleasure from inflicting it.

sadist: person who derives sexual pleasure from inflicting physical and emotional pain on others.

safe(ty): (*slang*) condom.

safe sex: (*colloquial*) using a condom, dental dam, or other protective device during sex to prevent the spread of STIs.

screwing: (*slang*) sexual intercourse.

scrotum: the pouch that hangs at the base of the penis and contains the testicles.

semen: thick, white, milky liquid ejaculated from the penis that contains sperm.

sex: characteristics that define humans as male or female; often refers to the anatomical structures involved in reproduction and sexual pleasure. Also refers to acts involving the sex organs, especially coitus.

sexism: gender-based prejudice.

sexual orientation: the direction of a person's sexual attraction, in terms of whether the person is attracted to members of the same and/or opposite gender. Sexual orientation can be described as heterosexual (straight), bisexual, or homosexual (gay or lesbian). This term is considered more appropriate than the term *sexual preference,* which implies that a person chooses to be straight, gay, lesbian, or bisexual.

sexuality: all the attitudes, feelings, and behavior associated with sex.

shaft: body of the penis that expands as a result of vasocongestion.

sissy: derogatory term for a male who is not manly or is girlish or effeminate.

sixty-nine (69): (*slang*) simultaneous oral sex of both sexual partners.

slut: (*vulgar slang*) prostitute, or a woman considered to be sexually promiscuous.

sodomy: definition varies by community; a range of sexual acts, which can include anal sex, intercourse with animals, oral sex, and homosexual acts.

Spanish fly: a dangerous aphrodisiac that irritates the digestive system, bladder, and urethra but promises to increase sexual drive.

sperm: the male reproductive cell. From the Greek *sperma,* meaning "seed."

statutory rape: legal term for sexual intercourse with a minor. The definition of *minor* varies from state to state.

STD: acronym for sexually transmitted disease; diseases such as gonorrhea and syphilis that are spread almost exclusively through vaginal intercourse, oral sex, and anal sex. Also known as STIs.

sterilization: surgical techniques such as vasectomy and tubal ligation that prevent sperm from reaching ova.

STI: acronym for sexually transmitted infection; an infection transmitted between partners through some form of sexual activity. While the acronyms STD and STI are often used interchangeably, they are not exactly the same thing. *Infection* refers to a germ, bacteria, or parasite; *disease* refers to a sickness. The term STI is a broader term, as it refers to infection with any germ.

straight: heterosexual.

stud: (*colloquial*) a man perceived as attractive and virile.

superego: in Freud's theory, the psychological structure that functions as a moral guardian and establishes high standards for behavior.

swinger: (*slang*) sexually active person who engages in sex with numerous partners.

syphilis: sexually transmitted bacterial disease, characterized by sores called *chancres.* If left untreated, the disease may render a person insane, blind, crippled or dead; the disease can be treated with antibiotics.

tampon: absorbent material inserted into the vagina that absorbs menstrual flow.

testicles: male sex glands that produce testosterone.

testosterone: primary hormone associated with sexual desire. While predominant in men, women also manufacture testosterone.

threesome: sexual relations between three persons; also see *ménage à trois.*

top: (*slang*) dominant partner in a sexual relationship.

transgender: term describing those whose gender identity differs from the sex they were assigned at birth.

transsexual: outdated term originating in the medical and psychological communities describing a person who identifies as a member of the gender opposite to the one assigned at birth; the term currently in use is *transgender.*

transvestite: person, usually heterosexual, who derives sexual pleasure from wearing garments of the opposite sex; not to be confused with a transsexual or transgender person.

tubal ligation: sterilization operation that involves cutting or tying the fallopian tubes.

tumescence: swelling or engorgement of the penis. From the Latin *tumere,* meaning "to swell."

umbilical cord: anatomical connection of the baby and placenta that is cut at birth.

uncut: (*colloquial*) describes an uncircumcised penis.

urethra: canal leading from the bladder to the urethral opening in both males and females. While this tube carries both urine and semen in men, it is not possible for both to be released during intercourse.

uterus: hollow, muscular, pear-shaped organ where fertilized ovum implants and develops until birth.

vagina: tubular organ connected to uterus. From the Latin *vagina,* for "sheath."

vas deferens: tube that extends from testicle to prostate gland, which is responsible for transporting sperm and ejaculatory fluid.

vasectomy: male sterilization in which vas deferens are cut or tied to block transport of sperm.

venereal disease: outdated term for disease transmitted by sexual contact. Term has been replaced by *sexually transmitted disease (STD)* or *sexually transmitted infection (STI).* Named after the Roman goddess of love, Venus.

Viagra: medication that enhances erection, which is prescribed to men who suffer from erectile dysfunction.

vibrator: electric or battery-operated vibrating device used for sexual stimulation.

virgin: person who has not had sexual relations. In colloquial parlance, a sexually inexperienced person.

virility: sexual potency in a man.

voyeur: person who derives sexual pleasure from observing unsuspecting individuals engaged in sexual activity.

vulva: external genitalia of women.

wet dream: (*colloquial*) nocturnal emission. This is often a boy's first experience with ejaculation.

whore: (*vulgar slang*) female prostitute. This can also be used as a derogatory term to verbally attack a woman.

withdrawal: ineffective contraceptive method of removing the penis from the vagina prior to ejaculation. See also *coitus interruptus.*

woman: adult female human; a person endowed with characteristics attributed to women, femininity, or womanliness. (*Slang*) wife. (*Vulgar slang*) used to describe a woman as an object.

womb: uterus.

X-rated media: media presenting pornography.

zoophilia: paraphilia characterized by sexual intercourse with animals.

Slang Expressions for Sex

As with the Glossary on the preceding pages, this list of slang expressions is intended to familiarize you with terms used in the popular vernacular. You may find some words or terms offensive or vulgar; keep in mind that its purpose is to equip you to understand common language so that you can explain these terms to your children as necessary.

All Variations of Sex

achieving Congress
banana split
banging
bed and breakfast
boinking
boning
boom boom
buzzing the horny hole
churning butter
the deed
doing the nasty

donating to the missionary
getting some
getting your rocks off
giving her the business
going all the way
hiding the salami
horizontal bone dance
hot beef injection
it
knockin' boots
knockin' uglies

making love
nookie
nooner
parking
poking
slamming
the sword in the stone
taking the skin boat to tuna town
two-backed beast
wild thing
wilding

Oral Sex

BJ
carpet cleaning
chowing bird/box
eating the Y
giving head
going downtown
having a box lunch

hummer
kneeling at the altar
lickety-split
making Johnny Walker red
muff diving
performing the big one

playing the skin flute
satisfying King Solomon
speaking in tongues
spelunking
sucking the salami
sweet smell of success

269

Penis

bratwurst
cannoli
cherry-splitter
cock-a-doodle-doo
dick
dickie
the general
giggle stick
hairy hot dog

hot dog
hot rod
johnson
love whistle
master of ceremonies
member
odie
one-eyed snake
pecker

prick
purple-headed monster
Russell the love muscle
schlong
shaft
unit
wanker
weiner (dog)

Vagina

bearded clam
beaver
Bermuda triangle
chinchilla
cooch
cooter
fur burger

Garfield
juice box
the juicy rough
muff pie
pearl
pink lips
puki

pussy (cat)
snatch
squirrel
strawberry fields
twat
yum-yum patch

Breasts

bazongas
bazookas
bodacious tatas
boobies
boobs
bosoms
cupcakes
enchiladas

fun bags
gagas
headphones
hooters
knobs
knockers
mammies
melons

nips
peepers
Pointer Sisters
sweater puffs
teats
tetons
tits
twins

Resources

Here is a list of resources to help you find more information about particular sexuality themes. Keep in mind that not all of these resources may align with your family's values. You may want to evaluate them before sharing them with your children.

Contraception, STIs, and Safer Sex Organizations

Planned Parenthood Federation of America

434 West 33rd St.
New York, NY 10001
800-230-7526 connects to affiliate in caller's service area
800-829-7732 National Office
www.plannedparenthood.org

Planned Parenthood is an international nonprofit organization that provides reproductive health care, family planning services, and sexuality education. Planned Parenthood centers provide a variety of resources to both teens and adults, from condoms and STI information to confidential consultation about all sexual health issues. The Web site offers an anonymous question forum as well as health research, news, and opportunities for social action.

National Prevention Information Network

P.O. Box 6003
Rockville, MD 20849
800-458-5231
919-361-4892 International
800-243-7012 TTY
919-361-4884 International TTY
Monday through Friday, 9 a.m.–8 p.m. (EST)
www.cdcpin.org

In addition to a help line that provides confidential and anonymous telephone support for questions about AIDS and STIs, the National Prevention Information Network Web site offers a full range of information about all aspects of STIs, from prevention to counseling, testing, and referral as well as information and educational programs for communities at risk. A Spanish-language version of the Web site is also available at www.cdcnpin.org/scripts/espanol/index.asp.

Gender Identity; Gay Males, Lesbians, Bisexuals, and Transgender Persons

Bisexual Resource Center

P.O. Box 1026
Boston, MA 02117
617-424-9595
www.biresource.org

The Bisexual Resource Center is a nonprofit organization that provides research and education about bisexuality to the general public as well as support, resources, and networking opportunities for bisexuals. This site is helpful for all those who want to learn more about bisexuality.

Children of Lesbians and Gays Everywhere (COLAGE)

1550 Bryant St.
Suite 830
San Francisco, CA 94103
415-861-KIDS (5437)
www.colage.org

COLAGE is a national network that provides education and support for families with gay, lesbian, bisexual, and/or transgendered members, advocating for their rights as well as providing community support. This is a helpful resource for same-sex parents, focusing on the issues of acceptance for children of same-sex partnerships.

Family Pride Coalition

P.O. Box 65327
Washington, DC 20035
202-331-5015
202-331-0080 (Fax)
www.familypride.org

Family Pride Coalition is another organization focusing on gay, lesbian, bisexual, and/or transgendered families, offering resources such as parenting groups, web-based communities, and educational materials. This site is helpful for families with same-sex parents and for learning about same-sex parenting.

Gay, Lesbian, and Straight Education Network

90 Broad St.
2nd Floor
New York, NY 10004
212-727-0135
212-727-0254 (Fax)
www.glsen.org

This is a national nonprofit organization dedicated to educating students about the acceptance of gay and lesbian students in public, private, and parochial K–12 schools. It offers educational resources, curricula, and training programs for teachers, parents, students, and families as well as networking and support to student-initiated Gay-Straight Alliances (GSA) in American high schools.

Parents, Families, and Friends of Lesbians and Gays (PFLAG)

1726 M St. NW
Suite 400
Washington, DC 20036
202-467-8180
202-467-8194 (Fax)
www.pflag.org

PFLAG is a national nonprofit organization that promotes the health and well-being of gay, lesbian, bisexual, and transgendered persons and families through support, education, and advocacy. The Web site offers special sections about coming out as well as sections for friends and family members of a person who has just come out. The frequently asked questions, "do's and don'ts," and support networks are helpful for gay, lesbian, bisexual, transgendered, and straight individuals.

Hotlines

Childhelp USA Hotline

800-4-A-CHILD (800-422-4453)
800-222-4453 (TTY)
24 hours/day, 7 days/week
Who they help: victims of sexual abuse—children, parents, friends, and concerned individuals.

This is the largest and oldest organization in the treatment, prevention, and research of child abuse and neglect in North America. The national hotline is staffed by crisis counselors who can speak through interpreters in 140 languages. In addition to crisis counseling, referrals, education, and support, referral resources are also available. All calls are anonymous and confidential.

Men Helping Men Create Peace—Men's Hotline

415-924-1070
24 hours/day, 7 days/week
www.maws.org/menssite

Who they help: men who are in danger of committing violence or abuse.

This is an anger management and crisis hotline for men who feel they are losing control and are in danger of abusing. It is staffed by professional counselors. The Web site includes ex-batterer testimonies and information about support groups. Operated by ManKind Program, 1435 4th St., Suite E, San Rafael, CA.

National Domestic Violence Hotline

800-799-SAFE (7233)
800-787-3224 (TTY)
24 hours/day, 7 days/week
Who they help: children, parents, friends, concerned individuals, offenders.

This large domestic violence hotline provides assistance in English and Spanish, with access to 140 languages through interpreters. Call if you or someone you know feels frightened about a relationship; hotline advocates provide crisis intervention, safety planning, information, and referrals to agencies and shelters across the United States, Puerto Rico, and the Virgin Islands. All calls are anonymous and confidential.

National Prevention Information Network—STI Hotline

800-458-5231
919-361-4892 International
800-243-7012 TTY
919-361-4884 International TTY
Monday through Friday, 9 a.m.–8 p.m. (EST)
Who they help: youth, adults, and anyone who has contracted or simply has a question about STIs and HIV/AIDS.

This hotline is staffed by counselors with accurate medical information to provide confidential and anonymous counseling to anybody concerned about sexually transmitted diseases, including prevention, referral, and treatment.

National Sexual Assault Hotline

800-656-HOPE (4673)

24 hours/day, 7 days/week

Who they help: children, parents, and individuals who are in danger of being assaulted or who have been victims of rape, incest, or sexual assault.

This national hotline provides confidential emergency counseling for sexual assault crises as well as post-traumatic stress disorder (PTSD) and depression counseling for people who have been abused in the past. The staff can also make referrals to local state agencies and support groups.

Stop It Now!

888-PREVENT (888-773-8368)

9:00 a.m.–6:00 p.m. (EST)

www.stopitnow.org

Who they help: adults who are at risk of sexually abusing a child, friends and family members of sexual abusers and/or victims, parents of children with sexual behavior problems, children or youth in need of help.

This organization educates about the risks that lead to sexual abuse of children. Its confidential helpline provides an outlet for adults to give voice to their struggles. It works up-close with communities to encourage a model of awareness and prevention, and it provides information about further resources for child abuse prevention and education.

Men's Health and Family Issues

American Coalition for Fathers and Children

1718 M St. NW, #187

Washington, DC 20036

800-978-3237

www.acfc.org

This is a membership-based nonprofit coalition that promotes the rights of fathers and grandparents to be involved with children and family after divorce. With membership, legal and educational resources are made available to fathers who are divorced or going through divorce.

Men's Health Network

P.O. Box 75972
Washington, DC 20013
202-543-MHN-1 (6461)
www.menshealthnetwork.org

This nonprofit educational organization of physicians, public health work-ers, and individuals recognizes men's health as a specific societal concern and promotes awareness and education about men's health. At this site you will find specific information covering all aspects of men's health as well as screening programs, news reports, and updates.

National Center for Fathering

P.O. Box 413888
Kansas City, MO 64141
800-593-DADS (3237) or 913-384-4661
913-384-4665 (Fax)
www.fathers.com

This nonprofit organization develops practical resources, education, and training for fathers. The Web site provides tips and advice on many dif-ferent types of fathering situations that adoptive, non-custodial, step-, sin-gle, stay-home, and traveling fathers will find useful. There is plenty of information for all dads on how to speak with sons and daughters about issues such as sex, drugs, and alcohol as well as helpful advice on disci-pline, marriage, education, and money. The site also gives advice on fathering through a child's developmental stages (infancy through adult-hood), and offers a variety of seminars and programs on how to be a more involved and confident father.

National Women's Health Information Center—Men's Health

Hosted by U.S. Department of Health and Human Services, Men's Health Home
200 Independence Ave. SW
Room 712E
Washington, DC 20201
800-994-9662 or 888-220-5446 (TDD)
Monday through Friday, 9:00 a.m.–6:00 p.m. (EST)
www.4woman.gov/mens

This branch of the women's health information center offers complete and comprehensive information on men's health, with topics such as aging male syndrome, testicular and prostate cancer, fertility issues, HIV/AIDS and STIs, diabetes, mental health, and violence prevention as well as guidelines for scheduling screenings and medical appointments.

Referrals

American Association of Sex Educators, Counselors, and Therapists

AASECT
P.O. Box 1960
Ashland, VA 23005-1960
804-752-0026
804-752-0056 (Fax)
www.aasect.org/directory.asp

This nonprofit professional group is the primary certifying organization for sex education, counseling, and therapy professionals, holding members to rigorous standards of ethics, academic preparation, and training. The Web site has a searchable directory to find certified professionals throughout the United States and Canada.

Sexual Violence and Abuse

Childhelp USA

15757 N. 78th Street
Scottsdale, Arizona 85260
480-922-8212
800-4-A-CHILD (Emergency)
480-922-7061 (Fax)
www.childhelpusa.org

This organization is dedicated to meeting the physical, emotional, educational, and spiritual needs of abused and neglected children; it focuses on treatment, prevention, and research. Childhelp USA operates a child abuse hotline (800-4-A-CHILD) for crisis counseling and referral and a Web site that includes information about child abuse, prevention, and education programs as well as a variety of online and other resources.

National Organization on Male Sexual Victimization

MaleSurvivor
PMB 103 5505 Connecticut Ave. NW
Washington, DC 20015-2601
800-738-4181
www.malesurvivor.org

This organization is dedicated to providing treatment for male survivors of sexual abuse. The Web site offers a directory of specially trained therapists as well as research and advocacy for male survivors of abuse.

Rape, Abuse & Incest National Network

2000 L St. NW
Suite 406
Washington, DC 20036
800-656-4673, extension 3
800-656-HOPE (Emergency)
202-544-3556 (Fax)
www.rainn.org

This national service operates a hotline (800-656-HOPE) and a Web site that contains valuable information about all aspects of sexual abuse, including rape, incest, prevention, recovery, post-traumatic stress disorder, flashbacks, and criminal justice. It is an excellent resource for learning about the pervasive problem of sexual abuse and violence. The Web site contains educational sections such as "Am I being abused?" and "Am I abusing?" along with information for friends and family and a variety of online and other resources.

Survivors of Incest Anonymous

P.O. Box 190
Benson, MD 21018-9998
410-893-3322
www.siawso.org

This community of male and female survivors of incest and child abuse meets in several different cities to move toward healing based on the twelve-step recovery program, which can be found on their Web site. Additionally, the Web site offers information on the effects of incest and sexual abuse, and it provides contacts for those interested in joining a regional group for meetings, discussion, and support.

Single Parenting

National Organization of Single Mothers

www.singlemothers.org

This nonprofit organization offers newsletters, networking, support groups, and practical publications for all single mothers. The Web site has a wealth of information as well as message boards, forums, and useful links addressing the day-to-day challenges of single motherhood.

Parents Without Partners

1650 South Dixie Highway
Suite 510
Boca Raton, FL 33432
561-391-8833
www.parentswithoutpartners.org

This is an international, nonprofit organization devoted to providing community and support for all single parents. Local chapters around the world allow single parents to meet to discuss issues of single parenting. A newsletter and online community also provide support for single mothers and fathers.

Single Parents Network

www.singleparentsnetwork.com

This Web site serves as a hub for Web sites, articles, information, government resources, online discussion forum support boards, and a variety of practical tips and information for single mothers and fathers.

Teen Sexuality

Kidshealth—for Parents

Hosted by the Nemours Foundation's Center for Children's Health Media
   4600 Touchton Rd. East
   Building 200, Suite 500
   Jacksonville, FL 32246
   904-232-4125 (Fax)
   www.kidshealth.org/parent/positive/index.html

This section within www.kidshealth.org offers a wealth of practical advice for all aspects of child rearing. In addition to offering tips on talking with your children about sex based on up-to-date medical research, the site addresses everything from child safety and education to fostering healthy communication with your child.

Kidshealth—for Teens

Hosted by the Nemours Foundation's Center for Children's Health Media
   4600 Touchton Rd. East
   Building 200, Suite 500
   Jacksonville, FL 32246
   904-232-4100
   904-232-4125 (Fax)
   www.kidshealth.org/teen/sexual_health/

Also under the www.kidshealth.org umbrella, this site speaks to teen issues such as body image, STIs, pregnancy, and questions of what's "normal" for teens going through the physical and emotional changes of puberty. It may also be helpful for parents looking for straightforward information about specific issues within sexuality.

Out Proud!

Hosted by the National Organization for Gay, Lesbian, Bisexual, and Transgendered Youth
   www.outproud.org

This organization provides information, advocacy, and community support for young gay, lesbian, bisexual, and transgendered people, including a magazine, online communities, and testimonials of young people coming out. The organization also provides services specifically for youth who are inquiring about their sexuality or considering coming out.

Sex, etc.

Hosted by Answer at Rutgers University

Answer
41 Gordon Rd.
Suite C
Piscataway, NJ 08854-8067
732-445-7929
www.sexetc.org

This Web site is written by and for teens about all aspects of sexuality, with information, articles, and an online magazine. Topics include girls' health, guys' health, pregnancy, STIs, testing, emotional health, love and relationships, abortion and adoption, sexual orientation, and what to do in a crisis. A great resource for teens to get honest and direct answers to questions about sexuality.

Women's and Girls' Health

International Council on Infertility Information Dissemination (INCIID)

P.O. Box 6836
Arlington, VA 22206
703-379-9178
www.inciid.org

This nonprofit organization provides information and support for infertility and related issues including pregnancy, pregnancy loss, adoption, parenting, insurance, and advocacy. More than 150 referrals and links are provided to nonprofit organizations that provide quality information on all aspects of infertility.

National Women's Health Information Center

Hosted by the Office of Women's Health, U.S. Department of Health and Human Services

200 Independence Ave. SW
Room 712E
Washington, DC 20201
800-994-9662 or 888-220-5446 (TDD)
Monday through Friday, 9:00 a.m.–6:00 p.m. (EST)
www.4women.gov

This government-sponsored organization offers free public service and information on all aspects of women's health, with topics such as pregnancy, breastfeeding, body image, HIV/AIDS, girls' health, heart health, menopause and hormone therapy, mental health, quitting smoking, and violence against women. The Web site also provides original health information and resources for special groups such as minority women, women with disabilities, girls, men, and Spanish speakers.

National Women's Health Information Center—Girls' Health

Hosted by the Office of Women's Health, U.S. Department of Health and Human Services

200 Independence Ave. SW
Room 712E
Washington, DC 20201
800-994-9662 or 888-220-5446 (TDD)
Monday through Friday, 9 a.m.–6 p.m. (EST)
www.girlshealth.gov

This branch of the National Women's Health Information Center is specifically for girls and their health. The site is designed to be accessible and appealing to young girls and covers important topics such as physical health, puberty and menstruation, body image and eating disorders, relationships, and drugs and alcohol. It also includes a section with articles written by girls for girls about everyday issues.

National Women's Health Resource Center

157 Broad St.
Suite 315
Red Bank, NJ 07701
877-986-9472
www.healthywomen.org

This national, nonprofit organization distributes independent, up-to-date women's health information based on the latest medical research and practices. The site provides an A–Z encyclopedia of women's health issues and topics, newsletters and special reports, and special forums on sexuality, aging, and lifestyle.

Reading List

As with the resources listed on the preceding pages, keep in mind that while all these books are useful, some may not align with your family's values. You may want to personally evaluate them before sharing them with your children.

Balter, Lawrence. *Not in Front of the Children: How to Talk with Your Child About Tough Family Matters*. New York: Viking Penguin, 1993.

> This book specifically addresses sexual privacy and boundaries with kids, taking on several interesting and difficult questions, ranging from when and how to manage nakedness and privacy to what to do if your kids walk in on you while you are having sex.

Berkenkamp, Lauri, Steven C. Atkins, and Charlie Woglom. *Talking to Your Kids about Sex: A Go Parents! Guide*. Chicago: Nomad Press, 2002.

> This playful guide assures parents about normal sexual activity for kids from birth to puberty. The cartoon layout is accessible to children, while parents get a user-friendly rundown on basic facts about sexuality.

Blake, Jeanne. *Risky Times: How to Be AIDS Smart and Stay Healthy: A Guide for Teenagers*. New York: Workman Publishing, 1990.

> This book features advice and comments from various youth, celebrities, and medical professionals on AIDS and contraception. This balanced and accurate discussion of the consequences of unprotected sex provides an in-depth look at a growing epidemic in language accessible to teens.

Brooks, Robert. Illustrated by Susan Perl. *So That's How I Was Born*. New York: Simon and Schuster, 1983.

Brooks opens with a conversation between a boy and a schoolmate about the facts of life. The boy then turns to his parents for straightforward talk about how babies are born. The book offers a sensitive, illustrated presentation on engaging in honest conversation with kids 5 to 8 years old. It's recommended for kids 3 to 7, but it's not quite appropriate for preschoolers.

Brown, Laurie K. and Marc Brown. *What's the Big Secret? Talking about Sex with Girls and Boys*. Boston: Little, Brown and Company, 1997.

This attractive and playful book about the differences between girls and boys establishes a natural tone for primary and middle school kids—getting into the sexual issues.

Casparian, Elisabeth and Eva S. Goldfarb. *Our Whole Lives: Sexuality Education for Grades 4–6*. Boston: Unitarian Universalist Association, 2000.

This prepubescent curriculum, prepared by the Unitarian Universalist Church, offers sound guidance regarding the sexual growth of middle school kids. Designed for classroom learning, the book offers useful exercises and information that is scientific, sound, and balanced, and may be easily adapted for family learning.

Chrisman, Kent and Donna Couchenour. *Healthy Sexual Development: A Guide for Early Childhood Educators and Families*. Washington, D.C.: National Association for the Education of Young Children, 2002.

This is a very useful guide about children's sexual development, directed at teachers and educators. This guidebook provides a systematic overview of sexuality that considers physical, emotional, and social factors, with directions on how parents and teachers may influence healthy sexual growth.

Cole, Joanna. Illustrated by Alan Tiegreen. *Asking about Sex and Growing Up: A Question and Answer Book for Girls and Boys*. New York: William Morrow and Co., Inc., 1988.

You can comfortably place this readable and nonprovocative book in your middle school kid's hands. No drama or hype—simple questions and clear, factual answers that young people can sit with and think about. It seems a good choice for middle school kids (ages 9 to 12)—not too complex and sowing the seeds covering fundamental issues about sexuality.

Eyre, Linda and Richard. *How to Talk to Your Child about Sex: It's Best to Start Early but It's Never Too Late*. New York: Golden Books, 1998.

Here's a book that presents basic sexual information and addresses moral and spiritual values directly. This husband and wife team provides a fresh and practical model for engaging your kids on this delicate topic.

Gitchel, Sam and Lorri Foster. *Let's Talk about Sex: A Read and Discussion Guide for Kids Ages 9–12 and Their Parents*. Fresno, Calif.: Planned Parenthood of Central California, 1992.

Created by Planned Parenthood, this objective presentation for talking about sex with kids—especially preteens and teens—helps parents open discussions about sexual feelings and love from a factual and direct approach. Most will find this book helpful in approaching difficult topics that are necessary to confront.

Gravelle, Karen with Nick and Chave Castro. Illustrated by Robert Leighton. *What's Going on Down There? Answers to Questions Boys Find Hard to Ask*. New York: Walker and Company, 1998.

This book is on target and is tastefully and appropriately written for adolescent boys. Though packaged for kids entering puberty, the book sometimes provides too much information for middle school kids (9–12 years old). Humorous, down-to-earth, and very informative, this book is appropriate for adolescents and young adults.

Harris, Robie H. Illustrated by Michael Emberley. *It's Perfectly Normal: Changing Bodies, Growing Up, Sex, and Sexual Health*. Cambridge, Mass.: Candlewick Press, 2004.

This clearly written and well-illustrated volume presents biological facts clearly, with clever diagrams and sensitivity to diverse groups. It has a nonjudgmental attitude toward various ways of being sexual as it addresses sexual orientation and the choices people make about their sexual behavior. The book is appropriate for kids nearing puberty and older.

Mayle, Peter. Illustrated by Arthur Robins. *"Where Did I Come From?" The Facts of Life without Any Nonsense and with Illustrations*. New York: Kensington Publishing Corp., 1987.

> Though the illustrations may be too basic for middle school kids, this book offers a mild, straightforward explanation about where we came from. This book needs parental guidance and supervision.

Mayle, Peter. *Will I Like It? Your First Sexual Experience: What to Expect, What to Avoid, and How Both of You Can Get the Most Out of It*. New York: Corwin Books, 1977.

> While many books discuss the sex act, few discuss the experience and feelings. Mayle's book is unusual because it helps the reader with pressing questions about sexual intercourse.

Morris, Makanah E. and Jerry Agate. *Sexuality and Our Faith: Grades 7–9: A Companion to Our Whole Lives*. Boston: Unitarian Universalist Association, 1999.

> Teachers and parents will appreciate this careful and thoughtful work by Morris and Agate. Blending psychological and physical facts with spiritual issues, this book guides instructors in presenting a wider picture for adolescents about how to understand sexuality.

Index

About the Author

John Chirban, PhD, ThD, serves as clinical instructor in psychology at Harvard Medical School at the Cambridge Hospital and as director of the Institute of Medicine, Psychology, and Religion in Cambridge, Massachusetts. He is also professor of psychology and chairman of the Department of Human Development at Hellenic College and Holy Cross School of Theology and has been a Senior Fellow at the Center for the Study of World Religions at Harvard University. As director of Cambridge Counseling Associates, LLP, a full-service psychotherapy practice in Massachusetts, Dr. Chirban provides psychotherapy for adolescents and adults concerning various developmental and relational concerns. Author of numerous books and articles, he recently authored *True Coming of Age—A Dynamic Process that Leads to Emotional Well-Being, Spiritual Growth, and Meaningful Relationship* and *Healing in Byzantium*. The Chirbans have three children: Alexis Georgia, Anthony Thomas, and Ariana Maria.

Sexual Pulse

For Information About:

- Issues and Needs Concerning Sexuality Throughout the Life Cycle

- Sexual Problems and Therapy

- Clinical Services and Referrals

Please Visit

www.sexualproblems.com